The Complete

Instant Pot

Cookbook for Beginners

1200 Days Simple, Delicious and Comprehensive Recipes to
Satisfy All Your Palate Needs

Isaac S. Murph

Table of Contents

Chapter 3   Beef, Pork, and Lamb   23

Chapter 4   Fish and Seafood   36

Chapter 5   Poultry   50

Chapter 6   Stews and Soups   64

Chapter 7   Vegetables and Sides   80

Chapter 8   Desserts   90

INTRODUCTION

Welcome to the Instant Pot Cookbook, the ultimate guide for anyone looking to make delicious and healthy meals using the revolutionary Instant Pot! If you're new to the Instant Pot craze, you're in for a real treat.

The Instant Pot is a kitchen appliance that has taken the world by storm, and for good reason. It's an all-in-one, versatile appliance that can replace a dozen different kitchen gadgets, saving you both time and space in the kitchen. With its various cooking functions, the Instant Pot is perfect for creating everything from soups and stews to rice, pasta, and even yogurt.

When I first heard about the Instant Pot, I was skeptical. I've tried countless kitchen gadgets that promised to make my life easier, only to end up collecting dust in the back of my cupboard. But the Instant Pot has truly been a game-changer for me. It's intuitive, easy to use, and delivers consistently delicious results.

In this cookbook, I've compiled a collection of my favorite Instant Pot recipes that have been optimized for this amazing appliance. From classic comfort foods like beef stew and chili to exotic curries and stews, you'll find something to suit every taste and occasion. And with the Instant Pot's various cooking functions, you can even create homemade yogurt, rice pudding, and perfectly cooked rice and grains at the touch of a button.

But before we dive into the recipes, I want to share some essential tips and tricks for using the Instant Pot. From understanding how the pressure cooking function works to properly cleaning and maintaining your Instant Pot, these tips will help you get the most out of your appliance and ensure that you can enjoy it for years to come.

Whether you're a seasoned cook or a newbie in the kitchen, the Instant Pot Cookbook has something for everyone. With easy-to-follow recipes and step-by-step instructions, you'll be able to create delicious meals in no time. And the best part? The Instant Pot does all the work for you, leaving you with

more time to spend with your loved ones or on your favorite hobbies.

So dust off your Instant Pot, plug it in, and get ready to embark on a culinary journey like no other. I guarantee that you won't be disappointed, and that the Instant Pot will quickly become your new favorite kitchen gadget. Happy cooking!

Chapter 1   Snacks and Appetizers

Stuffed Jalapeños with Bacon

Prep time: 10 minutes | Cook time: 6 minutes | Serves 2

1 ounce (28 g) bacon, chopped, fried
2 ounces (57 g) Cheddar cheese, shredded
1 tablespoon coconut cream
1 teaspoon chopped green onions
2 jalapeños, trimmed and seeded

1. Mix together the chopped bacon, cheese, coconut cream, and green onions in a mixing bowl and stir until well incorporated. 2. Stuff the jalapeños evenly with the bacon mixture. 3. Press the Sauté button to heat your Instant Pot. 4. Place the stuffed jalapeños in the Instant Pot and cook each side for 3 minutes until softened. 5. Transfer to a paper towel-lined plate and serve.

Per Serving:
calories: 216 | fat: 17.5g | protein: 12.9g | carbs: 1.7g | net carbs: 1.1g | fiber: 0.6g

Coconut Cajun Shrimp

Prep time: 10 minutes | Cook time: 6 minutes | Serves 2

4 Royal tiger shrimps
3 tablespoons coconut shred
2 eggs, beaten
½ teaspoon Cajun seasoning
1 teaspoon olive oil

1. Heat up olive oil in the instant pot on Sauté mode. 2. Meanwhile, mix up Cajun seasoning and coconut shred. 3. Dip the shrimps in the eggs and coat in the coconut shred mixture. 4. After this, place the shrimps in the hot olive oil and cook them on Sauté mode for 3 minutes from each side.

Per Serving:
calories: 292 | fat: 54g | protein: 40g | carbs: 2g | net carbs: 1g | fiber: 1g

Porcupine Meatballs

Prep time: 20 minutes | Cook time: 15 minutes | Serves 8

1 pound ground sirloin or turkey
½ cup raw brown rice, parboiled
1 egg
¼ cup finely minced onion
1 or 2 cloves garlic, minced
¼ teaspoon dried basil and/or oregano, optional
10¾-ounce can reduced-fat condensed tomato soup
½ soup can of water

1. Mix all ingredients, except tomato soup and water, in a bowl to combine well. 2. Form into balls about 1½-inch in diameter. 3. Mix tomato soup and water in the inner pot of the Instant Pot, then add the meatballs. 4. Secure the lid and make sure the vent is turned to sealing. 5. Press the Meat button and set for 15 minutes on high pressure. 6. Allow the pressure to release naturally after cook time is up.

Per Serving:
calories: 141 | fat: 2g | protein: 16g | carbs: 14g | sugars: 3g | fiber: 1g | sodium: 176mg

Chinese Spare Ribs

Prep time: 3 minutes | Cook time: 24 minutes | Serves 6

1½ pounds (680 g) spare ribs
Salt and ground black pepper, to taste
2 tablespoons sesame oil
½ cup chopped green onions
½ cup chicken stock
2 tomatoes, crushed
2 tablespoons sherry
1 tablespoon coconut aminos
1 teaspoon ginger-garlic paste
½ teaspoon crushed red pepper flakes
½ teaspoon dried parsley
2 tablespoons sesame seeds, for serving

1. Season the spare ribs with salt and black pepper to taste. 2. Set your Instant Pot to Sauté and heat the sesame oil. 3. Add the seasoned spare ribs and sear each side for about 3 minutes. 4. Add the remaining ingredients except the sesame seeds to the Instant Pot and stir well. 5. Secure the lid. Select the Meat/Stew mode and set the cooking time for 18 minutes at High Pressure. 6. When the timer beeps, perform a natural pressure release for 10 minutes, then release any remaining pressure. Carefully remove the lid. 7. Serve topped with the sesame seeds.

Per Serving:
calories: 336 | fat: 16.3g | protein: 42.6g | carbs: 3.0g | net carbs: 2.0g | fiber: 1.0g

Jalapeño Poppers with Bacon

Prep time: 10 minutes | Cook time: 3 minutes | Serves 4

6 jalapeños
4 ounces (113 g) cream cheese
¼ cup shredded sharp Cheddar
cheese
1 cup water
¼ cup cooked crumbled bacon

1. Cut jalapeños lengthwise and scoop out seeds and membrane, then set aside. 2. In small bowl, mix cream cheese and Cheddar. Spoon into emptied jalapeños. Pour water into Instant Pot and place steamer basket in bottom. 3. Place stuffed jalapeños on steamer rack. Click lid closed. Press the Manual button and adjust time for 3 minutes. When timer beeps, quick-release the pressure. Serve topped with crumbled bacon.

Per Serving:
calories: 185 | fat: 14g | protein: 7g | carbs: 3g | net carbs: 2g | fiber: 1g

Asparagus with Creamy Dip

Prep time: 5 minutes | Cook time: 1 minute | Serves 6

1 cup water
1½ pounds (680 g) asparagus spears, trimmed
Dipping Sauce:
½ cup mayonnaise
½ cup sour cream
2 tablespoons chopped scallions
2 tablespoons fresh chervil
1 teaspoon minced garlic
Salt, to taste

1. Pour the water into the Instant Pot and insert a steamer basket. Place the asparagus in the basket. 2. Lock the lid. Select the Manual mode and set the cooking time for 1 minute at High Pressure. 3. When the timer beeps, perform a quick pressure release. Carefully remove the lid. Transfer the asparagus to a plate. 4. Whisk together the remaining ingredients to make your dipping sauce. Serve the

asparagus with the dipping sauce on the side.
Per Serving:
calories: 119 | fat: 8.9g | protein: 4.8g | carbs: 6.6g | net carbs: 4.1g | fiber: 2.5g

Parmesan Artichoke

Prep time: 1 minute | Cook time: 30 minutes | Serves 2

1 large artichoke
1 cup water
¼ cup grated Parmesan cheese
¼ teaspoon salt
¼ teaspoon red pepper flakes

1. Trim artichoke. Remove stem, outer leaves and top. Gently spread leaves. 2. Add water to Instant Pot and place steam rack on bottom. Place artichoke on steam rack and sprinkle with Parmesan, salt, and red pepper flakes. Click lid closed. Press the Steam button and adjust time for 30 minutes. 3. When timer beeps, allow a 15-minute natural release and then quick-release the remaining pressure. Enjoy warm topped with additional Parmesan.
Per Serving:
calories: 90 | fat: 3g | protein: 6g | carbs: 10g | net carbs: 6g | fiber: 4g

Taco Beef Bites

Prep time: 10 minutes | Cook time: 15 minutes | Serves 6

10 ounces (283 g) ground beef
3 eggs, beaten
⅓ cup shredded Mozzarella
cheese
1 teaspoon taco seasoning
1 teaspoon sesame oil

1. In the mixing bowl mix up ground beef, eggs, Mozzarella, and taco seasoning. 2. Then make the small meat bites from the mixture. 3. Heat up sesame oil in the instant pot. 4. Put the meat bites in the hot oil and cook them for 5 minutes from each side on Sauté mode.
Per Serving:
calories: 132 | fat: 6g | protein: 17g | carbs: 1g | net carbs: 1g | fiber: 0g

Herbed Shrimp

Prep time: 5 minutes | Cook time: 5 minutes | Serves 4

2 tablespoons olive oil
¾ pound (340 g) shrimp, peeled and deveined
1 teaspoon paprika
1 teaspoon garlic powder
1 teaspoon onion powder
1 teaspoon dried parsley flakes
½ teaspoon dried oregano
½ teaspoon dried thyme
½ teaspoon dried basil
½ teaspoon dried rosemary
¼ teaspoon red pepper flakes
Coarse sea salt and ground black pepper, to taste
1 cup chicken broth

1. Set your Instant Pot to Sauté and heat the olive oil. 2. Add the shrimp and sauté for 2 to 3 minutes. 3. Add the remaining ingredients to the Instant Pot and stir to combine. 4. Secure the lid. Select the Manual mode and set the cooking time for 2 minutes at Low Pressure. 5. When the timer beeps, perform a quick pressure release. Carefully remove the lid. 6. Transfer the shrimp to a plate and serve.
Per Serving:
calories: 146 | fat: 7.7g | protein: 18.5g | carbs: 3.0g | net carbs: 2.3g | fiber: 0.7g

Cabbage and Broccoli Slaw

Prep time: 5 minutes | Cook time: 10 minutes | Serves 6

2 cups broccoli slaw
½ head cabbage, thinly sliced
¼ cup chopped kale
4 tablespoons butter
1 teaspoon salt
¼ teaspoon pepper

1. Press the Sauté button and add all ingredients to Instant Pot. Stir-fry for 7 to 10 minutes until cabbage softens. Serve warm.
Per Serving:
calories: 97 | fat: 7g | protein: 2g | carbs: 6g | net carbs: 3g | fiber: 3g

Parmesan Chicken Balls with Chives

Prep time: 10 minutes | Cook time: 15 minutes | Serves 4

1 teaspoon coconut oil, softened
1 cup ground chicken
¼ cup chicken broth
1 tablespoon chopped chives
1 teaspoon cayenne pepper
3 ounces (85 g) Parmesan cheese, grated

1. Set your Instant Pot to Sauté and heat the coconut oil. 2. Add the remaining ingredients except the cheese to the Instant Pot and stir to mix well. 3. Secure the lid. Select the Manual mode and set the cooking time for 15 minutes at High Pressure. 4. Once cooking is complete, do a quick pressure release. Carefully open the lid. 5. Add the grated cheese and stir until combined. Form the balls from the cooked chicken mixture and allow to cool for 10 minutes, then serve.
Per Serving:
calories: 154 | fat: 8.7g | protein: 17.5g | carbs: 1.0g | net carbs: 0.9g | fiber: 0.1g

Southern Boiled Peanuts

Prep time: 5 minutes | Cook time: 1 hour 20 minutes | Makes 8 cups

1 pound raw jumbo peanuts in the shell
3 tablespoons fine sea salt

1. Remove the inner pot from the Instant Pot and add the peanuts to it. Cover the peanuts with water and use your hands to agitate them, loosening any dirt. Drain the peanuts in a colander, rinse out the pot, and return the peanuts to it. Return the inner pot to the Instant Pot housing. 2. Add the salt and 9 cups water to the pot and stir to dissolve the salt. Select a salad plate just small enough to fit inside the pot and set it on top of the peanuts to weight them down, submerging them all in the water. 3. Secure the lid and set the Pressure Release to Sealing. Select the Steam setting and set the cooking time for 1 hour at low pressure. (The pot will take about 20 minutes to come up to pressure before the cooking program begins.) 4. When the cooking program ends, let the pressure release naturally (this will take about 1 hour). Open the pot and, wearing heat-resistant mitts, remove the inner pot from the housing. Let the peanuts cool to room temperature in the brine (this will take about 1½ hours). 5. Serve at room temperature or chilled. Transfer the peanuts with their brine to an airtight container and refrigerate for up to 1 week.
Per Serving:
calories: 306 | fat: 17g | protein: 26g | carbs: 12g | sugars: 2g | fiber: 4g | sodium: 303mg

Cayenne Beef Bites

Prep time: 5 minutes | Cook time: 23 minutes | Serves 6

2 tablespoons olive oil
1 pound (454 g) beef steak, cut
into cubes
1 cup beef bone broth
¼ cup dry white wine

1 teaspoon cayenne pepper
½ teaspoon dried marjoram
Sea salt and ground black
pepper, to taste

1. Set your Instant Pot to Sauté and heat the olive oil. 2. Add the beef and sauté for 2 to 3 minutes, stirring occasionally. 3. Add the remaining ingredients to the Instant Pot and combine well. 4. Lock the lid. Select the Manual mode and set the cooking time for 20 minutes at High Pressure. 5. When the timer beeps, perform a natural pressure release for 10 minutes, then release any remaining pressure. Carefully remove the lid. 6. Remove the beef from the Instant Pot to a platter and serve warm.
Per Serving:
calories: 173 | fat: 10.2g | protein: 18.6g | carbs: 1.0g | net carbs: 0.8g | fiber: 0.2g

Creamy Scallion Dip

Prep time: 10 minutes | Cook time: 11 minutes | Serves 4

5 ounces (142 g) scallions,
diced
4 tablespoons cream cheese
1 tablespoon chopped fresh
parsley

1 teaspoon garlic powder
2 tablespoons coconut cream
½ teaspoon salt
1 teaspoon coconut oil

1. Heat up the instant pot on Sauté mode. 2. Then add coconut oil and melt it. 3. Add diced scallions and sauté it for 6 to 7 minutes or until it is light brown. 4. Add cream cheese, parsley, garlic powder, salt, and coconut cream. 5. Close the instant pot lid and cook the scallions dip for 5 minutes on Manual mode (High Pressure). 6. Make a quick pressure release. Blend the dip will it is smooth if desired.
Per Serving:
calories: 76 | fat: 6g | protein: 2g | carbs: 4g | net carbs: 3g | fiber: 1g

Spicy Baked Feta in Foil

Prep time: 10 minutes | Cook time: 6 minutes | Serves 6

12 ounces (340 g) feta cheese
½ tomato, sliced
1 ounce (28 g) bell pepper,
sliced

1 teaspoon ground paprika
1 tablespoon olive oil
1 cup water, for cooking

1. Sprinkle the cheese with olive oil and ground paprika and place it on the foil. 2. Then top feta cheese with sliced tomato and bell pepper. Wrap it in the foil well. 3. After this, pour water and insert the steamer rack in the instant pot. 4. Put the wrapped cheese on the rack. Close and seal the lid. 5. Cook the cheese on Manual mode (High Pressure) for 6 minutes. Then make a quick pressure release. 6. Discard the foil and transfer the cheese on the serving plates.
Per Serving:
calories: 178 | fat: 14g | protein: 8g | carbs: 4g | net carbs: 3g | fiber: 1g

Rosemary Chicken Wings

Prep time: 10 minutes | Cook time: 16 minutes | Serves 4

4 boneless chicken wings
1 tablespoon olive oil
1 teaspoon dried rosemary

½ teaspoon garlic powder
¼ teaspoon salt

1. In the mixing bowl, mix up olive oil, dried rosemary, garlic powder, and salt. 2. Then rub the chicken wings with the rosemary mixture and leave for 10 minutes to marinate. 3. After this, put the chicken wings in the instant pot, add the remaining rosemary marinade and cook them on Sauté mode for 8 minutes from each side.
Per Serving:
calories: 222 | fat: 11g | protein: 27g | carbs: 2g | net carbs: 2g | fiber: 0g

Lemon-Cheese Cauliflower Bites

Prep time: 5 minutes | Cook time: 8 minutes | Serves 6

1 cup water
1 pound (454 g) cauliflower,
broken into florets
Sea salt and ground black
pepper, to taste

2 tablespoons extra-virgin olive
oil
2 tablespoons lemon juice
1 cup grated Cheddar cheese

1. Pour the water into the Instant Pot and insert a steamer basket. Place the cauliflower florets in the basket. 2. Lock the lid. Select the Manual mode and set the cooking time for 3 minutes at Low Pressure. 3. When the timer beeps, perform a quick pressure release. Carefully remove the lid. 4. Season the cauliflower with salt and pepper. Drizzle with olive oil and lemon juice. Sprinkle the grated cheese all over the cauliflower. 5. Press the Sauté button to heat the Instant Pot. Allow to cook for about 5 minutes, or until the cheese melts. Serve warm.
Per Serving:
calories: 136 | fat: 9.8g | protein: 7.2g | carbs: 5.0g | net carbs: 3.4g | fiber: 1.6g

Oregano Sausage Balls

Prep time: 10 minutes | Cook time: 16 minutes | Serves 10

15 ounces (425 g) ground pork
sausage
1 teaspoon dried oregano
4 ounces (113 g) Mozzarella,

shredded
1 cup coconut flour
1 garlic clove, grated
1 teaspoon coconut oil, melted

1. In the bowl mix up ground pork sausages, dried oregano, shredded Mozzarella, coconut flour, and garlic clove. 2. When the mixture is homogenous, make the balls. 3. After this, pour coconut oil in the instant pot. 4. Arrange the balls in the instant pot and cook them on Sauté mode for 8 minutes from each side.
Per Serving:
calories: 310 | fat: 23g | protein: 17g | carbs: 10g | net carbs: 5g | fiber: 5g

Red Wine Mushrooms

Prep time: 5 minutes | Cook time: 15 minutes | Serves 2

8 ounces (227 g) sliced mushrooms
¼ cup dry red wine
2 tablespoons beef broth
½ teaspoon garlic powder
¼ teaspoon Worcestershire sauce
Pinch of salt
Pinch of black pepper
¼ teaspoon xanthan gum

1. Add the mushrooms, wine, broth, garlic powder, Worcestershire sauce, salt, and pepper to the pot. 2. Close the lid and seal the vent. Cook on High Pressure for 13 minutes. Quick release the steam. Press Cancel. 3. Turn the pot to Sauté mode. Add the xanthan gum and whisk until the juices have thickened, 1 to 2 minutes.
Per Serving:
calories: 94 | fat: 1g | protein: 4g | carbs: 8g | net carbs: 6g | fiber: 2g

Brussels Sprouts with Aioli Sauce

Prep time: 5 minutes | Cook time: 7 minutes | Serves 4

1 tablespoon butter
½ cup chopped scallions
¾ pound (340 g) Brussels sprouts
Aioli Sauce:
¼ cup mayonnaise
1 tablespoon fresh lemon juice
1 garlic clove, minced
½ teaspoon Dijon mustard

1. Set your Instant Pot to Sauté and melt the butter. 2. Add the scallions and sauté for 2 minutes until softened. Add the Brussels sprouts and cook for another 1 minute. 3. Lock the lid. Select the Manual mode and set the cooking time for 4 minutes at High Pressure. 4. Meanwhile, whisk together all the ingredients for the Aioli sauce in a small bowl until well incorporated. 5. When the timer beeps, perform a quick pressure release. Carefully remove the lid. 6. Serve the Brussels sprouts with the Aioli sauce on the side.
Per Serving:
calories: 167 | fat: 13.8g | protein: 3.4g | carbs: 8.6g | net carbs: 5.4g | fiber: 3.2g

Mayo Chicken Celery

Prep time: 15 minutes | Cook time: 15 minutes | Serves 4

14 ounces (397 g) chicken breast, skinless, boneless
1 cup water
4 celery stalks
1 teaspoon salt
½ teaspoon onion powder
1 teaspoon mayonnaise

1. Combine all the ingredients except the mayo in the Instant Pot. 2. Secure the lid. Select the Manual mode and set the cooking time for 15 minutes at High Pressure. 3. Once cooking is complete, do a natural pressure release for 6 minutes, then release any remaining pressure. Carefully open the lid. 4. Remove the chicken and shred with two forks, then return to the Instant Pot. 5. Add the mayo and stir well. Serve immediately.
Per Serving:
calories: 119 | fat: 2.9g | protein: 21.4g | carbs: 0.7g | net carbs: 0.6g | fiber: 0.3g

Cauliflower Cheese Balls

Prep time: 5 minutes | Cook time: 21 minutes | Serves 8

1 cup water
1 head cauliflower, broken into florets
1 cup shredded Asiago cheese
½ cup grated Parmesan cheese
2 eggs, beaten
2 tablespoons butter
2 tablespoons minced fresh chives
1 garlic clove, minced
½ teaspoon cayenne pepper
Coarse sea salt and white pepper, to taste

1. Pour the water into the Instant Pot and insert a steamer basket. Place the cauliflower in the basket. 2. Lock the lid. Select the Manual mode and set the cooking time for 3 minutes at High Pressure. 3. When the timer beeps, perform a quick pressure release. Carefully remove the lid. 4. Transfer the cauliflower to a food processor, along with the remaining ingredients. Pulse until everything is well combined. 5. Form the mixture into bite-sized balls and place them on a baking sheet. 6. Bake in the preheated oven at 400ºF (205ºC) for 18 minutes until golden brown. Flip the balls halfway through the cooking time. Cool for 5 minutes before serving.
Per Serving:
calories: 161 | fat: 12.6g | protein: 9.3g | carbs: 3.8g | net carbs: 3g | fiber: 0.8g

Cheddar Chips

Prep time: 10 minutes | Cook time: 5 minutes | Serves 4

1 cup shredded Cheddar cheese
1 tablespoon almond flour

1. Mix up Cheddar cheese and almond flour. 2. Then preheat the instant pot on Sauté mode. 3. Line the instant pot bowl with baking paper. 4. After this, make the small rounds from the cheese in the instant pot (on the baking paper) and close the lid. 5. Cook them for 5 minutes on Sauté mode or until the cheese is melted. 6. Then switch off the instant pot and remove the baking paper with cheese rounds from it. 7. Cool the chips well and remove them from the baking paper.
Per Serving:
calories: 154 | fat: 13g | protein: 9g | carbs: 2g | net carbs: 1g | fiber: 1g

Italian Tomatillos

Prep time: 10 minutes | Cook time: 10 minutes | Serves 4

1 tablespoon Italian seasoning
4 tomatillos, sliced
4 teaspoons olive oil
4 tablespoons water

1. Sprinkle the tomatillos with Italian seasoning. 2. Then pour the olive oil in the instant pot and heat it up on Sauté mode for 1 minute. 3. Put the tomatillos in the instant pot in one layer and cook them for 2 minutes from each side. 4. Then add water and close the lid. 5. Sauté the vegetables for 3 minutes more.
Per Serving:
calories: 51 | fat: 5g | protein: 0g | carbs: 2g | net carbs: 1g | fiber: 1g

Garlic Meatballs

Prep time: 20 minutes | Cook time: 15 minutes | Serves 6

7 ounces (198 g) ground beef
7 ounces (198 g) ground pork
1 teaspoon minced garlic
3 tablespoons water

1 teaspoon chili flakes
1 teaspoon dried parsley
1 tablespoon coconut oil
¼ cup beef broth

1. In the mixing bowl, mix up ground beef, ground pork, minced garlic, water, chili flakes, and dried parsley. 2. Make the medium size meatballs from the mixture. 3. After this, heat up coconut oil in the instant pot on Sauté mode. 4. Put the meatballs in the hot coconut oil in one layer and cook them for 2 minutes from each side. 5. Then add beef broth and close the lid. 6. Cook the meatballs for 10 minutes on Manual mode (High Pressure). 7. Then make a quick pressure release and transfer the meatballs on the plate.

Per Serving:
calories: 131 | fat: 6g | protein: 19g | carbs: 0g | net carbs: 0g | fiber: 0g

Spinach and Artichoke Dip

Prep time: 5 minutes | Cook time: 4 minutes | Serves 11

8 ounces low-fat cream cheese
10-ounce box frozen spinach
½ cup no-sodium chicken broth
14-ounce can artichoke hearts, drained
½ cup low-fat sour cream
½ cup low-fat mayo

3 cloves of garlic, minced
1 teaspoon onion powder
16 ounces reduced-fat shredded Parmesan cheese
8 ounces reduced-fat shredded mozzarella

1. Put all ingredients in the inner pot of the Instant Pot, except the Parmesan cheese and the mozzarella cheese. 2. Secure the lid and set vent to sealing. Place on Manual high pressure for 4 minutes. 3. Do a quick release of steam. 4. Immediately stir in the cheeses.

Per Serving:
calories: 288 | fat: 18g | protein: 19g | carbs: 15g | sugars: 3g | fiber: 3g | sodium: 1007mg

Blackberry Baked Brie

Prep time: 5 minutes | Cook time: 15 minutes | Serves 5

8-ounce round Brie
1 cup water
¼ cup sugar-free blackberry

preserves
2 teaspoons chopped fresh mint

1. Slice a grid pattern into the top of the rind of the Brie with a knife. 2. In a 7-inch round baking dish, place the Brie, then cover the baking dish securely with foil. 3. Insert the trivet into the inner pot of the Instant Pot; pour in the water. 4. Make a foil sling and arrange it on top of the trivet. Place the baking dish on top of the trivet and foil sling. 5. Secure the lid to the locked position and turn the vent to sealing. 6. Press Manual and set the Instant Pot for 15 minutes on high pressure. 7. When cooking time is up, turn off the Instant Pot and do a quick release of the pressure. 8. When the valve has dropped, remove the lid, then remove the baking dish. 9. Remove the top rind of the Brie and top with the preserves. Sprinkle with the fresh mint.

Per Serving:
calorie: 133 | fat: 10g | protein: 8g | carbs: 4g | sugars: 0g | fiber: 0g | sodium: 238mg

Hummus with Chickpeas and Tahini Sauce

Prep time: 10 minutes | Cook time: 55 minutes | Makes 4 cups

4 cups water
1 cup dried chickpeas
2½ teaspoons fine sea salt
½ cup tahini

3 tablespoons fresh lemon juice
1 garlic clove
¼ teaspoon ground cumin

1. Combine the water, chickpeas, and 1 teaspoon of the salt in the Instant Pot and stir to dissolve the salt. 2. Secure the lid and set the Pressure Release to Sealing. Select the Bean/Chili, Pressure Cook, or Manual setting and set the cooking time for 40 minutes at high pressure. (The pot will take about 15 minutes to come up to pressure before the cooking program begins.) 3. When the cooking program ends, let the pressure release naturally for 15 minutes, then move the Pressure Release to Venting to release any remaining steam. 4. Place a colander over a bowl. Open the pot and, wearing heat-resistant mitts, lift out the inner pot and drain the beans in the colander. Return the chickpeas to the inner pot and place it back in the Instant Pot housing on the Keep Warm setting. Reserve the cooking liquid. 5. In a blender or food processor, combine 1 cup of the cooking liquid, the tahini, lemon juice, garlic, cumin, and 1 teaspoon salt. Blend or process on high speed, stopping to scrape down the sides of the container as needed, for about 30 seconds, until smooth and a little fluffy. Scoop out and set aside ½ cup of this sauce for the topping. 6. Set aside ½ cup of the chickpeas for the topping. Add the remaining chickpeas to the tahini sauce in the blender or food processor along with ½ cup of the cooking liquid and the remaining ½ teaspoon salt. Blend or process on high speed, stopping to scrape down the sides of the container as needed, for about 1 minute, until very smooth. 7. Transfer the hummus to a shallow serving bowl. Spoon the reserved tahini mixture over the top, then sprinkle on the reserved chickpeas. The hummus will keep in an airtight container in the refrigerator for up to 3 days. Serve at room temperature or chilled.

Per Serving:
calories: 107 | fat: 5g | protein: 4g | carbs: 10g | sugars: 3g | fiber: 4g | sodium: 753mg

Broccoli Cheese Dip

Prep time: 5 minutes | Cook time: 10 minutes | Serves 6

4 tablespoons butter
½ medium onion, diced
1½ cups chopped broccoli
8 ounces (227 g) cream cheese

½ cup mayonnaise
½ cup chicken broth
1 cup shredded Cheddar cheese

1. Press the Sauté button and then press the Adjust button to set heat to Less. Add butter to Instant Pot. Add onion and sauté until softened, about 5 minutes. Press the Cancel button. 2. Add broccoli, cream cheese, mayo, and broth to pot. Press the Manual button and adjust time for 4 minutes. 3. When timer beeps, quick-release the pressure and stir in Cheddar. Serve warm.

Per Serving:
calories: 411 | fat: 37g | protein: 8g | carbs: 4g | net carbs: 3g | fiber: 1g

Garlic Herb Butter

Prep time: 10 minutes | Cook time: 8 minutes | Serves 4

⅓ cup butter
1 teaspoon dried parsley
1 tablespoon dried dill

½ teaspoon minced garlic
¼ teaspoon dried thyme

1. Preheat the instant pot on Sauté mode. 2. Then add butter and melt it. 3. Add dried parsley, dill, minced garlic, and thyme. Stir the butter mixture well. 4. Transfer it in the butter mold and refrigerate until it is solid.
Per Serving:
calories: 138 | fat: 15g | protein: 0g | carbs: 1g | net carbs: 1g | fiber: 0g

Pancetta Pizza Dip

Prep time: 10 minutes | Cook time: 4 minutes | Serves 10

10 ounces (283 g) Pepper Jack cheese
10 ounces (283 g) cream cheese
10 ounces (283 g) pancetta, chopped
1 pound (454 g) tomatoes, puréed

1 cup green olives, pitted and halved
1 teaspoon dried oregano
½ teaspoon garlic powder
1 cup chicken broth
4 ounces (113 g) Mozzarella cheese, thinly sliced

1. Mix together the Pepper Jack cheese, cream cheese, pancetta, tomatoes, olives, oregano, and garlic powder in the Instant Pot. Pour in the chicken broth. 2. Lock the lid. Select the Manual mode and set the cooking time for 4 minutes at High Pressure. 3. When the timer beeps, perform a quick pressure release. Carefully remove the lid. 4. Scatter the Mozzarella cheese on top. Cover and allow to sit in the residual heat. Serve warm.
Per Serving:
calories: 287 | fat: 20.8g | protein: 20.8g | carbs: 3.4g | net carbs: 2.0g | fiber: 1.4g

Broccoli with Garlic-Herb Cheese Sauce

Prep time: 5 minutes | Cook time: 3 minutes | Serves 4

½ cup water
1 pound (454 g) broccoli (frozen or fresh)
½ cup heavy cream
1 tablespoon butter
½ cup shredded Cheddar

cheese
3 tablespoons garlic and herb cheese spread
Pinch of salt
Pinch of black pepper

1. Add the water to the pot and place the trivet inside. 2. Put the steamer basket on top of the trivet. Place the broccoli in the basket. 3. Close the lid and seal the vent. Cook on Low Pressure for 1 minute. Quick release the steam. Press Cancel. 4. Carefully remove the steamer basket from the pot and drain the water. If you steamed a full bunch of broccoli, pull the florets off the stem. (Chop the stem into bite-size pieces, it's surprisingly creamy.) 5. Turn the pot to Sauté mode. Add the cream and butter. Stir continuously while the butter melts and the cream warms up. 6. When the cream begins to bubble on the edges, add the Cheddar cheese, cheese spread, salt,

and pepper. Whisk continuously until the cheeses are melted and a sauce consistency is reached, 1 to 2 minutes. 7. Top one-fourth of the broccoli with 2 tablespoons cheese sauce.
Per Serving:
calories: 134 | fat: 12g | protein:4 g | carbs: 5g | net carbs: 3g | fiber: 2g

Creamy Spinach

Prep time: 5 minutes | Cook time: 4 minutes | Serves 4

2 cups chopped spinach
2 ounces (57 g) Monterey Jack cheese, shredded
1 cup almond milk

1 tablespoon butter
1 teaspoon minced garlic
½ teaspoon salt

1. Combine all the ingredients in the Instant Pot. 2. Secure the lid. Select the Manual mode and set the cooking time for 4 minutes at High Pressure. 3. Once cooking is complete, do a quick pressure release. Carefully open the lid. 4. Give the mixture a good stir and serve warm.
Per Serving:
calories: 101 | fat: 8.1g | protein: 4.2g | carbs: 2.6g | net carbs: 2.3g | fiber: 0.3g

Creamy Spinach Dip

Prep time: 13 minutes | Cook time: 5 minutes | Serves 11

8 ounces low-fat cream cheese
1 cup low-fat sour cream
½ cup finely chopped onion
½ cup no-sodium vegetable broth
5 cloves garlic, minced
½ teaspoon salt

¼ teaspoon black pepper
10 ounces frozen spinach
12 ounces reduced-fat shredded Monterey Jack cheese
12 ounces reduced-fat shredded Parmesan cheese

1. Add cream cheese, sour cream, onion, vegetable broth, garlic, salt, pepper, and spinach to the inner pot of the Instant Pot. 2. Secure lid, make sure vent is set to sealing, and set to the Bean/Chili setting on high pressure for 5 minutes. 3. When done, do a manual release. 4. Add the cheeses and mix well until creamy and well combined.
Per Serving:
calorie: 274 | fat: 18g | protein: 19g | carbs: 10g | sugars: 3g | fiber: 1g | sodium: 948mg

Buttered Cabbage

Prep time: 5 minutes | Cook time: 5 minutes | Serves 4

1 medium head white cabbage, sliced into strips
4 tablespoons butter

½ teaspoon salt
¼ teaspoon pepper
1 cup water

1. Place cabbage in 7-cup glass bowl with butter, salt, and pepper. 2. Pour water into Instant Pot and place steam rack on bottom. Place bowl on steam rack. Click lid closed. Press the Manual button and adjust time for 5 minutes. When timer beeps, quick-release the pressure.
Per Serving:
calories: 158 | fat: 10g | protein: 3g | carbs: 13g | net carbs: 8g | fiber: 5g

Buffalo Chicken Meatballs

Prep time: 5 minutes | Cook time: 10 minutes | Serves 4

1 pound (454 g) ground chicken	¼ teaspoon pepper
½ cup almond flour	¼ teaspoon garlic powder
2 tablespoons cream cheese	1 cup water
1 packet dry ranch dressing mix	2 tablespoons butter, melted
½ teaspoon salt	⅓ cup hot sauce
	¼ cup crumbled feta cheese
	¼ cup sliced green onion

1. In large bowl, mix ground chicken, almond flour, cream cheese, ranch, salt, pepper, and garlic powder. Roll mixture into 16 balls. 2. Place meatballs on steam rack and add 1 cup water to Instant Pot. Click lid closed. Press the Meat/Stew button and set time for 10 minutes. 3. Combine butter and hot sauce. When timer beeps, remove meatballs and place in clean large bowl. Toss in hot sauce mixture. Top with sprinkled feta and green onions to serve.

Per Serving:

calories: 367 | fat: 25g | protein: 25g | carbs: 9g | net carbs: 7g | fiber: 2g

Creole Pancetta and Cheese Balls

Prep time: 5 minutes | Cook time: 5 minutes | Serves 6

1 cup water	¼ cup mayonnaise
6 eggs	1 teaspoon Creole seasonings
4 slices pancetta, chopped	Sea salt and ground black pepper, to taste
⅓ cup grated Cheddar cheese	
¼ cup cream cheese	

1. Pour the water into the Instant Pot and insert a steamer basket. Place the eggs in the basket. 2. Lock the lid. Select the Manual mode and set the cooking time for 5 minutes at Low Pressure. 3. When the timer beeps, perform a quick pressure release. Carefully remove the lid. 4. Allow the eggs to cool for 10 to 15 minutes. Peel the eggs and chop them, then transfer to a bowl. Add the remaining ingredients and stir to combine well. 5. Shape the mixture into balls with your hands. Serve chilled.

Per Serving:

calories: 239 | fat: 19g | protein: 14g | carbs: 3g | net carbs: 3g | fiber: 0g

Colby Cheese and Pepper Dip

Prep time: 5 minutes | Cook time: 5 minutes | Serves 8

1 tablespoon butter	2 garlic cloves, minced
2 red bell peppers, sliced	1 teaspoon red Aleppo pepper flakes
2 cups shredded Colby cheese	
1 cup cream cheese, room temperature	1 teaspoon sumac
1 cup chicken broth	Salt and ground black pepper, to taste

1. Set your Instant Pot to Sauté and melt the butter. 2. Add the bell peppers and sauté for about 2 minutes until just tender. 3. Add the remaining ingredients to the Instant Pot and gently stir to incorporate. 4. Lock the lid. Select the Manual mode and set the cooking time for 3 minutes at High Pressure. 5. When the timer beeps, perform a quick pressure release. Carefully remove the lid. 6. Allow to cool for

5 minutes and serve warm.

Per Serving:

calories: 241 | fat: 20.8g | protein: 10.6g | carbs: 3.0g | net carbs: 2.6g | fiber: 0.4g

Creamy Mashed Cauliflower

Prep time: 3 minutes | Cook time: 1 minute | Serves 4

1 head cauliflower, chopped into florets	3 tablespoons butter
	2 tablespoons sour cream
1 cup water	½ teaspoon salt
1 clove garlic, finely minced	¼ teaspoon pepper

1. Place cauliflower on steamer rack. Add water and steamer rack to Instant Pot. Press the Steam button and adjust time to 1 minute. When timer beeps, quick-release the pressure. 2. Place cooked cauliflower into food processor and add remaining ingredients. Blend until smooth and creamy. Serve warm.

Per Serving:

calories: 125 | fat: 9g | protein: 3g | carbs: 8g | net carbs: 5g | fiber: 3g

Chicken and Cabbage Salad

Prep time: 15 minutes | Cook time: 10 minutes | Serves 4

12 ounces (340 g) chicken fillet, chopped	1 cup chopped Chinese cabbage
1 teaspoon Cajun seasoning	1 tablespoon avocado oil
1 tablespoon coconut oil	1 teaspoon sesame seeds

1. Sprinkle the chopped chicken with the Cajun seasoning. 2. Set your Instant Pot to Sauté and heat the coconut oil. Add the chicken and cook for 10 minutes, stirring occasionally. 3. When the chicken is cooked, transfer to a salad bowl. Add the cabbage, avocado oil, and sesame seeds and gently toss to combine. Serve immediately.

Per Serving:

calories: 207 | fat: 10.8g | protein: 25.3g | carbs: 0.6g | net carbs: 0.2g | fiber: 0.4g

Cheddar Cauliflower Rice

Prep time: 3 minutes | Cook time: 1 minute | Serves 4

1 head fresh cauliflower, chopped into florets	1 cup shredded sharp Cheddar cheese
1 cup water	½ teaspoon salt
3 tablespoons butter	¼ teaspoon pepper
1 tablespoon heavy cream	¼ teaspoon garlic powder

1. Place cauliflower in steamer basket. Pour water into Instant Pot and lower steamer rack into pot. Click lid closed. Press the Steam button and adjust time for 1 minute. When timer beeps, quick-release the pressure. 2. Remove steamer basket and place cauliflower in food processor. Pulse until cauliflower is broken into small pearls. Place cauliflower into large bowl, and add remaining ingredients. Gently fold until fully combined.

Per Serving:

calories: 241 | fat: 18g | protein: 10g | carbs: 8g | net carbs: 5g | fiber: 3g

7-Layer Dip

Prep time: 10 minutes | Cook time: 35 minutes | Serves 6

Cashew Sour Cream
1 cup raw whole cashews, soaked in water to cover for 1 to 2 hours and then drained
½ cup avocado oil
½ cup water
¼ cup fresh lemon juice
2 tablespoons nutritional yeast
1 teaspoon fine sea salt
Beans
½ cup dried black beans
2 cups water
½ teaspoon fine sea salt
½ teaspoon chili powder
¼ teaspoon garlic powder
½ cup grape or cherry tomatoes, halved
1 avocado, diced
¼ cup chopped yellow onion
1 jalapeño chile, sliced
2 tablespoons chopped cilantro
6 ounces baked corn tortilla chips
1 English cucumber, sliced
2 carrots, sliced
6 celery stalks, cut into sticks

1. To make the cashew sour cream: In a blender, combine the cashews, oil, water, lemon juice, nutritional yeast, and salt. Blend on high speed, stopping to scrape down the sides of the container as needed, for about 2 minutes, until very smooth. (The sour cream can be made in advance and stored in an airtight container in the refrigerator for up to 5 days.) 2. To make the beans: Pour 1 cup water into the Instant Pot. In a 1½-quart stainless-steel bowl, combine the beans, the 2 cups water, and salt and stir to dissolve the salt. Place the bowl on a long-handled silicone steam rack, then, holding the handles of the steam rack, lower it into the Instant Pot. (If you don't have the long-handled rack, use the wire metal steam rack and a homemade sling) 3. Secure the lid and set the Pressure Release to Sealing. Select the Bean/Chili, Pressure Cook, or Manual setting and set the cooking time for 25 minutes at high pressure. (The pot will take about 10 minutes to come up to pressure before the cooking program begins.) 4. When the cooking program ends, let the pressure release naturally for at least 20 minutes, then move the Pressure Release to Venting to release any remaining steam. 5. Place a colander over a bowl. Open the pot and, wearing heat-resistant mitts, lift out the inner pot and drain the beans in the colander. Transfer the liquid captured in the bowl to a measuring cup, and pour the beans into the bowl. Add ¼ cup of the cooking liquid to the beans and, using a potato masher or fork, mash the beans to your desired consistency, adding more cooking liquid as needed. Stir in the chili powder and garlic powder. 6. Using a rubber spatula, spread the black beans in an even layer in a clear-glass serving dish. Spread the cashew sour cream in an even layer on top of the beans. Add layers of the tomatoes, avocado, onion, jalapeño, and cilantro. (At this point, you can cover and refrigerate the assembled dip for up to 1 day.) Serve accompanied with the tortilla chips, cucumber, carrots, and celery on the side.
Per Serving:
calories: 259 | fat: 8g | protein: 8g | carbs: 41g | sugars: 3g | fiber: 8g | sodium: 811mg

Parmesan Zucchini Fries

Prep time: 15 minutes | Cook time: 5 minutes | Serves 4

1 zucchini
1 ounce (28 g) Parmesan, grated
1 tablespoon almond flour
½ teaspoon Italian seasoning
1 tablespoon coconut oil

1. Trim the zucchini and cut it into the French fries. 2. Then sprinkle them with grated Parmesan, almond flour, and Italian seasoning. 3. Put coconut oil in the instant pot and melt it on Sauté mode. 4. Put the zucchini in the hot oil in one layer and cook for 2 minutes from each side or until they are golden brown. 5. Dry the zucchini fries with paper towels.
Per Serving:
calories: 102 | fat: 9g | protein: 4g | carbs: 3g | net carbs: 2g | fiber: 1g

Lemon Artichokes

Prep time: 5 minutes | Cook time: 5 to 15 minutes | Serves 4

4 artichokes
1 cup water
2 tablespoons lemon juice
1 teaspoon salt

1. Wash and trim artichokes by cutting off the stems flush with the bottoms of the artichokes and by cutting ¾–1 inch off the tops. Stand upright in the bottom of the inner pot of the Instant Pot. 2. Pour water, lemon juice, and salt over artichokes. 3. Secure the lid and make sure the vent is set to sealing. On Manual, set the Instant Pot for 15 minutes for large artichokes, 10 minutes for medium artichokes, or 5 minutes for small artichokes. 4. When cook time is up, perform a quick release by releasing the pressure manually.
Per Serving:
calories: 60 | fat: 0g | protein: 4g | carbs: 13g | sugars: 1g | fiber: 6g | sodium: 397mg

Roasted Garlic Bulbs

Prep time: 2 minutes | Cook time: 25 minutes | Serves 4

4 bulbs garlic
1 tablespoon avocado oil
1 teaspoon salt
Pinch of black pepper
1 cup water

1. Slice the pointy tops off the bulbs of garlic to expose the cloves. 2. Drizzle the avocado oil on top of the garlic and sprinkle with the salt and pepper. 3. Place the bulbs in the steamer basket, cut-side up. Alternatively, you may place them on a piece of aluminum foil with the sides pulled up and resting on top of the trivet. Place the steamer basket in the pot. 4. Close the lid and seal the vent. Cook on High Pressure for 25 minutes. Quick release the steam. 5. Let the garlic cool completely before removing the bulbs from the pot. 6. Hold the stem end (bottom) of the bulb and squeeze out all the garlic. Mash the cloves with a fork to make a paste.
Per Serving:
calories: 44 | fat: 5g | protein: 0g | carbs: 1g | net carbs: 1g | fiber: 0g

Crispy Brussels Sprouts with Bacon

Prep time: 5 minutes | Cook time: 10 minutes | Serves 4

½ pound (227 g) bacon
1 pound (454 g) Brussels sprouts
4 tablespoons butter
1 teaspoon salt
½ teaspoon pepper
½ cup water

1. Press the Sauté button and press the Adjust button to lower heat to Less. Add bacon to Instant Pot and fry for 3 to 5 minutes or until fat begins to render. Press the Cancel button. 2. Press the Sauté button,

with heat set to Normal, and continue frying bacon until crispy. While bacon is frying, wash Brussels sprouts and remove damaged outer leaves. Cut in half or quarters. 3. When bacon is done, remove and set aside. Add Brussels sprouts to hot bacon grease and add butter. Sprinkle with salt and pepper. Sauté for 8 to 10 minutes until caramelized and crispy, adding a few tablespoons of water at a time as needed to deglaze pan. Serve warm.

Per Serving:
calories: 387 | fat: 32g | protein: 11g | carbs: 11g | net carbs: 7g | fiber: 4g

Sesame Mushrooms

Prep time: 2 minutes | Cook time: 10 minutes | Serves 6

3 tablespoons sesame oil
¾ pound (340 g) small button mushrooms
1 teaspoon minced garlic
½ teaspoon smoked paprika
½ teaspoon cayenne pepper
Salt and ground black pepper, to taste

1. Set your Instant Pot to Sauté and heat the sesame oil. 2. Add the mushrooms and sauté for 4 minutes until just tender, stirring occasionally. 3. Add the remaining ingredients to the Instant Pot and stir to mix well. 4. Lock the lid. Select the Manual mode and set the cooking time for 5 minutes at High Pressure. 5. When the timer beeps, perform a quick pressure release. Carefully remove the lid. 6. Serve warm.

Per Serving:
calories: 77 | fat: 7.6g | protein: 1.9g | carbs: 1.8g | net carbs: 1.0g | fiber: 0.8g

Candied Pecans

Prep time: 5 minutes | Cook time: 20 minutes | Serves 10

4 cups raw pecans
1½ teaspoons liquid stevia
½ cup plus 1 tablespoon water, divided
1 teaspoon vanilla extract
1 teaspoon cinnamon
¼ teaspoon nutmeg
⅛ teaspoon ground ginger
⅛ teaspoon sea salt

1. Place the raw pecans, liquid stevia, 1 tablespoon water, vanilla, cinnamon, nutmeg, ground ginger, and sea salt into the inner pot of the Instant Pot. 2. Press the Sauté button on the Instant Pot and sauté the pecans and other ingredients until the pecans are soft. 3. Pour in the ½ cup water and secure the lid to the locked position. Set the vent to sealing. 4. Press Manual and set the Instant Pot for 15 minutes. 5. Preheat the oven to 350°F. 6. When cooking time is up, turn off the Instant Pot, then do a quick release. 7. Spread the pecans onto a greased, lined baking sheet. 8. Bake the pecans for 5 minutes or less in the oven, checking on them frequently so they do not burn.

Per Serving:
calories: 275 | fat: 28g | protein: 4g | carbs: 6g | sugars: 2g | fiber: 4g | sodium: 20mg

Cheese Stuffed Mushrooms

Prep time: 15 minutes | Cook time: 8 minutes | Serves 4

1 cup cremini mushroom caps
1 tablespoon chopped scallions
1 tablespoon chopped chives
1 teaspoon cream cheese
1 teaspoon sour cream
1 ounce (28 g) Monterey Jack cheese, shredded
1 teaspoon butter, softened
½ teaspoon smoked paprika
1 cup water, for cooking

1. Trim the mushroom caps if needed and wash them well. 2. After this, in the mixing bowl, mix up scallions, chives, cream cheese, sour cream, butter, and smoked paprika. 3. Then fill the mushroom caps with the cream cheese mixture and top with shredded Monterey Jack cheese. 4. Pour water and insert the trivet in the instant pot. 5. Arrange the stuffed mushrooms caps on the trivet and close the lid. 6. Cook the meal on Manual (High Pressure) for 8 minutes. 7. Then make a quick pressure release.

Per Serving:
calories: 45 | fat: 4g | protein: 3g | carbs: 1g | net carbs: 1g | fiber: 0g

Herbed Mushrooms

Prep time: 5 minutes | Cook time: 10 minutes | Serves 4

2 tablespoons butter
2 cloves garlic, minced
20 ounces (567 g) button mushrooms
1 tablespoon coconut aminos
1 teaspoon dried rosemary
1 teaspoon dried basil
1 teaspoon dried sage
1 bay leaf
Sea salt, to taste
½ teaspoon freshly ground black pepper
½ cup chicken broth
½ cup water
1 tablespoon roughly chopped fresh parsley leaves, for garnish

1. Set your Instant Pot to Sauté and melt the butter. 2. Add the garlic and mushrooms and sauté for 3 to 4 minutes until the garlic is fragrant. 3. Add the remaining ingredients except the parsley to the Instant Pot and stir well. 4. Lock the lid. Select the Manual mode and set the cooking time for 5 minutes at High Pressure. 5. When the timer beeps, perform a quick pressure release. Carefully open the lid. 6. Remove the mushrooms from the pot to a platter. Serve garnished with the fresh parsley leaves.

Per Serving:
calories: 94 | fat: 6.8g | protein: 5.7g | carbs: 5.3g | net carbs: 3.6g | fiber: 1.7g

Chapter 2   Breakfasts

Southwestern Egg Casserole

Prep time: 10 minutes | Cook time: 20 minutes | Serves 12

1 cup water
2½ cups egg substitute
½ cup flour
1 teaspoon baking powder
⅛ teaspoon salt
⅛ teaspoon pepper
2 cups fat-free cottage cheese
1½ cups shredded 75%-less-fat sharp cheddar cheese
¼ cup no-trans-fat tub margarine, melted
2 (4-ounce) cans chopped green chilies

1. Place the steaming rack into the bottom of the inner pot and pour in 1 cup of water. 2. Grease a round springform pan that will fit into the inner pot of the Instant Pot. 3. Combine the egg substitute, flour, baking powder, salt and pepper in a mixing bowl. It will be lumpy. 4. Stir in the cheese, margarine, and green chilies then pour into the springform pan. 5. Place the springform pan onto the steaming rack, close the lid, and secure to the locking position. Be sure the vent is turned to sealing. Set for 20 minutes on Manual at high pressure. 6. Let the pressure release naturally. 7. Carefully remove the springform pan with the handles of the steaming rack and allow to stand 10 minutes before cutting and serving.

Per Serving:
calories: 130 | fat: 4g | protein: 14g | carbs: 9g | sugars: 1g | fiber: 1g | sodium: 450mg

Blackberry Vanilla Cake

Prep time: 10 minutes | Cook time: 25 minutes | Serves 8

1 cup almond flour
2 eggs
½ cup erythritol
2 teaspoons vanilla extract
1 cup blackberries
4 tablespoons melted butter
¼ cup heavy cream
½ teaspoon baking powder
1 cup water

1. In large bowl, mix all ingredients except water. Pour into 7-inch round cake pan or divide into two 4-inch pans, if needed. Cover with foil. 2. Pour water into Instant Pot and place steam rack in bottom. Place pan on steam rack and click lid closed. Press the Cake button and press the Adjust button to set heat to Less. Set time for 25 minutes. 3. When timer beeps, allow a 15-minute natural release then quick-release the remaining pressure. Let cool completely.

Per Serving:
calories: 174 | fat: 15g | protein: 10g | carbs: 17g | net carbs: 15g | fiber: 2g

Poached Eggs

Prep time: 5 minutes | Cook time: 5 minutes | Serves 4

Nonstick cooking spray   4 large eggs

1. Lightly spray 4 cups of a 7-count silicone egg bite mold with nonstick cooking spray. Crack each egg into a sprayed cup. 2. Pour 1 cup of water into the electric pressure cooker. Place the egg bite mold on the wire rack and carefully lower it into the pot. 3. Close and lock the lid of the pressure cooker. Set the valve to sealing. 4. Cook on high pressure for 5 minutes. 5. When the cooking is complete, hit Cancel and quick release the pressure. 6. Once the pin drops, unlock and remove the lid. 7. Run a small rubber spatula or spoon around each egg and carefully remove it from the mold. The white should be cooked, but the yolk should be runny. 8. Serve immediately.

Per Serving:
calories: 78 | fat: 5g | protein: 6g | carbs: 1g | sugars: 0g | fiber: 0g | sodium: 62mg

Fluffy Vanilla Pancake

Prep time: 5 minutes | Cook time: 50 minutes | Serves 6

3 eggs, beaten
½ cup coconut flour
¼ cup heavy cream
¼ cup almond flour
3 tablespoons Swerve
1 teaspoon vanilla extract
1 teaspoon baking powder
Cooking spray

1. In a bowl, stir together the eggs, coconut flour, heavy cream, almond flour, Swerve and vanilla extract. Whisk in the baking powder until smooth. 2. Spritz the bottom and sides of Instant Pot with cooking spray. Place the batter in the pot. 3. Set the lid in place. Select the Manual mode and set the cooking time for 50 minutes on Low Pressure. Once the timer goes off, perform a natural pressure release for 5 minutes, then release any remaining pressure. Carefully open the lid. 4. Let the pancake rest in the pot for 5 minutes before serving.

Per Serving:
calories: 121 | fat: 7.2g | protein: 5.3g | carbs: 9.4g | net carbs: 4.8g | fiber: 4.6g

Greek Frittata with Peppers, Kale, and Feta

Prep time: 5 minutes | Cook time: 45 minutes | Serves 6

8 large eggs
½ cup plain 2 percent Greek yogurt
Fine sea salt
Freshly ground black pepper
2 cups firmly packed finely shredded kale or baby kale leaves
One 12-ounce jar roasted red peppers, drained and cut into ¼ by 2-inch strips
2 green onions, white and green parts, thinly sliced
1 tablespoon chopped fresh dill
⅓ cup crumbled feta cheese
6 cups loosely packed mixed baby greens
¾ cup cherry or grape tomatoes, halved
2 tablespoons extra-virgin olive oil

1. Pour 1½ cups water into the Instant Pot. Lightly butter a 7-cup round heatproof glass dish or coat with nonstick cooking spray. 2. In a bowl, whisk together the eggs, yogurt, ¼ teaspoon salt, and ¼ teaspoon pepper until well blended, then stir in the kale, roasted peppers, green onions, dill, and feta cheese. 3. Pour the egg mixture into the prepared dish and cover tightly with aluminum foil. Place the dish on a long-handled silicone steam rack, then, holding the handles of the steam rack, lower it into the Instant Pot. (If you don't have the long-handled rack, use the wire metal steam rack and a homemade sling) 4. Secure the lid and set the Pressure Release to Sealing. Select the Pressure Cook or Manual setting and set the cooking time for 30 minutes at high pressure. (The pot will take about 15 minutes to come up to pressure before the cooking program begins.) 5. When the cooking program ends, let the pressure release naturally for 10 minutes, then move the Pressure Release to Venting to release any remaining steam. Open the pot and let the frittata sit for a minute

or two, until it deflates and settles into its dish. Then, wearing heat-resistant mitts, grasp the handles of the steam rack and lift it out of the pot. Uncover the dish, taking care not to get burned by the steam or to drip condensation onto the frittata. Let the frittata sit for 10 minutes, giving it time to reabsorb any liquid and set up. 6. In a medium bowl, toss together the mixed greens, tomatoes, and olive oil. Taste and adjust the seasoning with salt and pepper, if needed. 7. Cut the frittata into six wedges and serve warm, with the salad alongside.

Per Serving:

calories: 227 | fat: 13g | protein: 18g | carbs: 8g | sugars: 2g | fiber: 1g | sodium: 153mg

Cranberry Almond Grits

Prep time: 10 minutes | Cook time: 10 minutes | Serves 5

¾ cup stone-ground grits or polenta (not instant)
½ cup unsweetened dried cranberries
Pinch kosher salt

1 tablespoon unsalted butter or ghee (optional)
1 tablespoon half-and-half
¼ cup sliced almonds, toasted

1. In the electric pressure cooker, stir together the grits, cranberries, salt, and 3 cups of water. 2. Close and lock the lid. Set the valve to sealing. 3. Cook on high pressure for 10 minutes. 4. When the cooking is complete, hit Cancel and quick release the pressure. 5. Once the pin drops, unlock and remove the lid. 6. Add the butter (if using) and half-and-half. Stir until the mixture is creamy, adding more half-and-half if necessary. 7. Spoon into serving bowls and sprinkle with almonds.

Per Serving:

calories: 218 | fat: 10g | protein: 5g | carbs: 32g | sugars: 7g | fiber: 4g | sodium: 28mg

Tropical Steel Cut Oats

Prep time: 5 minutes | Cook time: 5 minutes | Serves 4

1 cup steel cut oats
1 cup unsweetened almond milk
2 cups coconut water or water
¾ cup frozen chopped peaches
¾ cup frozen mango chunks

1 (2-inch) vanilla bean, scraped (seeds and pod)
Ground cinnamon
¼ cup chopped unsalted macadamia nuts

1. In the electric pressure cooker, combine the oats, almond milk, coconut water, peaches, mango chunks, and vanilla bean seeds and pod. Stir well. 2. Close and lock the lid of the pressure cooker. Set the valve to sealing. 3. Cook on high pressure for 5 minutes. 4. When the cooking is complete, allow the pressure to release naturally for 10 minutes, then quick release any remaining pressure. Hit Cancel. 5. Once the pin drops, unlock and remove the lid. 6. Discard the vanilla bean pod and stir well. 7. Spoon the oats into 4 bowls. Top each serving with a sprinkle of cinnamon and 1 tablespoon of the macadamia nuts.

Per Serving:

calories: 127 | fat: 7g | protein: 2g | carbs: 14g | sugars: 8g | fiber: 3g | sodium: 167mg

Breakfast Burrito Bowls

Prep time: 10 minutes | Cook time: 15 minutes | Serves 4

6 eggs
3 tablespoons melted butter
1 teaspoon salt
¼ teaspoon pepper
½ pound (227 g) cooked breakfast sausage

½ cup shredded sharp Cheddar cheese
½ cup salsa
½ cup sour cream
1 avocado, cubed
¼ cup diced green onion

1. In large bowl, mix eggs, melted butter, salt, and pepper. Press the Sauté button and then press the Adjust button to set the heat to Less. 2. Add eggs to Instant Pot and cook for 5 to 7 minutes while gently moving with rubber spatula. When eggs begin to firm up, add cooked breakfast sausage and cheese and continue to cook until eggs are fully cooked. Press the Cancel button. 3. Divide eggs into four bowls and top with salsa, sour cream, avocado, and green onion.

Per Serving:

calories: 613 | fat: 50g | protein: 23g | carbs: 10g | net carbs: 6g | fiber: 4g

Bell Peppers Stuffed with Eggs

Prep time: 5 minutes | Cook time: 14 minutes | Serves 2

2 eggs, beaten
1 tablespoon coconut cream
¼ teaspoon dried oregano
¼ teaspoon salt

1 large bell pepper, cut into halves and deseeded
1 cup water

1. In a bowl, stir together the eggs, coconut cream, oregano and salt. 2. Pour the egg mixture in the pepper halves. 3. Pour the water and insert the trivet in the Instant Pot. Put the stuffed pepper halves on the trivet. 4. Set the lid in place. Select the Manual mode and set the cooking time for 14 minutes on High Pressure. When the timer goes off, do a quick pressure release. Carefully open the lid. 5. Serve warm.

Per Serving:

calories: 99 | fat: 6.2g | protein: 6.4g | carbs: 5.3g | net carbs: 4.2g | fiber: 1.2g

Blueberry Almond Cereal

Prep time: 5 minutes | Cook time: 2 minutes | Serves 4

⅓ cup crushed roasted almonds
¼ cup almond flour
¼ cup unsalted butter, softened
¼ cup vanilla-flavored egg

white protein powder
2 tablespoons Swerve
1 teaspoon blueberry extract
1 teaspoon ground cinnamon

1. Add all the ingredients to the Instant Pot and stir to combine. 2. Lock the lid, select the Manual mode and set the cooking time for 2 minutes on High Pressure. When the timer goes off, do a natural pressure release for 10 minutes, then release any remaining pressure. Open the lid. 3. Stir well and pour the mixture onto a sheet lined with parchment paper to cool. It will be crispy when completely cool. 4. Serve the cereal in bowls.

Per Serving:

calories: 282 | fat: 24.0g | protein: 10.1g | carbs: 6.9g | net carbs: 2.8g | fiber: 4.1g

Potato-Bacon Gratin

Prep time: 20 minutes | Cook time: 40 minutes | Serves 8

1 tablespoon olive oil
6-ounces bag fresh spinach
1 clove garlic, minced
4 large potatoes, peeled or unpeeled, divided
6-ounces Canadian bacon

slices, divided
5-ounces reduced-fat grated Swiss cheddar, divided
1 cup lower-sodium, lower-fat chicken broth

1. Set the Instant Pot to Sauté and pour in the olive oil. Cook the spinach and garlic in olive oil just until spinach is wilted (5 minutes or less). Turn off the instant pot. 2. Cut potatoes into thin slices about ¼" thick. 3. In a springform pan that will fit into the inner pot of your Instant Pot, spray it with nonstick spray then layer ⅓ the potatoes, half the bacon, ⅓ the cheese, and half the wilted spinach. 4. Repeat layers ending with potatoes. Reserve ⅓ cheese for later. 5. Pour chicken broth over all. 6. Wipe the bottom of your Instant Pot to soak up any remaining oil, then add in 2 cups of water and the steaming rack. Place the springform pan on top. 7. Close the lid and secure to the locking position. Be sure the vent is turned to sealing. Set for 35 minutes on Manual at high pressure. 8. Perform a quick release. 9. Top with the remaining cheese, then allow to stand 10 minutes before removing from the Instant Pot, cutting and serving.

Per Serving:
calories: 220 | fat: 7g | protein: 14g | carbs: 28g | sugars: 2g | fiber: 3g | sodium: 415mg

Cauliflower and Cheese Quiche

Prep time: 10 minutes | Cook time: 10 minutes | Serves 2

1 cup chopped cauliflower
¼ cup shredded Cheddar cheese
5 eggs, beaten

1 teaspoon butter
1 teaspoon dried oregano
1 cup water

1. Grease the instant pot baking pan with butter from inside. 2. Pour water in the instant pot. 3. Sprinkle the cauliflower with dried oregano and put it in the prepared baking pan. Flatten the vegetables gently. 4. After this, add eggs and stir the vegetables. 5. Top the quiche with shredded cheese and transfer it in the instant pot. Close and seal the lid. Cook the quiche on Manual mode (High Pressure) for 10 minutes. Make a quick pressure release.

Per Serving:
calories: 246 | fat: 18g | protein: 18g | carbs: 4g | net carbs: 2g | fiber: 2g

Coddled Huevos Rancheros

Prep time: 5 minutes | Cook time: 10 minutes | Serves 2

2 teaspoons unsalted butter
4 large eggs
1 cup drained cooked black beans, or two-thirds 15-ounce can black beans, rinsed and drained

Two 7-inch corn or whole-wheat tortillas, warmed
½ cup chunky tomato salsa (such as Pace brand)
2 cups shredded romaine lettuce

1 tablespoon chopped fresh cilantro

2 tablespoons grated Cotija cheese

1. Pour 1 cup water into the Instant Pot and place a long-handled silicone steam rack into the pot. (If you don't have the long-handled rack, use the wire metal steam rack and a homemade sling) 2. Coat each of four 4-ounce ramekins with ½ teaspoon butter. Crack an egg into each ramekin. Place the ramekins on the steam rack in the pot. 3. Secure the lid and set the Pressure Release to Sealing. Select the Steam setting and set the cooking time for 3 minutes at low pressure. (The pot will take about 5 minutes to come up to pressure before the cooking program begins.) 4. While the eggs are cooking, in a small saucepan over low heat, warm the beans for about 5 minutes, stirring occasionally. Cover the saucepan and remove from the heat. (Alternatively, warm the beans in a covered bowl in a microwave for 1 minute. Leave the beans covered until ready to serve.) 5. When the cooking program ends, let the pressure release naturally for 5 minutes, then move the Pressure Release to Venting to release any remaining steam. Open the pot and, wearing heat-resistant mitts, grasp the handles of the steam rack and carefully lift it out of the pot. 6. Place a warmed tortilla on each plate and spoon ½ cup of the beans onto each tortilla. Run a knife around the inside edge of each ramekin to loosen the egg and unmold two eggs onto the beans on each tortilla. Spoon the salsa over the eggs and top with the lettuce, cilantro, and cheese. Serve right away.

Per Serving:
calorie: 112 | fat: 8g | protein: 8g | carbs: 3g | sugars: 0g | fiber: 0g | sodium: 297mg

Cynthia's Yogurt

Prep time: 10 minutes | Cook time: 8 hours | Serves 16

1 gallon low-fat milk
¼ cup low-fat plain yogurt with

active cultures

1. Pour milk into the inner pot of the Instant Pot. 2. Lock lid, move vent to sealing, and press the yogurt button. Press Adjust till it reads "boil." 3. When boil cycle is complete (about 1 hour), check the temperature. It should be at 185°F. If it's not, use the Sauté function to warm to 185. 4. After it reaches 185°F, unplug Instant Pot, remove inner pot, and cool. You can place on cooling rack and let it slowly cool. If in a hurry, submerge the base of the pot in cool water. Cool milk to 110°F. 5. When mixture reaches 110, stir in the ¼ cup of yogurt. Lock the lid in place and move vent to sealing. 6. Press Yogurt. Use the Adjust button until the screen says 8:00. This will now incubate for 8 hours. 7. After 8 hours (when the cycle is finished), chill yogurt, or go immediately to straining in step 8. 8. After chilling, or following the 8 hours, strain the yogurt using a nut milk bag. This will give it the consistency of Greek yogurt.

Per Serving:
calories: 141 | fat: 5g | protein: 10g | carbs: 14g | sugars: 1g | fiber: 0g | sodium: 145mg

Keto Cabbage Hash Browns

Prep time: 5 minutes | Cook time: 8 minutes | Serves 3

1 cup shredded white cabbage
3 eggs, beaten
½ teaspoon ground nutmeg
½ teaspoon salt

½ teaspoon onion powder
½ zucchini, grated
1 tablespoon coconut oil

1. In a bowl, stir together all the ingredients, except for the coconut oil. Form the cabbage mixture into medium hash browns. 2. Press the Sauté button on the Instant Pot and heat the coconut oil. 3. Place the hash browns in the hot coconut oil. Cook for 4 minutes on each side, or until lightly browned. 4. Transfer the hash browns to a plate and serve warm.

Per Serving:
calories: 115 | fat: 9.0g | protein: 6.4g | carbs: 3.2g | net carbs: 2.1g | fiber: 1.1g

Breakfast Farro with Berries and Walnuts

Prep time: 8 minutes | Cook time: 10 minutes | Serves 6

1 cup farro, rinsed and drained	1 tablespoon pure maple syrup
1 cup unsweetened almond milk	1½ cups fresh blueberries, raspberries, or strawberries (or a combination)
¼ teaspoon kosher salt	
½ teaspoon pure vanilla extract	6 tablespoons chopped walnuts
1 teaspoon ground cinnamon	

1. In the electric pressure cooker, combine the farro, almond milk, 1 cup of water, salt, vanilla, cinnamon, and maple syrup. 2. Close and lock the lid. Set the valve to sealing. 3. Cook on high pressure for 10 minutes. 4. When the cooking is complete, allow the pressure to release naturally for 10 minutes, then quick release any remaining pressure. Hit Cancel. 5. Once the pin drops, unlock and remove the lid. 6. Stir the farro. Spoon into bowls and top each serving with ¼ cup of berries and 1 tablespoon of walnuts.

Per Serving:
calorie: 189 | fat: 5g | protein: 5g | carbs: 32g | sugars: 6g | fiber: 3g | sodium: 111mg

Mini Spinach Quiche

Prep time: 5 minutes | Cook time: 15 minutes | Serves 1

2 eggs	¼ cup chopped fresh spinach
1 tablespoon heavy cream	½ teaspoon salt
1 tablespoon diced green pepper	¼ teaspoon pepper
1 tablespoon diced red onion	1 cup water

1. In medium bowl whisk together all ingredients except water. Pour into 4-inch ramekin. Generally, if the ramekin is oven-safe, it is also safe to use in pressure cooking. 2. Pour water into Instant Pot. Place steam rack into pot. Carefully place ramekin onto steam rack. Click lid closed. Press the Manual button and set time for 15 minutes. When timer beeps, quick-release the pressure. Serve warm.

Per Serving:
calories: 201 | fat: 14g | protein: 13g | carbs: 3g | net carbs: 2g | fiber: 1g

Cheddar Broccoli Egg Bites

Prep time: 10 minutes | Cook time: 10 minutes | Serves 7

5 eggs, beaten	⅛ teaspoon black pepper
3 tablespoons heavy cream	1 ounce (28 g) finely chopped broccoli
⅛ teaspoon salt	

1 ounce (28 g) shredded Cheddar cheese ½ cup water

1. In a blender, combine the eggs, heavy cream, salt and pepper and pulse until smooth. 2. Divide the chopped broccoli among the egg cups equally. Pour the egg mixture on top of the broccoli, filling the cups about three-fourths of the way full. Sprinkle the Cheddar cheese on top of each cup. 3. Cover the egg cups tightly with aluminum foil. 4. Pour the water and insert the trivet in the Instant Pot. Put the egg cups on the trivet. 5. Lock the lid. Select the Manual mode and set the cooking time for 10 minutes on High Pressure. Once the timer goes off, perform a natural pressure release for 5 minutes, then release any remaining pressure. Carefully open the lid. 6. Serve immediately.

Per Serving:
calories: 89 | fat: 7.0g | protein: 5.8g | carbs: 0.7g | net carbs: 0.5g | fiber: 0.2g

Parmesan Baked Eggs

Prep time: 5 minutes | Cook time: 10 minutes | Serves 1

1 tablespoon butter, cut into small pieces	2 tablespoons grated Parmesan cheese
2 tablespoons keto-friendly low-carb Marinara sauce	¼ teaspoon Italian seasoning
3 eggs	1 cup water

1. Place the butter pieces on the bottom of the oven-safe bowl. Spread the marinara sauce over the butter. Crack the eggs on top of the marinara sauce and top with the cheese and Italian seasoning. 2. Cover the bowl with aluminum foil. Pour the water and insert the trivet in the Instant Pot. Put the bowl on the trivet. 3. Set the lid in place. Select the Manual mode and set the cooking time for 10 minutes on Low Pressure. When the timer goes off, do a quick pressure release. Carefully open the lid. 4. Let the eggs cool for 5 minutes before serving.

Per Serving:
calories: 375 | fat: 29.6g | protein: 23.0g | carbs: 2.4g | net carbs: 2.0g | fiber: 0.4g

Bacon Cheddar Bites

Prep time: 15 minutes | Cook time: 3 minutes | Serves 2

2 tablespoons coconut flour	2 bacon slices, cooked
½ cup shredded Cheddar cheese	½ teaspoon dried parsley
2 teaspoons coconut cream	1 cup water, for cooking

1. In the mixing bowl, mix up coconut flour, Cheddar cheese, coconut cream, and dried parsley. 2. Then chop the cooked bacon and add it in the mixture. 3. Stir it well. 4. Pour water and insert the trivet in the instant pot. 5. Line the trivet with baking paper. 6. After this, make the small balls (bites) from the cheese mixture and put them on the prepared trivet. 7. Cook the meal for 3 minutes on Manual mode (High Pressure). 8. Then make a quick pressure release and cool the cooked meal well.

Per Serving:
calories: 260 | fat: 19g | protein: 15g | carbs: 6g | net carbs: 3g | fiber: 3g

Mexican Breakfast Beef Chili

Prep time: 5 minutes | Cook time: 45 minutes | Serves 4

2 tablespoons coconut oil
1 pound (454 g) ground grass-fed beef
1 (14-ounce / 397-g) can sugar-free or low-sugar diced tomatoes
½ cup shredded full-fat Cheddar cheese (optional)

1 teaspoon hot sauce
½ teaspoon chili powder
½ teaspoon crushed red pepper
½ teaspoon ground cumin
½ teaspoon kosher salt
½ teaspoon freshly ground black pepper

1. Set the Instant Pot to Sauté and melt the oil. 2. Pour in ½ cup of filtered water, then add the beef, tomatoes, cheese, hot sauce, chili powder, red pepper, cumin, salt, and black pepper to the Instant Pot, stirring thoroughly. 3. Close the lid, set the pressure release to Sealing, and hit Cancel to stop the current program. Select Manual, set the Instant Pot to 45 minutes on High Pressure and let cook. 4. Once cooked, let the pressure naturally disperse from the Instant Pot for about 10 minutes, then carefully switch the pressure release to Venting. 5. Open the Instant Pot, serve, and enjoy!

Per Serving:
calories: 351 | fat: 19g | protein: 39g | carbs: 6g | net carbs: 4g | fiber: 2g

Spinach and Cheese Frittata

Prep time: 5 minutes | Cook time: 20 minutes | Serves 4 to 5

6 eggs
1 cup chopped spinach
1 cup shredded full-fat Cheddar cheese
1 cup shredded full-fat Monterey Jack cheese (optional)
2 tablespoons coconut oil

1 cup chopped bell peppers
½ teaspoon dried parsley
½ teaspoon dried basil
½ teaspoon ground turmeric
½ teaspoon freshly ground black pepper
½ teaspoon kosher salt

1. Pour 1 cup of filtered water into the inner pot of the Instant Pot, then insert the trivet. 2. In a large bowl, combine the eggs, spinach, Cheddar cheese, Monterey Jack cheese, coconut oil, bell peppers, parsley, basil, turmeric, black pepper, and salt, and stir thoroughly. Transfer this mixture into a well-greased Instant Pot-friendly dish. 3. Using a sling if desired, place the dish onto the trivet, and cover loosely with aluminum foil. Close the lid, set the pressure release to Sealing, and select Manual. Set the Instant Pot to 20 minutes on High Pressure, and let cook. 4. Once cooked, let the pressure naturally disperse from the Instant Pot for about 10 minutes, then carefully switch the pressure release to Venting. 5. Open the Instant Pot, serve, and enjoy!

Per Serving:
calories: 310 | fat: 25g | protein: 18g | carbs: 3g | net carbs: 2g | fiber: 1g

Nutty "Oatmeal"

Prep time: 5 minutes | Cook time: 4 minutes | Serves 4

2 tablespoons coconut oil
1 cup full-fat coconut milk

1 cup heavy whipping cream
½ cup macadamia nuts

½ cup chopped pecans
⅓ cup Swerve, or more to taste
¼ cup unsweetened coconut flakes

2 tablespoons chopped hazelnuts
2 tablespoons chia seeds
½ teaspoon ground cinnamon

1. Before you get started, soak the chia seeds for about 5 to 10 minutes (can be up to 20, if desired) in 1 cup of filtered water. After soaking, set the Instant Pot to Sauté and add the coconut oil. Once melted, pour in the milk, whipping cream, and 1 cup of filtered water. Then add the macadamia nuts, pecans, Swerve, coconut flakes, hazelnuts, chia seeds, and cinnamon. Mix thoroughly inside the Instant Pot. 2. Close the lid, set the pressure release to Sealing, and hit Cancel to stop the current program. Select Manual, set the Instant Pot to 4 minutes on High Pressure, and let cook. 3. Once cooked, carefully switch the pressure release to Venting. 4. Open the Instant Pot, serve, and enjoy!

Per Serving:
calories: 506 | fat: 53g | protein: 6g | carbs: 11g | net carbs: 5g | fiber: 6g

Cinnamon Roll Fat Bombs

Prep time: 5 minutes | Cook time: 5 minutes | Serves 5 to 6

2 tablespoons coconut oil
2 cups raw coconut butter
1 cup sugar-free chocolate chips
1 cup heavy whipping cream

½ cup Swerve, or more to taste
½ teaspoon ground cinnamon, or more to taste
½ teaspoon vanilla extract

1. Set the Instant Pot to Sauté and melt the oil. 2. Add the butter, chocolate chips, whipping cream, Swerve, cinnamon, and vanilla to the Instant Pot and cook. Stir occasionally until the mixture reaches a smooth consistency. 3. Pour mixture into a silicone mini-muffin mold. 4. Freeze until firm. Serve, and enjoy!

Per Serving:
calories: 372 | fat: 32g | protein: 4g | carbs: 15g | net carbs: 8g | fiber: 7g

Pecan and Walnut Granola

Prep time: 10 minutes | Cook time: 2 minutes | Serves 12

2 cups chopped raw pecans
1¾ cups vanilla-flavored egg white protein powder
1¼ cups unsalted butter, softened
1 cup sunflower seeds

½ cup chopped raw walnuts
½ cup slivered almonds
½ cup sesame seeds
½ cup Swerve
1 teaspoon ground cinnamon
½ teaspoon sea salt

1. Add all the ingredients to the Instant Pot and stir to combine. 2. Lock the lid, select the Manual mode and set the cooking time for 2 minutes on High Pressure. When the timer goes off, do a natural pressure release for 10 minutes, then release any remaining pressure. Open the lid. 3. Stir well and pour the granola onto a sheet of parchment paper to cool. It will become crispy when completely cool. Serve the granola in bowls.

Per Serving:
calories: 491 | fat: 43.7g | protein: 17.1g | carbs: 8.9g | net carbs: 3.8g | fiber: 5.1g

Lettuce Wrapped Chicken Sandwich

Prep time: 10 minutes | Cook time: 15 minutes | Serves 4

1 tablespoon butter	½ teaspoon ground nutmeg
3 ounces (85 g) scallions, chopped	1 tablespoon coconut flour
2 cups ground chicken	1 teaspoon salt
	1 cup lettuce

1. Press the Sauté button on the Instant Pot and melt the butter. Add the chopped scallions, ground chicken and ground nutmeg to the pot and sauté for 4 minutes. Add the coconut flour and salt and continue to sauté for 10 minutes. 2. Fill the lettuce with the ground chicken and transfer it on the plate. Serve immediately.
Per Serving:
calories: 176 | fat: 8.5g | protein: 21.2g | carbs: 3.1g | net carbs: 1.5g | fiber: 1.6g

Traditional Porridge

Prep time: 5 minutes | Cook time: 4 minutes | Serves 4

2 tablespoons coconut oil	½ cup chopped cashews
1 cup full-fat coconut milk	½ cup chopped pecans
2 tablespoons blanched almond flour	½ teaspoon ground cinnamon
2 tablespoons sugar-free chocolate chips	½ teaspoon erythritol, or more to taste
1 cup heavy whipping cream	¼ cup unsweetened coconut flakes

1. Set the Instant Pot to Sauté and melt the coconut oil. 2. Pour in the coconut milk, 1 cup of filtered water, then combine and mix the flour, chocolate chips, whipping cream, cashews, pecans, cinnamon, erythritol, and coconut flakes, inside the Instant Pot. 3. Close the lid, set the pressure release to Sealing, and hit Cancel to stop the current program. Select Manual, set the Instant Pot to 4 minutes on High Pressure, and let cook. 4. Once cooked, perform a quick release by carefully switching the pressure valve to Venting. 5. Open the Instant Pot, serve, and enjoy!
Per Serving:
calories: 533 | fat: 51g | protein: 7g | carbs: 16g | net carbs: 11g | fiber: 5g

Kale and Egg Bake

Prep time: 10 minutes | Cook time: 10 minutes | Serves 2

½ cup chopped kale	1 teaspoon coconut oil, melted
3 eggs, beaten	¼ teaspoon ground black pepper
1 tablespoon organic almond milk	1 cup water, for cooking

1. In the mixing bowl, mix up chopped kale, eggs, almond milk, and ground black pepper. 2. Grease the ramekins with coconut oil. 3. Pour the kale-egg mixture in the ramekins and flatten it with the help of the spatula, if needed. 4. Pour water and insert the trivet in the instant pot. 5. Put the ramekins with egg mixture on the trivet and close the lid. 6. Cook the breakfast on Manual mode (High Pressure) for 10 minutes. Make a quick pressure release.
Per Serving:

calories: 126 | fat: 9g | protein: 9g | carbs: 3g | net carbs: 3g | fiber: 0g

Bacon Spaghetti Squash Fritters

Prep time: 20 minutes | Cook time: 15 minutes | Serves 4

½ cooked spaghetti squash	¼ teaspoon pepper
2 tablespoons cream cheese	1 stalk green onion, sliced
½ cup shredded whole-milk Mozzarella cheese	4 slices cooked bacon, crumbled
1 egg	2 tablespoons coconut oil
½ teaspoon salt	

1. Remove seeds from cooked squash and use fork to scrape strands out of shell. Place strands into cheesecloth or kitchen towel and squeeze to remove as much excess moisture as possible. 2. Place cream cheese and Mozzarella in small bowl and microwave for 45 seconds to melt together. Mix with spoon and place in large bowl. Add all ingredients except coconut oil to bowl. Mixture will be wet like batter. 3. Press the Sauté button and then press the Adjust button to set heat to Less. Add coconut oil to Instant Pot. When fully preheated, add 2 to 3 tablespoons of batter to pot to make a fritter. Let fry until firm and completely cooked through.
Per Serving:
calories: 202 | fat: 16g | protein: 9g | carbs: 2g | net carbs: 1g | fiber: 1g

Bacon and Spinach Eggs

Prep time: 5 minutes | Cook time: 9 minutes | Serves 4

2 tablespoons unsalted butter, divided	Pinch of black pepper
½ cup diced bacon	½ cup water
⅓ cup finely diced shallots	¼ cup heavy whipping cream
⅓ cup chopped spinach, leaves only	8 large eggs
Pinch of sea salt	1 tablespoon chopped fresh chives, for garnish

1. Set the Instant Pot on the Sauté mode and melt 1 tablespoon of the butter. Add the bacon to the pot and sauté for about 4 minutes, or until crispy. Using a slotted spoon, transfer the bacon bits to a bowl and set aside. 2. Add the remaining 1 tablespoon of the butter and shallots to the pot and sauté for about 2 minutes, or until tender. Add the spinach leaves and sauté for 1 minute, or until wilted. Season with sea salt and black pepper and stir. Transfer the spinach to a separate bowl and set aside. 3. Drain the oil from the pot into a bowl. Pour in the water and put the trivet inside. 4. With a paper towel, coat four ramekins with the bacon grease. In each ramekin, place 1 tablespoon of the heavy whipping cream, reserved bacon bits and sautéed spinach. Crack two eggs without breaking the yolks in each ramekin. Cover the ramekins with aluminum foil. Place two ramekins on the trivet and stack the other two on top. 5. Lock the lid. Select the Manual mode and set the cooking time for 2 minutes at Low Pressure. When the timer goes off, use a natural pressure release for 5 minutes, then release any remaining pressure. Carefully open the lid. 6. Carefully take out the ramekins and serve garnished with the chives.
Per Serving:
calories: 320 | fat: 25.8g | protein: 17.2g | carbs: 4.0g | net carbs: 3.9g | fiber: 0.1g

Cinnamon French Toast

Prep time: 10 minutes | Cook time: 20 minutes | Serves 8

3 eggs
2 cups low-fat milk
2 tablespoons maple syrup
15 drops liquid stevia
2 teaspoons vanilla extract
2 teaspoons cinnamon

Pinch salt
16-ounces whole wheat bread,
cubed and left out overnight to
go stale
1½ cups water

1. In a medium bowl, whisk together the eggs, milk, maple syrup, Stevia, vanilla, cinnamon, and salt. Stir in the cubes of whole wheat bread. 2. You will need a 7-inch round baking pan for this. Spray the inside with nonstick spray, then pour the bread mixture into the pan. 3. Place the trivet in the bottom of the inner pot, then pour in the water. 4. Make foil sling and insert it onto the trivet. Carefully place the 7-inch pan on top of the foil sling/trivet. 5. Secure the lid to the locked position, then make sure the vent is turned to sealing. 6. Press the Manual button and use the "+/-" button to set the Instant Pot for 20 minutes. 7. When cook time is up, let the Instant Pot release naturally for 5 minutes, then quick release the rest

Per Serving:
calories: 75 | fat: 3g | protein: 4g | carbs: 7g | sugars: 6g | fiber: 0g | sodium: 74mg

Egg Bites with Sausage and Peppers

Prep time: 5 minutes | Cook time: 15 minutes | Serves 7

4 large eggs
¼ cup vegan cream cheese
(such as Tofutti brand) or
cream cheese
¼ teaspoon fine sea salt
¼ teaspoon freshly ground
black pepper
3 ounces lean turkey sausage,
cooked and crumbled, or 1
vegetarian sausage (such as

Beyond Meat brand), cooked
and diced
½ red bell pepper, seeded and
chopped
2 green onions, white and
green parts, minced, plus more
for garnish (optional)
¼ cup vegan cheese shreds or
shredded sharp Cheddar cheese

1. In a blender, combine the eggs, cream cheese, salt, and pepper. Blend on medium speed for about 20 seconds, just until combined. Add the sausage, bell pepper, and green onions and pulse for 1 second once or twice. You want to mix in the solid ingredients without grinding them up very much. 2. Pour 1 cup water into the Instant Pot. Generously grease a 7-cup egg-bite mold or seven 2-ounce silicone baking cups with butter or coconut oil, making sure to coat each cup well. Place the prepared mold or cups on a long-handled silicone steam rack. (If you don't have the long-handled rack, use the wire metal steam rack and a homemade sling) 3. Pour ¼ cup of the egg mixture into each prepared mold or cup. Holding the handles of the steam rack, carefully lower the egg bites into the pot. 4. Secure the lid and set the Pressure Release to Sealing. Select the Steam setting and set the cooking time for 8 minutes at low pressure. (The pot will take about 5 minutes to come up to pressure before the cooking program begins.) 5. When the cooking program ends, let the pressure release naturally for 5 minutes, then move the Pressure Release to Venting to release any remaining steam. Open the pot. The egg muffins will have puffed up quite a bit during cooking, but they will deflate and settle as they cool. Wearing heat-resistant mitts,

grasp the handles of the steam rack and carefully lift the egg bites out of the pot. Sprinkle the egg bites with the cheese, then let them cool for about 5 minutes, until the cheese has fully melted and you are able to handle the mold or cups comfortably. 6. Pull the sides of the egg mold or cups away from the egg bites, running a butter knife around the edge of each bite to loosen if necessary. Transfer the egg bites to plates, garnish with more green onions (if desired), and serve warm. To store, let cool to room temperature, transfer to an airtight container, and refrigerate for up to 3 days; reheat gently in the microwave for about 1 minute before serving.

Per Serving:
calories: 112 | fat: 8g | protein: 8g | carbs: 3g | sugars: 0g | fiber: 0g | sodium: 297mg

Mini Chocolate Chip Muffins

Prep time: 5 minutes | Cook time: 20 minutes | Serves 7

1 cup blanched almond flour
2 eggs
¾ cup sugar-free chocolate
chips
1 tablespoon vanilla extract

½ cup Swerve, or more to taste
2 tablespoons salted grass-fed
butter, softened
½ teaspoon salt
¼ teaspoon baking soda

1. Pour 1 cup of filtered water into the inner pot of the Instant Pot, then insert the trivet. Using an electric mixer, combine flour, eggs, chocolate chips, vanilla, Swerve, butter, salt, and baking soda. Mix thoroughly. Transfer this mixture into a well-greased Instant Pot-friendly muffin (or egg bites) mold. 2. Using a sling if desired, place the pan onto the trivet and cover loosely with aluminum foil. Close the lid, set the pressure release to Sealing, and select Manual. Set the Instant Pot to 20 minutes on High Pressure and let cook. 3. Once cooked, let the pressure naturally disperse from the Instant Pot for about 10 minutes, then carefully switch the pressure release to Venting. 4. Open the Instant Pot and remove the pan. Let cool, serve, and enjoy!

Per Serving:
calories: 204 | fat: 17g | protein: 3g | carbs: 10g | net carbs: 9g | fiber: 1g

Coddled Eggs and Smoked Salmon Toasts

Prep time: 5 minutes | Cook time: 10 minutes | Serves 4

2 teaspoons unsalted butter
4 large eggs
4 slices gluten-free or whole-
grain rye bread
½ cup plain 2 percent Greek
yogurt
4 ounces cold-smoked salmon,
or 1 medium avocado, pitted,

peeled, and sliced
2 radishes, thinly sliced
1 Persian cucumber, thinly
sliced
1 tablespoon chopped fresh
chives
¼ teaspoon freshly ground
black pepper

1. Pour 1 cup water into the Instant Pot and place a long-handled silicone steam rack into the pot. (If you don't have the long-handled rack, use the wire metal steam rack and a homemade sling) 2. Coat each of four 4-ounce ramekins with ½ teaspoon butter. Crack an egg into each ramekin. Place the ramekins on the steam rack in the pot. 3. Secure the lid and set the Pressure Release to Sealing. Select the Steam setting and set the cooking time for 3 minutes at low pressure. (The pot will take about 5 minutes to come up to pressure before the cooking program begins.) 4. While eggs are cooking, toast the

bread in a toaster until golden brown. Spread the yogurt onto the toasted slices, put the toasts onto plates, and then top each toast with the smoked salmon, radishes, and cucumber. 5. When the cooking program ends, let the pressure release naturally for 5 minutes, then move the Pressure Release to Venting to release any remaining steam. Open the pot and, wearing heat-resistant mitts, grasp the handles of the steam rack and lift it out of the pot. 6. Run a knife around the inside edge of each ramekin to loosen the egg and unmold one egg onto each toast. Sprinkle the chives and pepper on top and serve right away. 7. Note 8. The yolks of these eggs are fully cooked through. If you prefer the yolks slightly less solid, perform a quick pressure release rather than letting the pressure release naturally for 5 minutes.

Per Serving:

calories: 275 | fat: 12g | protein: 21g | carbs: 21g | sugars: 4g | fiber: 5g | sodium: 431mg

Three-Cheese Quiche

Prep time: 10 minutes | Cook time: 6 minutes | Serves 6

6 eggs, beaten
2 tablespoon cream cheese
1 teaspoon Italian seasoning
¼ cup shredded Cheddar cheese

3 ounces (85 g) Monterey Jack cheese, shredded
2 ounces (57 g) Mozzarella, shredded
1 cup water, for cooking

1. Pour water in the instant pot. 2. In the mixing bowl, mix up eggs cream cheese, Italian seasoning, and all types of cheese. 3. Pour the mixture in the baking cups (molds) and place them in the instant pot. 4. Close and seal the lid. 5. Cook the quiche cups for 6 minutes on Manual mode (High Pressure). 6. Make a quick pressure release.

Per Serving:

calories: 175 | fat: 13g | protein: 13g | carbs: 1g | net carbs: 0g | fiber: 1g

Classic Cinnamon Roll Coffee Cake

Prep time: 10 minutes | Cook time: 45 minutes | Serves 8

Cake:
2 cups almond flour
1 cup granulated erythritol
1 teaspoon baking powder
Pinch of salt
2 eggs
½ cup sour cream
4 tablespoons butter, melted
2 teaspoons vanilla extract
2 tablespoons Swerve

1½ teaspoons ground cinnamon
Cooking spray
½ cup water
Icing:
2 ounces (56 g) cream cheese, softened
1 cup powdered erythritol
1 tablespoon heavy cream
½ teaspoon vanilla extract

1. In the bowl of a stand mixer, combine the almond flour, granulated erythritol, baking powder and salt. Mix until no lumps remain. Add the eggs, sour cream, butter and vanilla to the mixer bowl and mix until well combined. 2. In a separate bowl, mix together the Swerve and cinnamon. 3. Spritz the baking pan with cooking spray. Pour in the cake batter and use a knife to make sure it is level around the pan. Sprinkle the cinnamon mixture on top. Cover the pan tightly with aluminum foil. 4. Pour the water and insert the trivet in the Instant Pot. Put the pan on the trivet. 5. Set the lid in place. Select the Manual mode and set the cooking time for 45 minutes on High

Pressure. When the timer goes off, do a quick pressure release. Carefully open the lid. 6. Remove the cake from the pot and remove the foil. Blot off any moisture on top of the cake with a paper towel, if necessary. Let rest in the pan for 5 minutes. 7. Meanwhile, make the icing: In a small bowl, use a mixer to whip the cream cheese until it is light and fluffy. Slowly fold in the powdered erythritol and mix until well combined. Add the heavy cream and vanilla extract and mix until thoroughly combined. 8. When the cake is cooled, transfer it to a platter and drizzle the icing all over.

Per Serving:

calories: 313 | fat: 27.0g | protein: 8.7g | carbs: 6.8g | net carbs: 3.5g | fiber: 3.3g

Avocado Green Power Bowl

Prep time: 10 minutes | Cook time: 10 minutes | Serves 1

1 cup water
2 eggs
1 tablespoon coconut oil
1 tablespoon butter
1 ounce (28 g) sliced almonds
1 cup fresh spinach, sliced into strips

½ cup kale, sliced into strips
½ clove garlic, minced
½ teaspoon salt
⅛ teaspoon pepper
½ avocado, sliced
⅛ teaspoon red pepper flakes

1. Pour water into Instant Pot and place steam rack on bottom. Place eggs on steam rack. Click lid closed. Press the Manual button and adjust time for 6 minutes. When timer beeps, quick-release the pressure. Set eggs aside. 2. Pour water out, clean pot, and replace. Press the Sauté button and add coconut oil, butter, and almonds. Sauté for 2 to 3 minutes until butter begins to turn golden and almonds soften. Add spinach, kale, garlic, salt, and pepper to Instant Pot. Sauté for 4 to 6 minutes until greens begin to wilt. Press the Cancel button. Place greens in bowl for serving. Peel eggs, cut in half, and add to bowl. Slice avocado and place in bowl. Sprinkle red pepper flakes over all. Serve warm.

Per Serving:

calories: 650 | fat: 55g | protein: 21g | carbs: 15g | net carbs: 6g | fiber: 9g

Vegetable and Cheese Bake

Prep time: 7 minutes | Cook time: 9 minutes | Serves 3

3 eggs, beaten
¼ cup coconut cream
¼ teaspoon salt
3 ounces (85 g) Brussel sprouts, chopped
2 ounces (57 g) tomato,

chopped
3 ounces (85 g) provolone cheese, shredded
1 teaspoon butter
1 teaspoon smoked paprika

1. Grease the instant pot pan with the butter. 2. Put eggs in the bowl, add salt, and smoked paprika. Whisk the eggs well. 3. After this, add chopped Brussel sprouts and tomato. 4. Pour the mixture into the instant pot pan and sprinkle over with the shredded cheese. 5. Pour 1 cup of the water in the instant pot. Then place the pan with the egg mixture and close the lid. 6. Cook the meal on Manual (High Pressure) for 4 minutes. Then make naturally release for 5 minutes.

Per Serving:

calories: 237 | fat: 18g | protein: 14g | carbs: 6g | net carbs: 4g | fiber: 2g

Soft-Scrambled Eggs

Prep time: 5 minutes | Cook time: 7 minutes | Serves 4

6 eggs
2 tablespoons heavy cream
1 teaspoon salt
¼ teaspoon pepper
2 tablespoons butter
2 ounces (57 g) cream cheese, softened

1. In large bowl, whisk eggs, heavy cream, salt, and pepper. Press the Sauté button and then press the Adjust button to set heat to Less. 2. Gently push eggs around pot with rubber spatula. When they begin to firm up, add butter and softened cream cheese. Continue stirring slowly in a figure-8 pattern until eggs are fully cooked, approximately 7 minutes total.
Per Serving:
calories: 232 | fat: 18g | protein: 10g | carbs: 2g | net carbs: 2g | fiber: 0g

Pumpkin Mug Muffin

Prep time: 5 minutes | Cook time: 9 minutes | Serves 1

½ cup Swerve
½ cup blanched almond flour
2 tablespoons organic pumpkin purée
1 teaspoon sugar-free chocolate chips
1 tablespoon organic coconut flour
1 egg
1 tablespoon coconut oil
½ teaspoon pumpkin pie spice
½ teaspoon ground nutmeg
½ teaspoon ground cinnamon
⅛ teaspoon baking soda

1. Mix the Swerve, almond flour, pumpkin purée, chocolate chips, coconut flour, egg, coconut oil, pumpkin pie spice, nutmeg, cinnamon, and baking soda in a large bowl. Transfer this mixture into a well-greased, Instant Pot-friendly mug. 2. Pour 1 cup of filtered water into the inner pot of the Instant Pot, and insert the trivet. Cover the mug in foil and place on top of the trivet. 3. Close the lid, set the pressure release to Sealing, and select Manual. Set the Instant Pot to 9 minutes on High Pressure. 4. Once cooked, release the pressure immediately by switching the valve to Venting. Be sure your muffin is done by inserting a toothpick into the cake and making sure it comes out clean, as cook times may vary. 5. Remove mug and enjoy!
Per Serving:
calories: 297 | fat: 22g | protein: 9g | carbs: 17g | net carbs: 9g | fiber: 8g

Kale Omelet

Prep time: 5 minutes | Cook time: 10 minutes | Serves 2

2 eggs
1 cup chopped kale
1 teaspoon heavy cream
⅔ teaspoon white pepper
½ teaspoon butter

1. Grease the instant pot pan with butter. 2. Beat the eggs in the separated bowl and whisk them well. 3. After this, add heavy cream and white pepper. Stir it gently. 4. Place the chopped kale in the greased pan and add the whisked eggs. 5. Pour 1 cup of water in the instant pot. 6. Place the trivet in the instant pot and transfer the egg mixture pan on the trivet. 7. Close the instant pot and set the Manual (High Pressure) program and cook the frittata for 5 minutes. Do a natural pressure release for 5 minutes.

Per Serving:
calories: 98 | fat: 6g | protein: 7g | carbs: 5g | net carbs: 4g | fiber: 1g

Chocolate Chip Pancake

Prep time: 5 minutes | Cook time: 37 minutes | Serves 5 to 6

4 tablespoons salted grass-fed butter, softened
2 cups blanched almond flour
½ cup Swerve, or more to taste
1 ¼ cups full-fat coconut milk
¼ cup sugar-free chocolate chips
¼ cup organic coconut flour
2 eggs
1 tablespoon chopped walnuts
¼ teaspoon baking soda
½ teaspoon salt
½ cup dark berries, for serving (optional)

1. Grease the bottom and sides of your Instant Pot with the butter. Make sure you coat it very liberally. 2. In a large bowl, mix together the almond flour, Swerve, milk, chocolate chips, coconut flour, eggs, walnuts, baking soda, and salt. Add this mixture to the Instant Pot. Close the lid, set the pressure release to Sealing, and select Multigrain. Set the Instant Pot to 37 minutes on Low Pressure, and let cook. 3. Switch the pressure release to Venting and open the Instant Pot. Confirm your pancake is cooked, then carefully remove it using a spatula. Serve with the berries (if desired), and enjoy!
Per Serving:
calories: 369 | fat: 31g | protein: 7g | carbs: 16g | net carbs: 9g | fiber: 7g

Gouda Egg Casserole with Canadian Bacon

Prep time: 12 minutes | Cook time: 20 minutes | Serves 4

Nonstick cooking spray
1 slice whole grain bread, toasted
½ cup shredded smoked Gouda cheese
3 slices Canadian bacon, chopped
6 large eggs
¼ cup half-and-half
¼ teaspoon kosher salt
¼ teaspoon freshly ground black pepper
¼ teaspoon dry mustard

1. Spray a 6-inch cake pan with cooking spray, or if the pan is nonstick, skip this step. If you don't have a 6-inch cake pan, any bowl or pan that fits inside your pressure cooker should work. 2. Crumble the toast into the bottom of the pan. Sprinkle with the cheese and Canadian bacon. 3. In a medium bowl, whisk together the eggs, half-and-half, salt, pepper, and dry mustard. 4. Pour the egg mixture into the pan. Loosely cover the pan with aluminum foil. 5. Pour 1½ cups water into the electric pressure cooker and insert a wire rack or trivet. Place the covered pan on top of the rack. 6. Close and lock the lid of the pressure cooker. Set the valve to sealing. 7. Cook on high pressure for 20 minutes. 8. When the cooking is complete, hit Cancel and quick release the pressure. 9. Once the pin drops, unlock and remove the lid. 10. Carefully transfer the pan from the pressure cooker to a cooling rack and let it sit for 5 minutes. 11. Cut into 4 wedges and serve.
Per Serving:
calories: 247 | fat: 15g | protein: 20g | carbs: 8g | sugars: 1g | fiber: 1g | sodium: 717mg

Chicken, Mozzarella, and Tomato Pizza

Prep time: 5 minutes | Cook time: 20 minutes | Serves 4 to 5

Crust:
2 eggs
2 tablespoons salted grass-fed butter, softened
1 pound (454 g) ground chicken
1 cup grated full-fat Parmesan cheese
⅓ cup blanched almond flour
Topping:
1 (14-ounce / 397-g) can fire

roasted sugar-free or low-sugar tomatoes, drained
2 cups shredded full-fat Mozzarella cheese
1 cup chopped spinach
½ teaspoon dried basil
½ teaspoon crushed red pepper
½ teaspoon dried oregano
½ teaspoon dried cilantro

1. Pour 1 cup of filtered water into the inner pot of the Instant Pot, then insert the trivet. In a large bowl, combine the eggs, butter, chicken, cheese, and flour. Mix thoroughly. Transfer this mixture into a greased, Instant Pot-friendly dish. Cover loosely with aluminum foil. Using a sling, place this dish on top of the trivet. 2. Close the lid, set the pressure release to Sealing, and select Manual. Set the Instant Pot to 10 minutes on High Pressure and let cook. 3. Meanwhile, in a small bowl, mix together basil, red pepper, oregano, and cilantro, and set aside. 4. Once the crust is cooked, carefully switch the pressure release to Venting. Open the Instant Pot and add the tomatoes in an even layer, followed by the Mozzarella cheese and the spinach. Sprinkle the spice and herb mixture over the top of the pizza. Loosely re-cover dish with aluminum foil. 5. Close the lid to the Instant Pot, set the pressure release to Sealing, and select Manual. Set the Instant Pot to 10 minutes on High Pressure and let cook again. 6. Once cooked, let the pressure naturally disperse from the Instant Pot for about 10 minutes, then carefully switch the pressure release to Venting. 7. Open the Instant Pot, serve, and enjoy!
Per Serving:
calories: 405 | fat: 22g | protein: 47g | carbs: 5g | net carbs: 4g | fiber: 1g

Baked Eggs

Prep time: 15 minutes | Cook time: 20 minutes | Serves 8

1 cup water
2 tablespoons no-trans-fat tub margarine, melted
1 cup reduced-fat buttermilk baking mix
1½ cups fat-free cottage cheese
2 teaspoons chopped onion

1 teaspoon dried parsley
½ cup grated reduced-fat cheddar cheese
1 egg, slightly beaten
1¼ cups egg substitute
1 cup fat-free milk

1. Place the steaming rack into the bottom of the inner pot and pour in 1 cup of water. 2. Grease a round springform pan that will fit into the inner pot of the Instant Pot. 3. Pour melted margarine into springform pan. 4. Mix together buttermilk baking mix, cottage cheese, onion, parsley, cheese, egg, egg substitute, and milk in large mixing bowl. 5. Pour mixture over melted margarine. Stir slightly to distribute margarine. 6. Place the springform pan onto the steaming rack, close the lid, and secure to the locking position. Be sure the vent is turned to sealing. Set for 20 minutes on Manual at high pressure. 7. Let the pressure release naturally. 8. Carefully remove

the springform pan with the handles of the steaming rack and allow to stand 10 minutes before cutting and serving.
Per Serving:
calories: 155 | fat: 5g | protein: 12g | carbs: 15g | sugars: 4g | fiber: 0g | sodium: 460mg

Spinach and Chicken Casserole

Prep time: 5 minutes | Cook time: 15 minutes | Serves 5

1 tablespoon avocado oil
1 tablespoon coconut oil
1 tablespoon unflavored MCT oil
1 avocado, mashed
½ cup shredded full-fat Cheddar cheese
½ cup chopped spinach
½ teaspoon dried basil

½ teaspoon kosher salt
½ teaspoon freshly ground black pepper
¼ cup sugar-free or low-sugar salsa
¼ cup heavy whipping cream
1 pound (454 g) ground chicken

1. Pour 1 cup of filtered water inside the inner pot of the Instant Pot, then insert the trivet. 2. In a large bowl, combine and mix the avocado oil, coconut oil, MCT oil, avocado, cheese, spinach, basil, salt, black pepper, salsa, and whipping cream. 3. In a greased Instant Pot-safe dish, add the ground chicken in an even layer. Pour the casserole mixture over the chicken and cover with aluminum foil. Using a sling, place this dish on top of the trivet. 4. Close the lid, set the pressure release to Sealing, and select Manual. Set the Instant Pot to 15 minutes on High Pressure, and let cook. 5. Once cooked, carefully switch the pressure release to Venting. Open the Instant Pot, serve, and enjoy!
Per Serving:
calories: 405 | fat: 30g | protein: 30g | carbs: 5g | net carbs: 2g | fiber: 3g

Almond Pancakes

Prep time: 10 minutes | Cook time: 15 minutes per batch | Serves 6

4 eggs, beaten
2 cups almond flour
½ cup butter, melted
2 tablespoons granulated erythritol

1 tablespoon avocado oil
1 teaspoon baking powder
1 teaspoon vanilla extract
Pinch of salt
¾ cup water, divided

1. In a blender, combine all the ingredients, except for the ½ cup of the water. Pulse until fully combined and smooth. Let the batter rest for 5 minutes before cooking. 2. Fill each cup with 2 tablespoons of the batter, about two-thirds of the way full. Cover the cups with aluminum foil. 3. Pour the remaining ½ cup of the water and insert the trivet in the Instant Pot. Place the cups on the trivet. 4. Set the lid in place. Select the Manual mode and set the cooking time for 15 minutes on High Pressure. When the timer goes off, do a quick pressure release. Carefully open the lid. 5. Repeat with the remaining batter, until all the batter is used. Add more water to the pot before cooking each batch, if needed. 6. Serve warm.
Per Serving:
3 bites: calories: 423 | fat: 38.7g | protein: 12.3g | carbs: 8.2g | net carbs: 4.0g | fiber: 4.2g

Gruyère Asparagus Frittata

Prep time: 10 minutes | Cook time: 22 minutes | Serves 6

6 eggs
6 tablespoons heavy cream
½ teaspoon salt
½ teaspoon black pepper
1 tablespoon butter
2½ ounces (71 g) asparagus, chopped
1 clove garlic, minced
1¼ cup shredded Gruyère cheese, divided
Cooking spray
3 ounces (85 g) halved cherry tomatoes
½ cup water

1. In a large bowl, stir together the eggs, cream, salt, and pepper. 2. Set the Instant Pot on the Sauté mode and melt the butter. Add the asparagus and garlic to the pot and sauté for 2 minutes, or until the garlic is fragrant. The asparagus should still be crisp. 3. Transfer the asparagus and garlic to the bowl with the egg mixture. Stir in 1 cup of the cheese. Clean the pot. 4. Spritz a baking pan with cooking spray. Spread the tomatoes in a single layer in the pan. Pour the egg mixture on top of the tomatoes and sprinkle with the remaining ¼ cup of the cheese. Cover the pan tightly with aluminum foil. 5. Pour the water in the Instant Pot and insert the trivet. Place the pan on the trivet. 6. Set the lid in place. Select the Manual mode and set the cooking time for 20 minutes on High Pressure. When the timer goes off, perform a quick pressure release. Carefully open the lid. 7. Remove the pan from the pot and remove the foil. Blot off any excess moisture with a paper towel. Let the frittata cool for 5 to 10 minutes before transferring onto a plate.

Per Serving:
calories: 204 | fat: 16.6g | protein: 11.3g | carbs: 2.2g | net carbs: 1.6g | fiber: 0.6g

Avocado Breakfast Sandwich

Prep time: 5 minutes | Cook time: 15 minutes | Serves 1

2 slices bacon
2 eggs
1 avocado

1. Press the Sauté button. Press the Adjust button to set heat to Low. Add bacon to Instant Pot and cook until crispy. Remove and set aside. 2. Crack egg over Instant Pot slowly, into bacon grease. Repeat with second egg. When edges become golden, after 2 to 3 minutes, flip. Press the Cancel button. 3. Cut avocado in half and scoop out half without seed. Place in small bowl and mash with fork. Spread on one egg. Place bacon on top and top with second egg. Let cool 5 minutes before eating.

Per Serving:
calories: 489 | fat: 39g | protein: 21g | carbs: 7g | net carbs: 2g | fiber: 5g

Pork and Quill Egg Cups

Prep time: 15 minutes | Cook time: 15 minutes | Serves 4

10 ounces (283 g) ground pork
1 jalapeño pepper, chopped
1 tablespoon butter, softened
1 teaspoon dried dill
½ teaspoon salt
1 cup water
4 quill eggs

1. In a bowl, stir together all the ingredients, except for the quill eggs and water. Transfer the meat mixture to the silicone muffin molds and press the surface gently. 2. Pour the water and insert the trivet in the Instant Pot. Put the meat cups on the trivet. 3. Crack the eggs over the meat mixture. 4. Set the lid in place. Select the Manual mode and set the cooking time for 15 minutes on High Pressure. When the timer goes off, do a quick pressure release. Carefully open the lid. 5. Serve warm.

Per Serving:
calories: 142 | fat: 6.3g | protein: 20.0g | carbs: 0.3g | net carbs: 0.1g | fiber: 0.2g

3 Beef, Pork, and Lamb

Lamb Koobideh

Prep time: 15 minutes | Cook time: 30 minutes | Serves 4

1 pound (454 g) ground lamb
1 egg, beaten
1 tablespoon lemon juice
1 teaspoon ground turmeric
½ teaspoon garlic powder
1 teaspoon chives, chopped
½ teaspoon ground black pepper
1 cup water

1. In a mixing bowl, combine all the ingredients except for water. 2. Shape the mixture into meatballs and press into ellipse shape. 3. Pour the water and insert the trivet in the Instant Pot. 4. Put the prepared ellipse meatballs in a baking pan and transfer on the trivet. 5. Close the lid and select Manual mode. Set cooking time for 30 minutes on High Pressure. 6. When timer beeps, make a quick pressure release. Open the lid. 7. Serve immediately

Per Serving:
calories: 231 | fat: 9.5g | protein: 33.4g | carbs: 1.0g | net carbs: 0.7g | fiber: 0.3g

Filipino Pork Loin

Prep time: 10 minutes | Cook time: 40 minutes | Serves 4

1 pound (454 g) pork loin, chopped
½ cup apple cider vinegar
1 cup chicken broth
1 chili pepper, chopped
1 tablespoon coconut oil
1 teaspoon salt

1. Melt the coconut oil on Sauté mode. 2. When it is hot, and chili pepper and cook it for 2 minutes. Stir it. 3. Add chopped pork loin and salt. Cook the ingredients for 5 minutes. 4. After this, add apple cider vinegar and chicken broth. 5. Close and seal the lid and cook the Filipino pork for 30 minutes on High Pressure (Manual mode). Then make a quick pressure release.

Per Serving:
calories: 320 | fat:19 g | protein: 32g | carbs: 0g | net carbs: 0g | fiber: 0g

Bacon-Wrapped Pork Bites

Prep time: 15 minutes | Cook time: 20 minutes | Serves 4

3 tablespoons butter
10 ounces (283 g) pork tenderloin, cubed
6 ounces (170 g) bacon, sliced
½ teaspoon white pepper
¾ cup chicken stock

1. Melt the butter on Sauté mode in the Instant Pot. 2. Meanwhile, wrap the pork tenderloin cubes in the sliced bacon and sprinkle with white pepper. Secure with toothpicks, if necessary. 3. Put the wrapped pork tenderloin in the melted butter and cook for 3 minutes on each side. 4. Add the chicken stock and close the lid. 5. Select Manual mode and set cooking time for 14 minutes on High Pressure. 6. When timer beeps, use a natural pressure release for 5 minutes, then release any remaining pressure. Open the lid. 7. Discard the toothpicks and serve immediately.

Per Serving:
calories: 410 | fat: 29.0g | protein: 34.6g | carbs: 0.9g | net carbs: 0.8g | fiber: 0.1g

Salisbury Steaks with Seared Cauliflower

Prep time: 5 minutes | Cook time: 30 minutes | Serves 4

Salisbury Steaks
1 pound 95 percent lean ground beef
⅓ cup almond flour
1 large egg
½ teaspoon fine sea salt
¼ teaspoon freshly ground black pepper
2 tablespoons cold-pressed avocado oil
1 small yellow onion, sliced
1 garlic clove, chopped
8 ounces cremini or button mushrooms, sliced
½ teaspoon fine sea salt
2 tablespoons tomato paste
1½ teaspoons yellow mustard
1 cup low-sodium roasted beef bone broth
Seared Cauliflower
1 tablespoon olive oil
1 head cauliflower, cut into bite-size florets
2 tablespoons chopped fresh flat-leaf parsley
¼ teaspoon fine sea salt
2 teaspoons cornstarch
2 teaspoons water

1. To make the steaks: In a bowl, combine the beef, almond flour, egg, salt, and pepper and mix with your hands until all of the ingredients are evenly distributed. Divide the mixture into four equal portions, then shape each portion into an oval patty about ½ inch thick. 2. Select the Sauté setting on the Instant Pot and heat the oil for 2 minutes. Swirl the oil to coat the bottom of the pot, then add the patties and sear for 3 minutes, until browned on one side. Using a thin, flexible spatula, flip the patties and sear the second side for 2 to 3 minutes, until browned. Transfer the patties to a plate. 3. Add the onion, garlic, mushrooms, and salt to the pot and sauté for 4 minutes, until the onion is translucent and the mushrooms have begun to give up their liquid. Add the tomato paste, mustard, and broth and stir with a wooden spoon, using it to nudge any browned bits from the bottom of the pot. Return the patties to the pot in a single layer and spoon a bit of the sauce over each one. 4. Secure the lid and set the Pressure Release to Sealing. Press the Cancel button to reset the cooking program, then select the Pressure Cook or Manual setting and set the cooking time for 10 minutes at high pressure. (The pot will take about 5 minutes to come up to pressure before the cooking program begins.) 5. When the cooking program ends, let the pressure release naturally for at least 10 minutes, then move the Pressure Release to Venting to release any remaining steam. 6. To make the cauliflower: While the pressure is releasing, in a large skillet over medium heat, warm the oil. Add the cauliflower and stir or toss to coat with the oil, then cook, stirring every minute or two, until lightly browned, about 8 minutes. Turn off the heat, sprinkle in the parsley and salt, and stir to combine. Leave in the skillet, uncovered, to keep warm. 7. Open the pot and, using a slotted spatula, transfer the patties to a serving plate. In a small bowl, stir together the cornstarch and water. Press the Cancel button to reset the cooking program, then select the Sauté setting. When the sauce comes to a simmer, stir in the cornstarch mixture and let the sauce boil for about 1 minute, until thickened. Press the Cancel button to turn off the Instant Pot. 8. Spoon the sauce over the patties. Serve right away, with the cauliflower.

Per Serving:
calorie: 362 | fat: 21g | protein: 33g | carbs: 21g | sugars: 4g | fiber: 6g | sodium: 846mg

Buttery Beef and Spinach

Prep time: 2 minutes | Cook time: 10 minutes | Serves 4

1 pound (454 g) 85% lean ground beef
1 cup water
4 cups fresh spinach
¾ teaspoon salt
¼ cup butter
¼ teaspoon pepper
¼ teaspoon garlic powder

1. Press the Sauté button and add ground beef to Instant Pot. Brown beef until fully cooked and spoon into 7-cup glass bowl. Drain grease and replace pot. 2. Pour water into pot and place steam rack in bottom. Place baking dish on steam rack and add fresh spinach, salt, butter, pepper, and garlic powder to ground beef. Cover with aluminum foil. Click lid closed. 3. Press the Manual button and adjust time for 2 minutes. When timer beeps, quick-release the pressure. Remove aluminum foil and stir.

Per Serving:
calories: 272 | fat: 19g | protein: 18g | carbs: 1g | net carbs: 0g | fiber: 1g

Paprika Pork Ribs

Prep time: 10 minutes | Cook time: 30 minutes | Serves 4

1 pound (454 g) pork ribs
1 tablespoon ground paprika
1 teaspoon ground turmeric
3 tablespoons avocado oil
1 teaspoon salt
½ cup beef broth

1. Rub the pork ribs with ground paprika, turmeric, salt, and avocado oil. 2. Then pour the beef broth in the instant pot. 3. Arrange the pork ribs in the instant pot. Close and seal the lid. 4. Cook the pork ribs for 30 minutes on Manual mode (High Pressure). 5. When the time is finished, make a quick pressure release and chop the ribs into servings.

Per Serving:
calories: 335 | fat: 22g | protein: 31g | carbs: 2g | net carbs: 1g | fiber: 1g

Balsamic Roast Beef

Prep time: 5 minutes | Cook time: 20 minutes | Serves 4

1 pound (454 g) chuck roast
2 cloves garlic, minced
1 cup grass-fed bone broth
½ teaspoon ground rosemary
½ teaspoon freshly ground black pepper
½ teaspoon kosher salt
½ teaspoon ground thyme
½ teaspoon crushed red pepper
¼ cup balsamic vinegar
4 tablespoons grass-fed butter, softened
1 cup chopped broccoli

1. Pour ½ cup filtered water into the Instant Pot, then add the chuck roast. Close the lid, set the pressure release to Sealing, and select Manual. Set the Instant Pot to 20 minutes on High Pressure, and let cook. 2. In a large bowl, combine the garlic, bone broth, rosemary, black pepper, salt, thyme, red pepper, vinegar, and 2 tablespoons of butter. Mix thoroughly. 3. Once cooked, let the pressure naturally disperse from the Instant Pot for about 10 minutes, then carefully switch the pressure release to Venting. 4. Open the Instant Pot, and remove the dish. Set the Instant Pot to Sauté mode, add in the broccoli, and mix in 2 additional tablespoons of grass-fed butter.

Cook the broccoli, stirring continuously, until cooked. 5. Remove the broccoli, and serve alongside the roast. Spoon your prepared sauce over both, to taste.

Per Serving:
calories: 323 | fat: 16g | protein: 40g | carbs: 3g | net carbs: 2g | fiber: 1g

Beef Ribs with Radishes

Prep time: 20 minutes | Cook time: 56 minutes | Serves 4

¼ teaspoon ground coriander
¼ teaspoon ground cumin
1 teaspoon kosher salt, plus more to taste
½ teaspoon smoked paprika
Pinch of ground allspice (optional)
4 (8-ounce / 227-g) bone-in beef short ribs
2 tablespoons avocado oil
1 cup water
2 radishes, ends trimmed, leaves rinsed and roughly chopped
Freshly ground black pepper, to taste

1. In a small bowl, mix together the coriander, cumin, salt, paprika, and allspice. Rub the spice mixture all over the short ribs. 2. Set the Instant Pot to Sauté mode and add the oil to heat. Add the short ribs, bone side up. Brown for 4 minutes on each side. 3. Pour the water into the Instant Pot. Secure the lid. Press the Manual button and set cooking time for 45 minutes on High Pressure. 4. When timer beeps, allow the pressure to release naturally for 10 minutes, then release any remaining pressure. Open the lid. 5. Remove the short ribs to a serving plate. 6. Add the radishes to the sauce in the pot. Place a metal steaming basket directly on top of the radishes and place the radish leaves in the basket. 7. Secure the lid. Press the Manual button and set cooking time for 3 minutes on High Pressure. 8. When timer beeps, quick release the pressure. Open the lid. Transfer the leaves to a serving bowl. Sprinkle with with salt and pepper. 9. Remove the radishes and place on top of the leaves. Serve hot with the short ribs.

Per Serving:
calories: 450 | fat: 25g | protein: 45g | carbs: 12g | net carbs: 9g | fiber: 3g

Beef Clod Vindaloo

Prep time: 15 minutes | Cook time: 15 minutes | Serves 2

½ Serrano pepper, chopped
¼ teaspoon cumin seeds
¼ teaspoon minced ginger
¼ teaspoon cayenne pepper
¼ teaspoon salt
¼ teaspoon ground paprika
1 cup water
9 ounces (255 g) beef clod, chopped

1. Put Serrano pepper, cumin seeds, minced ginger, cayenne pepper, salt, ground paprika, and water in a food processor. Blend the mixture until smooth. 2. Transfer the mixture in a bowl and add the chopped beef clod. Toss to coat well. 3. Transfer the beef clod and the mixture in the Instant Pot and close the lid. 4. Select Manual mode and set cooking time for 15 minutes on High Pressure. 5. When timer beeps, use a natural pressure release for 10 minutes, then release any remaining pressure. Open the lid. 6. Serve immediately.

Per Serving:
calories: 376 | fat: 27.4g | protein: 29.9g | carbs: 0.7g | net carbs: 0.4g | fiber: 0.3g

Pork Chops in Creamy Mushroom Gravy

Prep time: 5 minutes | Cook time: 15 minutes | Serves 4

4 (5-ounce / 142-g) pork chops
1 teaspoon salt
½ teaspoon pepper
2 tablespoons avocado oil
1 cup chopped button
mushrooms
½ medium onion, sliced

1 clove garlic, minced
1 cup chicken broth
¼ cup heavy cream
4 tablespoons butter
¼ teaspoon xanthan gum
1 tablespoon chopped fresh
parsley

1. Sprinkle pork chops with salt and pepper. Place avocado oil and mushrooms in Instant Pot and press the Sauté button. Sauté 3 to 5 minutes until mushrooms begin to soften. Add onions and pork chops. Sauté additional 3 minutes until pork chops reach a golden brown. 2. Add garlic and broth to Instant Pot. Click lid closed. Press the Manual button and adjust time for 15 minutes. When timer beeps, allow a 10-minute natural release. Quick-release the remaining pressure. 3. Remove lid and place pork chops on plate. Press the Sauté button and add heavy cream, butter, and xanthan gum. Reduce for 5 to 10 minutes or until sauce begins to thicken. Add pork chops back into pot. Serve warm topped with mushroom sauce and parsley.
Per Serving:
calories: 516 | fat: 40g | protein: 32g | carbs: 3g | net carbs: 2g | fiber: 1g

Fajita Pork Shoulder

Prep time: 5 minutes | Cook time: 45 minutes | Serves 2

11 ounces (312 g) pork
shoulder, boneless, sliced
1 teaspoon fajita seasoning

2 tablespoons butter
½ cup water

1. Sprinkle the meat with fajita seasoning and put in the instant pot. 2. Add butter and cook it on Sauté mode for 5 minutes. 3. Then stir the pork strips and add water. 4. Seal the instant pot lid and set the Manual mode (High Pressure). 5. Set timer for 40 minutes. 6. When the time is running out, make the natural pressure release for 10 minutes.
Per Serving:
calories: 375 | fat: 30g | protein: 24g | carbs: 1g | net carbs: 1g | fiber: 0g

Albóndigas Sinaloenses

Prep time: 15 minutes | Cook time: 10 minutes | Serves 6

1 pound (454 g) ground pork
½ pound (227 g) Italian
sausage, crumbled
2 tablespoons yellow onion,
finely chopped
½ teaspoon dried oregano
1 sprig fresh mint, finely
minced
½ teaspoon ground cumin
2 garlic cloves, finely minced

¼ teaspoon fresh ginger, grated
Seasoned salt and ground black
pepper, to taste
1 tablespoon olive oil
½ cup yellow onions, finely
chopped
2 chipotle chilies in adobo
2 tomatoes, puréed
2 tablespoons tomato passata
1 cup chicken broth

1. In a mixing bowl, combine the pork, sausage, 2 tablespoons of yellow onion, oregano, mint, cumin, garlic, ginger, salt, and black pepper. 2. Roll the mixture into meatballs and reserve. 3. Press the Sauté button to heat up the Instant Pot. Heat the olive oil and cook the meatballs for 4 minutes, stirring continuously. 4. Stir in ½ cup of yellow onions, chilies in adobo, tomatoes passata, and broth. Add reserved meatballs. 5. Secure the lid. Choose the Manual mode and set cooking time for 6 minutes at High pressure. 6. Once cooking is complete, use a quick pressure release. Carefully remove the lid. 7. Serve immediately.
Per Serving:
calories: 408 | fat: 31.1g | protein: 26.5g | carbs: 4.7g | net carbs: 2.4g | fiber: 2.3g

Marjoram Beef Ribs

Prep time: 10 minutes | Cook time: 40 minutes | Serves 2

10 ounces (283 g) beef ribs
¾ cup water
2 tablespoons coconut oil

1 teaspoon dried marjoram
½ teaspoon salt
½ cup chicken broth

1. Rub the beef ribs with the dried marjoram and salt. 2. Place the beef ribs in the instant pot bowl. 3. Add chicken broth and water. 4. Then add coconut oil. 5. Close the lid and set the Meat/Stew mode. Cook the ribs for 40 minutes.
Per Serving:
calories: 391 | fat: 23g | protein: 44g | carbs: 0g | net carbs: 0g | fiber: 0g

Garlic Beef Roast

Prep time: 2 minutes | Cook time: 70 minutes | Serves 6

2 pounds (907 g) top round
roast
½ cup beef broth
2 teaspoons salt

1 teaspoon black pepper
3 whole cloves garlic
1 bay leaf

1. Add the roast, broth, salt, pepper, garlic, and bay leaf to the pot. 2. Close the lid and seal the vent. Cook on High Pressure for 15 minutes. Let the steam naturally release for 15 minutes before Manually releasing. 3. Remove the beef from the pot and slice or shred it. Store it in an airtight container in the fridge or freezer.
Per Serving:
calories: 178 | fat: 4g | protein: 32g | carbs: 1g | net carbs: 1g | fiber: 0g

Creamed Beef Brisket

Prep time: 6 minutes | Cook time: 20 minutes | Serves 3

½ teaspoon salt
14 ounces (397 g) beef brisket,
cut into the strips
½ cup water

½ cup heavy cream
½ teaspoon ground black
pepper
1 tablespoon avocado oil

1. Preheat the instant pot on the Sauté mode. 2. When it is displayed "Hot", pour avocado oil inside and heat it up. 3. Add the meat. 4. Sprinkle the meat with the ground black pepper and salt. 5. Sauté it for 5 minutes. Stir it once per cooking time. 6. Add water and heavy cream. 7. Seal the lid and set the Manual mode. 8. Put the timer on 15

minutes (High Pressure). 9. Make a quick pressure release.

Per Serving:
calories: 322 | fat: 16g | protein: 41g | carbs: 1g | net carbs: 1g | fiber: 0g

Egg Meatloaf

Prep time: 20 minutes | Cook time: 25 minutes | Serves 6

1 tablespoon avocado oil	pepper
1½ cup ground pork	2 tablespoons coconut flour
1 teaspoon chives	3 eggs, hard-boiled, peeled
1 teaspoon salt	1 cup water
½ teaspoon ground black	

1. Brush a loaf pan with avocado oil. 2. In the mixing bowl, mix the ground pork, chives, salt, ground black pepper, and coconut flour. 3. Transfer the mixture in the loaf pan and flatten with a spatula. 4. Fill the meatloaf with hard-boiled eggs. 5. Pour water and insert the trivet in the Instant Pot. 6. Lower the loaf pan over the trivet in the Instant Pot. Close the lid. 7. Select Manual mode and set cooking time for 25 minutes on High Pressure. 8. When timer beeps, use a natural pressure release for 10 minutes, then release any remaining pressure. Open the lid. 9. Serve immediately.

Per Serving:
calories: 277 | fat: 19.0g | protein: 23.3g | carbs: 2.1g | net carbs: 0.9g | fiber: 1.2g

Italian Sausage Stuffed Bell Peppers

Prep time: 15 minutes | Cook time: 17 minutes | Serves 4

4 medium bell peppers, tops and seeds removed

1 pound (454 g) ground pork sausage	½ teaspoon sea salt
1 large egg	¼ teaspoon ground black pepper
3 tablespoons unsweetened tomato purée	½ teaspoon onion powder
2 garlic cloves, minced	⅓ cup tomato, puréed
½ tablespoon Italian seasoning blend	1 cup water
	4 slices Mozzarella cheese

1. Using a fork, pierce small holes into the bottoms of the peppers. Set aside. 2. In a large mixing bowl, combine the sausage, egg, tomato purée, garlic, Italian seasoning, sea salt, black pepper, and onion powder. Mix to combine. 3. Stuff each bell pepper with the meat mixture. 4. Place the trivet in the Instant Pot and add the water. 5. Place the stuffed peppers on the trivet. Pour the puréed tomato over. 6. Lock the lid. Select Manual mode and set cooking time for 15 minutes on High Pressure. 7. When cooking is complete, allow the pressure to release naturally for 5 minutes and then release the remaining pressure. 8. Open the lid and top each pepper with 1 slice of the Mozzarella. Secure the lid, select Keep Warm / Cancel, and set cooking time for 2 minutes to melt the cheese. 9. Open the lid and use tongs to carefully transfer the peppers to a large serving platter. Serve warm.

Per Serving:
calories: 369 | fat: 22.0g | protein: 17.0g | carbs: 25.8g | net carbs: 8.0g | fiber: 17.8g

Beef Tenderloin with Red Wine Sauce

Prep time: 30 minutes | Cook time: 10 minutes | Serves 5

2 pounds (907 g) beef tenderloin	1 teaspoon Worcestershire sauce
Salt and black pepper, to taste	1½ teaspoons dried rosemary
2 tablespoons avocado oil	¼ teaspoon xanthan gum
½ cup beef broth	Chopped fresh rosemary, for garnish (optional)
½ cup dry red wine	
2 cloves garlic, minced	

1. Thirty minutes prior to cooking, take the tenderloin out of the fridge and let it come to room temperature. Crust the outside of the tenderloin in salt and pepper. 2. Turn the pot to Sauté mode and add the avocado oil. Once hot, add the tenderloin and sear on all sides, about 5 minutes. Press Cancel. 3. Add the broth, wine, garlic, Worcestershire sauce, and rosemary to the pot around the beef. 4. Close the lid and seal the vent. Cook on High Pressure for 8 minutes. Quick release the steam. 5. Remove the tenderloin to a platter, tent with aluminum foil, and let it rest for 10 minutes. Press Cancel. 6. Turn the pot to Sauté mode. Once the broth has begun a low boil, add the xanthan gum and whisk until a thin sauce has formed, 2 to 3 minutes. 7. Slice the tenderloin against the grain into thin rounds. Top each slice with the red wine glaze. Garnish with rosemary, if desired.

Per Serving:
calories: 575 | fat: 44g | protein: 33g | carbs: 2g | net carbs: 1g | fiber: 1g

Pork Steaks with Pico de Gallo

Prep time: 15 minutes | Cook time: 12 minutes | Serves 6

1 tablespoon butter	black pepper, or more to taste
2 pounds (907 g) pork steaks	Pico de Gallo:
1 bell pepper, deseeded and sliced	1 tomato, chopped
½ cup shallots, chopped	1 chili pepper, seeded and minced
2 garlic cloves, minced	½ cup red onion, chopped
¼ cup dry red wine	2 garlic cloves, minced
1 cup chicken bone broth	1 tablespoon fresh cilantro, finely chopped
¼ cup water	Sea salt, to taste
Salt, to taste	
¼ teaspoon freshly ground	

1. Press the Sauté button to heat up the Instant Pot. Melt the butter and sear the pork steaks about 4 minutes or until browned on both sides. 2. Add bell pepper, shallot, garlic, wine, chicken bone broth, water, salt, and black pepper to the Instant Pot. 3. Secure the lid. Choose the Manual mode and set cooking time for 8 minutes at High pressure. 4. Meanwhile, combine the ingredients for the Pico de Gallo in a small bowl. Refrigerate until ready to serve. 5. Once cooking is complete, use a quick pressure release. Carefully remove the lid. 6. Serve warm pork steaks with the chilled Pico de Gallo on the side.

Per Serving:
calories: 448 | fat: 29g | protein: 39g | carbs: 4g | net carbs: 2g | fiber: 2g

Spicy Beef Stew with Butternut Squash

1½ tablespoons smoked paprika
2 teaspoons ground cinnamon
1½ teaspoons kosher salt
1 teaspoon ground ginger
1 teaspoon red pepper flakes
½ teaspoon freshly ground black pepper
2 pounds beef shoulder roast, cut into 1-inch cubes
2 tablespoons avocado oil, divided

1 cup low-sodium beef or vegetable broth
1 medium red onion, cut into wedges
8 garlic cloves, minced
1 (28-ounce) carton or can no-salt-added diced tomatoes
2 pounds butternut squash, peeled and cut into 1-inch pieces
Chopped fresh cilantro or parsley, for serving

1. In a zip-top bag or medium bowl, combine the paprika, cinnamon, salt, ginger, red pepper, and black pepper. Add the beef and toss to coat. 2. Set the electric pressure cooker to the Sauté setting. When the pot is hot, pour in 1 tablespoon of avocado oil. 3. Add half of the beef to the pot and cook, stirring occasionally, for 3 to 5 minutes or until the beef is no longer pink. Transfer it to a plate, then add the remaining 1 tablespoon of avocado oil and brown the remaining beef. Transfer to the plate. Hit Cancel. 4. Stir in the broth and scrape up any brown bits from the bottom of the pot. Return the beef to the pot and add the onion, garlic, tomatoes and their juices, and squash. Stir well. 5. Close and lock lid of pressure cooker. Set the valve to sealing. 6. Cook on high pressure for 30 minutes. 7. When cooking is complete, hit Cancel. Allow the pressure to release naturally for 10 minutes, then quick release any remaining pressure. 8. Unlock and remove lid. 9. Spoon into serving bowls, sprinkle with cilantro or parsley, and serve.

Per Serving:
calorie: 275 | fat: 9g | protein: 28g | carbs: 24g | sugars: 7g | fiber: 6g | sodium: 512mg

Italian Beef Meatloaf

1 pound (454 g) ground beef
1 cup crushed pork rinds
1 egg
¼ cup grated Parmesan cheese
¼ cup Italian dressing
2 teaspoons Italian seasoning

½ cup water
½ cup sugar-free tomato sauce
1 tablespoon chopped fresh herbs (such as parsley or basil)
1 clove garlic, minced

1. In large bowl, combine the beef, pork rinds, egg, cheese, dressing, and Italian seasoning. Use a wooden spoon to incorporate everything into the meat, but do not overwork the meat or it will turn out tough. 2. Turn the meat mixture out onto a piece of aluminum foil. Use your hands to shape into a loaf. Wrap the foil up around the meat like a packet, but do not cover the top. Place the trivet in the pot and add the water. Place the meatloaf on top of the trivet. 3. Close the lid and seal the vent. Cook on High Pressure 20 minutes. Quick release the steam. 4. While the meat is cooking, whisk together the tomato sauce, herbs, and garlic in a small bowl. Heat the broiler. 5. Remove the meat and foil packet from the pot. Place on a baking sheet and spread the tomato sauce mixture on top. Broil until the glaze becomes sticky, about 5 minutes. Slice into six equal pieces.

Per Serving:
calories: 358 | fat: 25g | protein: 29g | carbs: 2g | net carbs: 2g | fiber: 0g

Wine-Braised Short Ribs with Potatoes

2 pounds (907 g) bone-in English-style beef short ribs, trimmed
¾ teaspoon table salt, divided
¼ teaspoon pepper
1 tablespoon extra-virgin olive oil
1 onion, chopped fine
6 garlic cloves, minced
2 tablespoons tomato paste
1 tablespoon minced fresh

oregano or 1 teaspoon dried
1 (14½-ounce / 411-g) can whole peeled tomatoes, drained with ¼ cup juice reserved, chopped coarse
½ cup dry red wine
1 pound (454 g) small red potatoes, unpeeled, halved
2 tablespoons minced fresh parsley

1. Pat short ribs dry with paper towels and sprinkle with ½ teaspoon salt and pepper. Using highest sauté function, heat oil in Instant Pot for 5 minutes (or until just smoking). Brown short ribs on all sides, 6 to 8 minutes; transfer to plate. 2. Add onion and remaining ¼ teaspoon salt to fat left in pot and cook, using highest sauté function, until onion is softened, about 3 minutes. Stir in garlic, tomato paste, and oregano and cook until fragrant, about 30 seconds. Stir in tomatoes and reserved juice and wine, scraping up any browned bits. Nestle short ribs meat side down into pot and add any accumulated juices. Lock lid in place and close pressure release valve. Select high pressure cook function and cook for 60 minutes. 3. Turn off Instant Pot and let pressure release naturally for 15 minutes. Quick-release any remaining pressure, then carefully remove lid, allowing steam to escape away from you. Transfer short ribs to serving dish, tent with aluminum foil, and let rest while preparing potatoes. 4. Strain braising liquid through fine-mesh strainer into fat separator; transfer solids to now-empty pot. Let braising liquid settle for 5 minutes, then pour 1½ cups defatted liquid and any accumulated juices into pot with solids; discard remaining liquid. Add potatoes. Lock lid in place and close pressure release valve. Select high pressure cook function and cook for 4 minutes. Turn off Instant Pot and quick-release pressure. Carefully remove lid, allowing steam to escape away from you. 5. Using slotted spoon, transfer potatoes to serving dish. Season sauce with salt and pepper to taste. Spoon sauce over short ribs and potatoes and sprinkle with parsley. Serve.

Per Serving:
calories: 340 | fat: 13g | protein: 21g | carbs: 29g | fiber: 3g | sodium: 700mg

Beef Masala Curry

2 tomatoes, quartered
1 small onion, quartered
4 garlic cloves, chopped
½ cup fresh cilantro leaves
1 teaspoon garam masala
½ teaspoon ground coriander

1 teaspoon ground cumin
½ teaspoon cayenne
1 teaspoon salt
1 pound (454 g) beef chuck roast, cut into 1-inch cubes

1. In a blender, combine the tomatoes, onion, garlic, and cilantro. 2. Process until the vegetables are puréed. Add the garam masala, coriander, cumin, cayenne, and salt. Process for several more seconds. 3. To the Instant Pot, add the beef and pour the vegetable purée on top. 4. Lock the lid. Select Manual mode and set cooking time for 20 minutes on High Pressure. 5. When timer beeps, let the pressure release naturally for 10 minutes, then release any remaining pressure. Unlock the lid. 6. Stir and serve immediately.
Per Serving:
calories: 309 | fat: 21.0g | protein: 24.0g | carbs: 6.0g | net carbs: 4.0g | fiber: 2.0g

Cilantro Lime Shredded Pork

Prep time: 5 minutes | Cook time: 30 minutes | Serves 4

1 tablespoon chili adobo sauce	1 (2½ to 3 pounds / 1.1 to 1.4
1 tablespoon chili powder	kg) cubed pork butt
2 teaspoons salt	1 tablespoon coconut oil
1 teaspoon garlic powder	2 cups beef broth
1 teaspoon cumin	1 lime, cut into wedges
½ teaspoon pepper	¼ cup chopped cilantro

1. In a small bowl, mix adobo sauce, chili powder, salt, garlic powder, cumin, and pepper. 2. Press the Sauté button on Instant Pot and add coconut oil to pot. Rub spice mixture onto cubed pork butt. Place pork into pot and sear for 3 to 5 minutes per side. Add broth. 3. Press the Cancel button. Lock Lid. Press the Manual button and adjust time to 30 minutes. 4. When timer beeps, let pressure naturally release until the float valve drops, and unlock lid. 5. Shred pork with fork. Pork should easily fall apart. For extra-crispy pork, place single layer in skillet on stove over medium heat. Cook for 10 to 15 minutes or until water has cooked out and pork becomes brown and crisp. Serve warm with fresh lime wedges and cilantro garnish.
Per Serving:
calories: 570 | fat: 36g | protein: 55g | carbs: 3g | net carbs: 2g | fiber: 1g

Bo Ssäm

Prep time: 10 minutes | Cook time: 8 minutes | Serves 6

1 tablespoon vegetable oil	1 tablespoon minced garlic
1 pound (454 g) ground pork	1 tablespoon coconut aminos
2 tablespoons gochujang	1 teaspoon hot sesame oil
1 tablespoon Doubanjiang	1 teaspoon salt
½ teaspoon ground Sichuan	¼ cup water
peppercorns	1 bunch bok choy, chopped
1 tablespoon minced fresh	(about 4 to 6 cups)
ginger	

1. Preheat the Instant Pot on Sauté mode. Add the oil and heat until it is shimmering. 2. Add the ground pork, breaking up all lumps, and cook for 4 minutes or until the pork is no longer pink. 3. Add the gochujang, doubanjiang, peppercorns, ginger, garlic, coconut aminos, sesame oil, and salt. Stir to combine. 4. Add the water and bok choy. 5. Lock the lid. Select Manual mode. Set cooking time for 4 minutes on High Pressure. 6. When cooking is complete, quick-release the pressure. Unlock the lid. 7. Serve immediately.
Per Serving:
calories: 239 | fat: 19.0g | protein: 14.0g | carbs: 2.0g | net carbs: 1.0g | fiber: 1.0g

Osso Buco with Gremolata

Prep time: 35 minutes | Cook time: 1 hour 2 minutes | Serves 6

4 bone-in beef shanks	1 cup chicken broth
Sea salt, to taste	1 sprig fresh rosemary
2 tablespoons avocado oil	2 sprigs fresh thyme
1 small turnip, diced	3 Roma tomatoes, diced
1 medium onion, diced	For the Gremolata:
1 medium stalk celery, diced	½ cup loosely packed parsley
4 cloves garlic, smashed	leaves
1 tablespoon unsweetened	1 clove garlic, crushed
tomato purée	Grated zest of 2 lemons
½ cup dry white wine	

1. On a clean work surface, season the shanks all over with salt. 2. Set the Instant Pot to Sauté and add the oil. When the oil shimmers, add 2 shanks and sear for 4 minutes per side. Remove the shanks to a bowl and repeat with the remaining shanks. Set aside. 3. Add the turnip, onion, and celery to the pot and cook for 5 minutes or until softened. 4. Add the garlic and unsweetened tomato purée and cook 1 minute more, stirring frequently. 5. Deglaze the pot with the wine, scraping the bottom with a wooden spoon to loosen any browned bits. Bring to a boil. 6. Add the broth, rosemary, thyme, and shanks, then add the tomatoes on top of the shanks. 7. Secure the lid. Press the Manual button and set cooking time for 40 minutes on High Pressure. 8. Meanwhile, for the gremolata: In a small food processor, combine the parsley, garlic, and lemon zest and pulse until the parsley is finely chopped. Refrigerate until ready to use. 9. When timer beeps, allow the pressure to release naturally for 20 minutes, then release any remaining pressure. Open the lid. 10. To serve, transfer the shanks to large, shallow serving bowl. Ladle the braising sauce over the top and sprinkle with the gremolata.
Per Serving:
calories: 605 | fat: 30.1g | protein: 69.1g | carbs: 7.7g | net carbs: 6.0g | fiber: 1.7g

Eggplant Pork Lasagna

Prep time: 20 minutes | Cook time: 30 minutes | Serves 6

2 eggplants, sliced	1 tablespoon unsweetened
1 teaspoon salt	tomato purée
10 ounces (283 g) ground pork	1 teaspoon butter, softened
1 cup Mozzarella, shredded	1 cup chicken stock

1. Sprinkle the eggplants with salt and let sit for 10 minutes, then pat dry with paper towels. 2. In a mixing bowl, mix the ground pork, butter, and tomato purée. 3. Make a layer of the sliced eggplants in the bottom of the Instant Pot and top with ground pork mixture. 4. Top the ground pork with Mozzarella and repeat with remaining ingredients. 5. Pour in the chicken stock. Close the lid. Select Manual mode and set cooking time for 30 minutes on High Pressure. 6. When timer beeps, use a natural pressure release for 10 minutes, then release the remaining pressure and open the lid. 7. Cool for 10 minutes and serve.
Per Serving:
calories: 136 | fat: 3.6g | protein: 15.7g | carbs: 11.5g | net carbs: 4.9g | fiber: 6.6g

Cilantro Pork Meatballs

Prep time: 10 minutes | Cook time: 15 minutes | Serves 3

1 cup ground pork	½ teaspoon salt
1 ounce (28 g) fresh cilantro, chopped	1 teaspoon ground coriander
	2 tablespoons butter
1 garlic clove, diced	1 tablespoon coconut cream

1. Blend the fresh cilantro until it is smooth and mix it up with ground pork, diced garlic, salt, and ground coriander. 2. Make the small meatballs and press them gently with the help of the hand palms. 3. Then melt the butter in the instant pot on Sauté mode and add the meatballs. 4. Cook them for 3 minutes from each side. Add coconut cream and close the lid. 5. Cook the meal on Sauté mode for 5 minutes.

Per Serving:

calories: 393 | fat: 30g | protein: 27g | carbs: 1g | net carbs: 1g | fiber: 0g

esty Swiss Steak

Prep time: 35 minutes | Cook time: 35 minutes | Serves 6

3–4 tablespoons flour	1 cup sliced onions
½ teaspoon salt	1 pound carrots, sliced
¼ teaspoon pepper	14½-ounce can whole tomatoes
1½ teaspoons dry mustard	⅓ cup water
1½–2 pounds round steak, trimmed of fat	1 tablespoon brown sugar
	1½ tablespoons Worcestershire sauce
1 tablespoon canola oil	

1. Combine flour, salt, pepper, and dry mustard. 2. Cut steak in serving pieces. Dredge in flour mixture. 3. Set the Instant Pot to Sauté and add in the oil. Brown the steak pieces on both sides in the oil. Press Cancel. 4. Add onions and carrots into the Instant Pot. 5. Combine the tomatoes, water, brown sugar, and Worcestershire sauce. Pour into the Instant Pot. 6. Secure the lid and make sure the vent is set to sealing. Press Manual and set the time for 35 minutes. 7. When cook time is up, let the pressure release naturally for 15 minutes, then perform a quick release.

Per Serving:

calories: 236 | fat: 8g | protein: 23g | carbs: 18g | sugars: 9g | fiber: 3g | sodium: 426mg

5-Ingredient Mexican Lasagna

Prep time: 15 minutes | Cook time: 15 minutes | Serves 4

Nonstick cooking spray	1½ cups cooked shredded beef, pork, or chicken
½ (15-ounce) can light red kidney beans, rinsed and drained	
	1⅓ cups salsa
4 (6-inch) gluten-free corn tortillas	1⅓ cups shredded Mexican cheese blend

1. Spray a 6-inch springform pan with nonstick spray. Wrap the bottom in foil. 2. In a medium bowl, mash the beans with a fork. 3. Place 1 tortilla in the bottom of the pan. Add about ⅓ of the beans, ½ cup of meat, ⅓ cup of salsa, and ⅓ cup of cheese. Press down. Repeat for 2 more layers. Add the remaining tortilla and press down. Top with the remaining salsa and cheese. There are no beans or meat on the top layer. 4. Tear off a piece of foil big enough to cover the pan, and spray it with nonstick spray. Line the pan with the foil, sprayed-side down. 5. Pour 1 cup of water into the electric pressure cooker. 6. Place the pan on the wire rack and carefully lower it into the pot. Close and lock the lid of the pressure cooker. Set the valve to sealing. 7. Cook on high pressure for 15 minutes. 8. When the cooking is complete, hit Cancel. Allow the pressure to release naturally for 10 minutes, then quick release any remaining pressure. 9. Once the pin drops, unlock and remove the lid. 10. Using the handles of the wire rack, carefully remove the pan from the pot. Let the lasagna sit for 5 minutes. Carefully remove the ring. 11. Slice into quarters and serve.

Per Serving:

calorie: 380 | fat: 18g | protein: 32g | carbs: 22g | sugars: 4g | fiber: 4g | sodium: 594mg

Braised Pork Belly

Prep time: 15 minutes | Cook time: 37 minutes | Serves 4

1 pound (454 g) pork belly	1 clove garlic, minced
1 tablespoon olive oil	1 cup dry white wine
Salt and ground black pepper to taste	Rosemary sprig

1. Select the Sauté mode on the Instant Pot and heat the oil. 2. Add the pork belly and sauté for 2 minutes per side, until starting to brown. 3. Season the meat with salt and pepper, add the garlic. 4. Pour in the wine and add the rosemary sprig. Bring to a boil. 5. Select the Manual mode and set the cooking time for 35 minutes at High pressure. 6. Once cooking is complete, use a natural pressure release for 10 minutes, then release any remaining pressure. Open the lid. 7. Slice the meat and serve.

Per Serving:

calories: 666 | fat: 63.5g | protein: 10.7g | carbs: 1.5g | net carbs: 1.4g | fiber: 0.1g

Beef Steak with Cheese Mushroom Sauce

Prep time: 6 minutes | Cook time: 30 minutes | Serves 6

1 tablespoon olive oil	Sauce:
1½ pounds (680 g) beef blade steak	1 tablespoon butter, softened
	2 cups sliced Porcini mushrooms
1 cup stock	
2 garlic cloves, minced	½ cup thinly sliced onions
Sea salt and ground black pepper, to taste	½ cup sour cream
	4 ounces (113 g) goat cheese, crumbled
½ teaspoon cayenne pepper	
1 tablespoon coconut aminos	

1. Press the Sauté button to heat up the Instant Pot. Then, heat the olive oil until sizzling. Once hot, cook the blade steak approximately 3 minutes or until delicately browned. 2. Add the stock, garlic, salt, black pepper, cayenne pepper, and coconut aminos. 3. Secure the lid. Choose Manual mode and High Pressure; cook for 20 minutes. Once cooking is complete, use a quick pressure release; carefully remove the lid. 4. Take the meat out of the Instant Pot. Allow it to

cool slightly and then, slice it into strips. 5. Press the Sauté button again and add the butter, mushrooms and onions to the Instant Pot. Let it cook for 5 minutes longer or until the mushrooms are fragrant and the onions are softened. 6. Add sour cream and goat cheese; continue to simmer for a couple of minutes more or until everything is thoroughly heated. 7. Return the meat to the Instant Pot and serve. Bon appétit!

Per Serving:
calories: 311 | fat: 20g | protein: 31g | carbs: 3g | net carbs: 3g | fiber: 0g

Pork Cubes with Fennel

Prep time: 8 minutes | Cook time: 30 minutes | Serves 2

1 teaspoon lemon juice
10 ounces (283 g) pork loin, chopped
½ cup water
1 ounce (28 g) fennel, chopped
1 teaspoon salt
½ teaspoon peppercorns

1. Sprinkle the chopped pork loin with the lemon juice. 2. Then strew the meat with the salt. 3. Place the meat in the meat mold. 4. Insert the meat mold in the instant pot. 5. Add water, fennel, and peppercorns. 6. Close the lid and lock it. 7. Set the Meat/Stew mode and put a timer on 30 minutes. 8. Serve the pork cubes with hot gravy.

Per Serving:
calories: 349 | fat: 20g | protein: 39g | carbs: 2g | net carbs: 1g | fiber: 1g

Pork Chops Pomodoro

Prep time: 0 minutes | Cook time: 30 minutes | Serves 6

2 pounds boneless pork loin chops, each about 5⅓ ounces and ½ inch thick
¾ teaspoon fine sea salt
½ teaspoon freshly ground black pepper
2 tablespoons extra-virgin olive oil
2 garlic cloves, chopped
½ cup low-sodium chicken broth or vegetable broth
½ teaspoon Italian seasoning
1 tablespoon capers, drained
2 cups cherry tomatoes
2 tablespoons chopped fresh basil or flat-leaf parsley
Spiralized zucchini noodles, cooked cauliflower "rice," or cooked whole-grain pasta for serving
Lemon wedges for serving

1. Pat the pork chops dry with paper towels, then season them all over with the salt and pepper. 2. Select the Sauté setting on the Instant Pot and heat 1 tablespoon of the oil for 2 minutes. Swirl the oil to coat the bottom of the pot. Using tongs, add half of the pork chops in a single layer and sear for about 3 minutes, until lightly browned on the first side. Flip the chops and sear for about 3 minutes more, until lightly browned on the second side. Transfer the chops to a plate. Repeat with the remaining 1 tablespoon oil and pork chops. 3. Add the garlic to the pot and sauté for about 1 minute, until bubbling but not browned. Stir in the broth, Italian seasoning, and capers, using a wooden spoon to nudge any browned bits from the bottom of the pot and working quickly so not too much liquid evaporates. Using the tongs, transfer the pork chops to the pot. Add the tomatoes in an even layer on top of the chops. 4. Secure the lid and set the Pressure Release to Sealing. Press the Cancel button to reset the cooking program, then select the Pressure Cook or Manual setting and set the cooking time for 10 minutes at high pressure. (The pot will take

about 5 minutes to come up to pressure before the cooking program begins.) 5. When the cooking program ends, let the pressure release naturally for at least 10 minutes, then move the Pressure Release to Venting to release any remaining steam. Open the pot and, using the tongs, transfer the pork chops to a serving dish. 6. Spoon the tomatoes and some of the cooking liquid on top of the pork chops. Sprinkle with the basil and serve right away, with zucchini noodles and lemon wedges on the side.

Per Serving:
calorie: 265 | fat: 13g | protein: 31g | carbs: 3g | sugars: 2g | fiber: 1g | sodium: 460mg

Cider-Herb Pork Tenderloin

Prep time: 15 minutes | Cook time: 18 minutes | Serves 4

¼ teaspoon ground cumin
½ teaspoon ground nutmeg
½ teaspoon dried thyme
½ teaspoon ground coriander
1 tablespoon sesame oil
1 pound (454 g) pork tenderloin
2 tablespoons apple cider vinegar
1 cup water

1. In the mixing bowl, mix up ground cumin, ground nutmeg, thyme, ground coriander, and apple cider vinegar. 2. Then rub the meat with the spice mixture. 3. Heat up sesame oil on Sauté mode for 2 minutes. 4. Put the pork tenderloin in the hot oil and cook it for 5 minutes from each side or until meat is light brown. 5. Add water. 6. Close and seal the lid. Cook the meat on Manual mode (High Pressure) for 5 minutes. 7. When the time is finished, allow the natural pressure release for 15 minutes.

Per Serving:
calories: 196 | fat: 7g | protein: 29g | carbs: 0g | net carbs: 0g | fiber: 0g

Korean Short Rib Lettuce Wraps

Prep time: 7 minutes | Cook time: 25 minutes | Serves 4

¼ cup coconut aminos, or 1 tablespoon wheat-free tamari
2 tablespoons coconut vinegar
2 tablespoons sesame oil
3 green onions, thinly sliced, plus more for garnish
2 teaspoons peeled and grated fresh ginger
2 teaspoons minced garlic
½ teaspoon fine sea salt
½ teaspoon red pepper flakes, plus more for garnish
1 pound (454 g) boneless beef short ribs, sliced ½ inch thick
For Serving:
1 head radicchio, thinly sliced
Butter lettuce leaves

1. Place the coconut aminos, vinegar, sesame oil, green onions, ginger, garlic, salt, and red pepper flakes in the Instant Pot and stir to combine. Add the short ribs and toss to coat well. 2. Seal the lid, press Manual, and set the timer for 20 minutes. Once finished, let the pressure release naturally. 3. Remove the ribs from the Instant Pot and set aside on a warm plate, leaving the sauce in the pot. 4. Press Sauté and cook the sauce, whisking often, until thickened to your liking, about 5 minutes. 5. Put the sliced radicchio on a serving platter, then lay the short ribs on top. Pour the thickened sauce over the ribs. Garnish with more sliced green onions and red pepper flakes. Serve wrapped in lettuce leaves.

Per Serving:
calories: 547 | fat: 48g | protein: 18g | carbs: 9g | net carbs: 0g | fiber: 9g

Beef Brisket with Cabbage

Prep time: 15 minutes | Cook time: 1 hour 7 minutes | Serves 8

3 pounds (1.4 kg) corned beef brisket
4 cups water
3 garlic cloves, minced
2 teaspoons yellow mustard seed

2 teaspoons black peppercorns
3 celery stalks, chopped
½ large white onion, chopped
1 green cabbage, cut into quarters

1. Add the brisket to the Instant Pot. Pour the water into the pot. Add the garlic, mustard seed, and black peppercorns. 2. Lock the lid. Select Meat/Stew mode and set cooking time for 50 minutes on High Pressure. 3. When cooking is complete, allow the pressure to release naturally for 20 minutes, then release any remaining pressure. Open the lid and transfer only the brisket to a platter. 4. Add the celery, onion, and cabbage to the pot. 5. Lock the lid. Select Soup mode and set cooking time for 12 minutes on High Pressure. 6. When cooking is complete, quick release the pressure. Open the lid, add the brisket back to the pot and let warm in the pot for 5 minutes. 7. Transfer the warmed brisket back to the platter and thinly slice. Transfer the vegetables to the platter. Serve hot.

Per Serving:
calories: 357 | fat: 25.5g | protein: 26.3g | carbs: 7.3g | net carbs: 5.3g | fiber: 2.0g

Mary's Sunday Pot Roast

Prep time: 10 minutes | Cook time:1 hour 30 minutes | Serves 10

1 (3- to 4-pound) beef rump roast
2 teaspoons kosher salt, divided
2 tablespoons avocado oil
1 large onion, coarsely chopped (about 1½ cups)
4 large carrots, each cut into 4

pieces
1 tablespoon minced garlic
3 cups low-sodium beef broth
1 teaspoon freshly ground black pepper
1 tablespoon dried parsley
2 tablespoons all-purpose flour

1. Rub the roast all over with 1 teaspoon of the salt. 2. Set the electric pressure cooker to the Sauté setting. When the pot is hot, pour in the avocado oil. 3. Carefully place the roast in the pot and sear it for 6 to 9 minutes on each side. (You want a dark caramelized crust.) Hit Cancel. 4. Transfer the roast from the pot to a plate. 5. In order, put the onion, carrots, and garlic in the pot. Place the roast on top of the vegetables along with any juices that accumulated on the plate. 6. In a medium bowl, whisk together the broth, remaining 1 teaspoon of salt, pepper, and parsley. Pour the broth mixture over the roast. 7. Close and lock the lid of the pressure cooker. Set the valve to sealing. 8. Cook on high pressure for 1 hour and 30 minutes. 9. When the cooking is complete, hit Cancel and allow the pressure to release naturally. 10. Once the pin drops, unlock and remove the lid. 11. Using large slotted spoons, transfer the roast and vegetables to a serving platter while you make the gravy. 12. Using a large spoon or fat separator, remove the fat from the juices in the pot. Set the electric pressure cooker to the Sauté setting and bring the liquid to a boil. 13. In a small bowl, whisk together the flour and 4 tablespoons of water to make a slurry. Pour the slurry into the pot, whisking occasionally, until the gravy is the thickness you like. Season with salt and pepper, if necessary. 14. Serve the meat and carrots with the gravy.

Per Serving:
calories: 245 | fat: 10g | protein: 33g | carbs: 6g | sugars: 2g | fiber: 1g | sodium: 397mg

Beef Shawarma and Veggie Salad Bowls

Prep time: 10 minutes | Cook time: 19 minutes | Serves 4

2 teaspoons olive oil
1½ pounds (680 g) beef flank steak, thinly sliced
Sea salt and freshly ground black pepper, to taste
1 teaspoon cayenne pepper
½ teaspoon ground bay leaf
½ teaspoon ground allspice
½ teaspoon cumin, divided

½ cup Greek yogurt
2 tablespoons sesame oil
1 tablespoon fresh lime juice
2 English cucumbers, chopped
1 cup cherry tomatoes, halved
1 red onion, thinly sliced
½ head romaine lettuce, chopped

1. Press the Sauté button to heat up the Instant Pot. Then, heat the olive oil and cook the beef for about 4 minutes. 2. Add all seasonings, 1½ cups of water, and secure the lid. 3. Choose Manual mode. Set the cook time for 15 minutes on High Pressure. 4. Once cooking is complete, use a natural pressure release. Carefully remove the lid. 5. Allow the beef to cool completely. 6. To make the dressing, whisk Greek yogurt, sesame oil, and lime juice in a mixing bowl. 7. Then, divide cucumbers, tomatoes, red onion, and romaine lettuce among four serving bowls. Dress the salad and top with the reserved beef flank steak. Serve warm.

Per Serving:
calories: 367 | fat: 19.1g | protein: 39.5g | carbs: 8.4g | net carbs: 5.0g | fiber: 3.4g

Cilantro Pork

Prep time: 10 minutes | Cook time: 85 minutes | Serves 4

1 pound (454 g) boneless pork shoulder
¼ cup chopped fresh cilantro
1 cup water

1 teaspoon salt
1 teaspoon coconut oil
½ teaspoon mustard seeds

1. Pour water in the instant pot. 2. Add pork shoulder, fresh cilantro, salt, coconut oil, and mustard seeds. 3. Close and seal the lid. Cook the meat on High Pressure (Manual mode) for 85 minutes. 4. Then make a quick pressure release and open the lid. 5. The cooked meat has to be served with the remaining liquid from the instant pot.

Per Serving:
calories: 343 | fat: 25g | protein: 26g | carbs: 0g | net carbs: 0g | fiber: 0g

Blade Pork with Sauerkraut

Prep time: 15 minutes | Cook time: 37 minutes | Serves 6

2 pounds (907 g) blade pork steaks
Sea salt and ground black pepper, to taste
½ teaspoon cayenne pepper

½ teaspoon dried parsley flakes
1 tablespoon butter
1½ cups water
2 cloves garlic, thinly sliced
2 pork sausages, casing

removed and sliced   4 cups sauerkraut

1. Season the blade pork steaks with salt, black pepper, cayenne pepper, and dried parsley. 2. Press the Sauté button to heat up the Instant Pot. Melt the butter and sear blade pork steaks for 5 minutes or until browned on all sides. 3. Clean the Instant Pot. Add water and trivet to the bottom of the Instant Pot. 4. Place the blade pork steaks on the trivet. Make small slits over entire pork with a knife. Insert garlic pieces into each slit. 5. Secure the lid. Choose the Meat/Stew mode and set cooking time for 30 minutes on High pressure. 6. Once cooking is complete, use a natural pressure release for 15 minutes, then release any remaining pressure. Carefully remove the lid. 7. Add the sausage and sauerkraut. Press the Sauté button and cook for 2 minutes more or until heated through. 8. Serve immediately

Per Serving:
calories: 471 | fat: 27.3g | protein: 47.7g | carbs: 8.4g | net carbs: 2.0g | fiber: 6.4g

BBQ Ribs and Broccoli Slaw

Prep time: 10 minutes | Cook time: 50 minutes | Serves 6

BBQ Ribs
4 pounds baby back ribs
1 teaspoon fine sea salt
1 teaspoon freshly ground black pepper
Broccoli Slaw
½ cup plain 2 percent Greek yogurt
1 tablespoon olive oil
1 tablespoon fresh lemon juice
½ teaspoon fine sea salt
¼ teaspoon freshly ground black pepper
1 pound broccoli florets (or

florets from 2 large crowns), chopped
10 radishes, halved and thinly sliced
1 red bell pepper, seeded and cut lengthwise into narrow strips
1 large apple (such as Fuji, Jonagold, or Gala), thinly sliced
½ red onion, thinly sliced
¾ cup low-sugar or unsweetened barbecue sauce

1. To make the ribs: Pat the ribs dry with paper towels, then cut the racks into six sections (three to five ribs per section, depending on how big the racks are). Season the ribs all over with the salt and pepper. 2. Pour 1 cup water into the Instant Pot and place the wire metal steam rack into the pot. Place the ribs on top of the wire rack (it's fine to stack them up). 3. Secure the lid and set the Pressure Release to Sealing. Select the Pressure Cook or Manual setting and set the cooking time for 20 minutes at high pressure. (The pot will take about 15 minutes to come up to pressure before the cooking program begins.) 4. To make the broccoli slaw: While the ribs are cooking, in a small bowl, stir together the yogurt, oil, lemon juice, salt, and pepper, mixing well. In a large bowl, combine the broccoli, radishes, bell pepper, apple, and onion. Drizzle with the yogurt mixture and toss until evenly coated. 5. When the ribs have about 10 minutes left in their cooking time, preheat the oven to 400°F. Line a sheet pan with aluminum foil. 6. When the cooking program ends, perform a quick pressure release by moving the Pressure Release to Venting. Open the pot and, using tongs, transfer the ribs in a single layer to the prepared sheet pan. Brush the barbecue sauce onto both sides of the ribs, using 2 tablespoons of sauce per section of ribs. Bake, meaty-side up, for 15 to 20 minutes, until lightly browned. 7. Serve the ribs warm, with the slaw on the side.

Per Serving:
calories: 392 | fat: 15g | protein: 45g | carbs: 19g | sugars: 9g | fiber:

4g | sodium: 961mg

Herbed Lamb Shank

Prep time: 15 minutes | Cook time: 35 minutes | Serves 2

2 lamb shanks
1 rosemary spring
1 teaspoon coconut flour
¼ teaspoon onion powder

¼ teaspoon chili powder
¾ teaspoon ground ginger
½ cup beef broth
½ teaspoon avocado oil

1. Put all ingredients in the Instant Pot. Stir to mix well. 2. Close the lid. Select Manual mode and set cooking time for 35 minutes on High Pressure. 3. When timer beeps, use a natural pressure release for 15 minutes, then release any remaining pressure. Open the lid. 4. Discard the rosemary sprig and serve warm.

Per Serving:
calories: 179 | fat: 7.0g | protein: 25.4g | carbs: 2.0g | net carbs: 1.2g | fiber: 0.8g

Greek Lamb Leg

Prep time: 10 minutes | Cook time: 50 minutes | Serves 4

1 pound (454 g) lamb leg
½ teaspoon dried thyme
1 teaspoon paprika powder
¼ teaspoon cumin seeds

1 tablespoon softened butter
2 garlic cloves
¼ cup water

1. Rub the lamb leg with dried thyme, paprika powder, and cumin seeds on a clean work surface. 2. Brush the leg with softened butter and transfer to the Instant Pot. Add garlic cloves and water. 3. Close the lid. Select Manual mode and set cooking time for 50 minutes on High Pressure. 4. When timer beeps, use a quick pressure release. Open the lid. 5. Serve warm.

Per Serving:
calories: 239 | fat: 11.2g | protein: 32.0g | carbs: 0.6g | net carbs: 0.5g | fiber: 0.1g

Pork Meatballs with Thyme

Prep time: 15 minutes | Cook time: 16 minutes | Serves 8

2 cups ground pork
1 teaspoon dried thyme
½ teaspoon chili flakes
½ teaspoon garlic powder

1 tablespoon coconut oil
¼ teaspoon ground ginger
3 tablespoons almond flour
¼ cup water

1. In the mixing bowl, mix up ground pork, dried thyme, chili flakes, garlic powder, ground ginger, and almond flour. 2. Make the meatballs. 3. Melt the coconut oil in the instant pot on Sauté mode. 4. Arrange the meatballs in the instant pot in one layer and cook them for 3 minutes from each side. 5. Then add water and cook the meatballs for 10 minutes.

Per Serving:
calories: 264 | fat: 19g | protein: 20g | carbs: 1g | net carbs: 1g | fiber: 0g

Shepherd's Pie with Cauliflower-Carrot Mash

Prep time: 10 minutes | Cook time: 35 minutes | Serves 6

1 tablespoon coconut oil
2 garlic cloves, minced
1 large yellow onion, diced
1 pound ground lamb
1 pound 95 percent lean ground beef
½ cup low-sodium vegetable broth
1 teaspoons dried thyme
1 teaspoon dried sage
1 teaspoon freshly ground black pepper
1¾ teaspoons fine sea salt
2 tablespoons Worcestershire sauce
One 12-ounce bag frozen baby lima beans, green peas, or shelled edamame
3 tablespoons tomato paste
1 pound cauliflower florets
1 pound carrots, halved lengthwise and then crosswise (or quartered if very large)
¼ cup coconut milk or other nondairy milk
½ cup sliced green onions, white and green parts

1. Select the Sauté setting on the Instant Pot and heat the oil and garlic for 2 minutes, until the garlic is bubbling but not browned. Add the onion and sauté for 3 minutes, until it begins to soften. Add the lamb and beef and sauté, using a wooden spoon or spatula to break up the meat as it cooks, for 6 minutes, until cooked through and no streaks of pink remain. 2. Stir in the broth, using the spoon or spatula to nudge any browned bits from the bottom of the pot. Add the thyme, sage, pepper, ¾ teaspoon of the salt, the Worcestershire sauce, and lima beans and stir to mix. Dollop the tomato paste on top. Do not stir it in. 3. Place a tall steam rack in the pot, then place the cauliflower and carrots on top of the rack. 4. Secure the lid and set the Pressure Release to Sealing. Press the Cancel button to reset the cooking program, then select the Pressure Cook or Manual setting and set the cooking time for 4 minutes at low pressure. (The pot will take about 15 minutes to come up to pressure before the cooking program begins.) 5. Position an oven rack 4 to 6 inches below the heat source and preheat the broiler. 6. When the cooking program ends, perform a quick pressure release by moving the Pressure Release to Venting. Open the pot and, using tongs, transfer the cauliflower and carrots to a bowl. Add the coconut milk and remaining 1 teaspoon salt to the bowl. Using an immersion blender, blend the vegetables until smooth. 7. Wearing heat-resistant mitts, remove the steam rack from the pot. Stir ½ cup of the mashed vegetables into the filling mixture in the pot, incorporating the tomato paste at the same time. Remove the inner pot from the housing. Transfer the mixture to a broiler-safe 9 by 13-inch baking dish, spreading it in an even layer. Dollop the mashed vegetables on top and spread them out evenly with a fork. Broil, checking often, for 5 to 8 minutes, until the mashed vegetables are lightly browned. 8. Spoon the shepherd's pie onto plates, sprinkle with the green onions, and serve hot.

Per Serving:
calories: 437 | fat: 18g | protein: 39g | carbs: 33g | sugars: 8g | fiber: 9g | sodium: 802mg

Korean Ground Beef Bowl

Prep time: 5 minutes | Cook time: 10 minutes | Serves 4

1 tablespoon sesame oil
1½ pounds (680 g) ground
sirloin
1 teaspoon dried basil
½ teaspoon oregano
Sea salt and ground black pepper, to taste
½ cup diced onion
1 teaspoon minced garlic
¼ teaspoon ground ginger
1 teaspoon red pepper flakes
¼ teaspoon allspice
1 tablespoon coconut aminos
½ cup roughly chopped fresh cilantro leaves

1. Press the Sauté button to heat up the Instant Pot. Then, heat the sesame oil until sizzling. 2. Add ground sirloin and cook for a few minutes or until browned. Add the remaining ingredients, except for cilantro. 3. Secure the lid. Choose Manual mode and High Pressure; cook for 5 minutes. Once cooking is complete, use a natural pressure release; carefully remove the lid. 4. Divide among individual bowls and serve garnished with fresh cilantro. Bon appétit!

Per Serving:
calories: 307 | fat: 17g | protein: 34g | carbs: 4g | net carbs: 3g | fiber: 1g

Bacon Cheddar Cheese Stuffed Burgers

Prep time: 10 minutes | Cook time: 9 minutes | Serves 4

1 pound (454 g) ground beef
6 ounces (170 g) shredded Cheddar cheese
5 slices bacon, coarsely chopped
2 teaspoons Worcestershire
sauce
1 teaspoon salt
½ teaspoon liquid smoke
½ teaspoon black pepper
½ teaspoon garlic powder
1 cup water

1. In a large bowl, add the beef, cheese, bacon, Worcestershire sauce, salt, liquid smoke, pepper, and garlic powder. Gently work everything into the meat. Do not overwork the meat, or it will become tough when it cooks. 2. Separate the meat into four equal portions. Use a food scale to measure evenly. 3. Shape each piece into a ball. Use your thumb to make a crater in the middle of the patty but make sure the round shape is retained. 4. Wrap each patty loosely in aluminum foil. Place them on top of the trivet in the pot. They will overlap. 5. Add the water to the bottom of the pot. Close the lid and seal the vent. Cook on High Pressure for 9 minutes. Quick release the steam. Remove the foil packets from the pot and set them on a large plate. Carefully unwrap the burgers. There will be juices in the bottom of the foil.

Per Serving:
calories: 454 | fat: 33g | protein: 39g | carbs: 2g | net carbs: 0g | fiber: 2g

Blue Cheese Stuffed Steak Roll-Ups

Prep time: 5 minutes | Cook time: 15 minutes | Serves 6

1 (1½-pound / 680-g) beef round tip roast, sliced into 6 steaks of equal thickness
6 ounces (170 g) blue cheese, crumbled
½ cup beef broth
¼ cup coconut aminos, or 1
tablespoon wheat-free tamari
4 cloves garlic, minced
Chopped fresh Italian parsley, for garnish
Cracked black pepper, for garnish

1. Place each steak in a resealable plastic bag and pound with a rolling pin or meat mallet until it is ½ inch thick. Lay the pounded steaks flat on a cutting board or other work surface. 2. Divide the blue cheese evenly among the steaks, placing the cheese on one side.

Roll up each steak, starting at a shorter end, and secure with toothpicks. 3. Combine the broth, coconut aminos, and garlic in the Instant Pot. Add the steak roll-ups to the broth mixture. 4. Seal the lid, press Manual, and set the timer for 15 minutes. Once finished, turn the valve to venting for a quick release. 5. Remove the toothpicks from the steak roll-ups before serving. Garnish the roll-ups with chopped parsley and cracked black pepper.

Per Serving:

calories: 417 | fat: 28g | protein: 37g | carbs: 3g | net carbs: 1g | fiber: 2g

Chipotle Pork Chops with Tomatoes

Prep time: 7 minutes | Cook time: 15 minutes | Serves 4

2 tablespoons coconut oil
3 chipotle chilies
2 tablespoons adobo sauce
2 teaspoons cumin
1 teaspoon dried thyme
1 teaspoon salt

4 (5-ounce / 142-g) boneless pork chops
½ medium onion, chopped
2 bay leaves
1 cup chicken broth
½ (7-ounce / 198-g) can fire-roasted diced tomatoes
⅓ cup chopped cilantro

1. Press the Sauté button and add coconut oil to Instant Pot. While it heats, add chilies, adobo sauce, cumin, thyme, and salt to food processor. Pulse to make paste. Rub paste into pork chops. Place in Instant Pot and sear each side 5 minutes or until browned. 2. Press the Cancel button and add onion, bay leaves, broth, tomatoes, and cilantro to Instant Pot. Click lid closed. Press the Manual button and adjust time for 15 minutes. When timer beeps, allow a 10-minute natural release, then quick-release the remaining pressure. Serve warm with additional cilantro as garnish if desired.

Per Serving:

calories: 375 | fat: 24g | protein: 31g | carbs: 5g | net carbs: 3g | fiber: 2g

Chapter 4   Fish and Seafood

Chunky Fish Soup with Tomatoes

Prep time: 10 minutes | Cook time: 8 minutes | Serves 4

2 teaspoons olive oil
1 yellow onion, chopped
1 bell pepper, sliced
1 celery, diced
2 garlic cloves, minced
3 cups fish stock
2 ripe tomatoes, crushed
¾ pound (340 g) haddock

fillets
1 cup shrimp
1 tablespoon sweet Hungarian paprika
1 teaspoon hot Hungarian paprika
½ teaspoon caraway seeds

1. Set the Instant Pot to Sauté. Add and heat the oil. Once hot, add the onions and sauté until soft and fragrant. 2. Add the pepper, celery, and garlic and continue to sauté until soft. 3. Stir in the remaining ingredients. 4. Lock the lid. Select the Manual mode and set the cooking time for 5 minutes at High Pressure. 5. When the timer beeps, perform a quick pressure release. Carefully remove the lid. 6. Divide into serving bowls and serve hot.
Per Serving:
calories: 177 | fat: 4.7g | protein: 25.8g | carbs: 8.0g | net carbs: 5.6g | fiber: 2.4g

Crispy Fish Nuggets

Prep time: 15 minutes | Cook time: 9 minutes | Serves 4

1 pound (454 g) tilapia fillet
½ cup almond flour
3 eggs, beaten

¼ cup avocado oil
1 teaspoon salt

1. Cut the fish into the small pieces (nuggets) and sprinkle withs alt. 2. Then dip the fish nuggets in the eggs and coat in the almond flour. 3. Heat up avocado oil for 3 minutes on Sauté mode. 4. Put the prepared fish nuggets in the hot oil and cook them on Sauté mode for 3 minutes from each side or until they are golden brown.
Per Serving:
calories: 179 | fat: 8g | protein: 26g | carbs: 2g | net carbs: 1g | fiber: 1g

Herb-Crusted Cod Steaks

Prep time: 5 minutes | Cook time: 4 minutes | Serves 4

1½ cups water
2 tablespoons garlic-infused oil
4 cod steaks, 1½-inch thick
Sea salt, to taste
½ teaspoon mixed peppercorns,

crushed
2 sprigs thyme
1 sprig rosemary
1 yellow onion, sliced

1. Pour the water into your Instant Pot and insert a trivet. 2. Rub the garlic-infused oil into the cod steaks and season with the salt and crushed peppercorns. 3. Lower the cod steaks onto the trivet, skin-side down. Top with the thyme, rosemary, and onion. 4. Lock the lid. Select the Manual mode and set the cooking time for 4 minutes at High Pressure. 5. When the timer beeps, perform a quick pressure release. Carefully remove the lid. 6. Serve immediately.
Per Serving:
calories: 149 | fat: 7.3g | protein: 18.0g | carbs: 2.0g | net carbs: 1.5g | fiber: 0.5g

Cayenne Cod

Prep time: 10 minutes | Cook time: 10 minutes | Serves 2

2 cod fillets
¼ teaspoon chili powder
½ teaspoon cayenne pepper

½ teaspoon dried oregano
1 tablespoon lime juice
2 tablespoons avocado oil

1. Rub the cod fillets with chili powder, cayenne pepper, dried oregano, and sprinkle with lime juice. 2. Then pour the avocado oil in the instant pot and heat it up on Sauté mode for 2 minutes. 3. Put the cod fillets in the hot oil and cook for 5 minutes. 4. Then flip the fish on another side and cook for 5 minutes more.
Per Serving:
calories: 144 | fat: 3g | protein: 20g | carbs: 2g | net carbs: 1g | fiber: 1g

Rosemary Catfish

Prep time: 10 minutes | Cook time: 20 minutes | Serves 4

16 ounces (454 g) catfish fillet
1 tablespoon dried rosemary
1 teaspoon garlic powder

1 tablespoon avocado oil
1 teaspoon salt
1 cup water, for cooking

1. Cut the catfish fillet into 4 steaks. 2. Then sprinkle them with dried rosemary, garlic powder, avocado oil, and salt. 3. Place the fish steak in the baking mold in one layer. 4. After this, pour water and insert the steamer rack in the instant pot. 5. Put the baking mold with fish on the rack. Close and seal the lid. 6. Cook the meal on Manual (High Pressure) for 20 minutes. Make a quick pressure release.
Per Serving:
calories: 163 | fat: 9g | protein: 18g | carbs: 1g | net carbs: 1g | fiber: 0g

Caprese Salmon

Prep time: 10 minutes | Cook time: 15 minutes | Serves 2

10 ounces (283 g) salmon fillet (2 fillets)
4 ounces (113 g) Mozzarella, sliced
4 cherry tomatoes, sliced
1 teaspoon erythritol
1 teaspoon dried basil

½ teaspoon ground black pepper
1 tablespoon apple cider vinegar
1 tablespoon butter
1 cup water, for cooking

1. Grease the mold with butter and put the salmon inside. 2. Sprinkle the fish with erythritol, dried basil, ground black pepper, and apple cider vinegar. 3. Then top the salmon with tomatoes and Mozzarella. 4. Pour water and insert the steamer rack in the instant pot. 5. Put the fish on the rack. 6. Close and seal the lid. 7. Cook the meal on Manual mode at High Pressure for 15 minutes. Make a quick pressure release.
Per Serving:
calories: 447 | fat: 25g | protein: 46g | carbs: 15g | net carbs: 12g | fiber: 3g

Parmesan Salmon Loaf

Prep time: 15 minutes | Cook time: 25 minutes | Serves 6

12 ounces (340 g) salmon, boiled and shredded
3 eggs, beaten
½ cup almond flour
1 teaspoon garlic powder
¼ cup grated Parmesan
1 teaspoon butter, softened
1 cup water, for cooking

1. Pour water in the instant pot. 2. Mix up the rest of the ingredients in the mixing bowl and stir until smooth. 3. After this, transfer the salmon mixture in the loaf pan and flatten; insert the pan in the instant pot. Close and seal the lid. 4. Cook the meal on Manual mode (High Pressure) for 25 minutes. 5. When the cooking time is finished, make a quick pressure release and cool the loaf well before serving.
Per Serving:
calories: 172 | fat: 10g | protein: 19g | carbs: 2g | net carbs: 2g | fiber: 0g

Basil Cod Fillets

Prep time: 5 minutes | Cook time: 12 minutes | Serves 4

½ cup water
4 frozen cod fillets (about 6 ounces / 170 g each)
1 teaspoon dried basil
Pinch of salt
Pinch of black pepper
4 lemon slices
¼ cup heavy cream
2 tablespoons butter, softened
1 ounce (28 g) cream cheese, softened
2 teaspoons lemon juice
1½ teaspoons chopped fresh basil, plus more for garnish (optional)
Lemon wedges, for garnish (optional)

1. Place the trivet inside the pot and add the water. Lay a piece of aluminum foil on top of the trivet and place the cod on top. 2. Sprinkle the fish with the dried basil, salt, and pepper. Set a lemon slice on top of each fillet. 3. Close the lid and seal the vent. Cook on High Pressure for 9 minutes. Quick release the steam. Press Cancel. 4. Remove the trivet and fish from the pot. Rinse the pot if needed and turn to Sauté mode. 5. Add the cream and butter and whisk as the butter melts and the cream warms up. Add the cream cheese and whisk until thickened, 2 to 3 minutes. Add the lemon juice and another pinch of salt and pepper. Once the sauce is thickened and well combined, 1 to 2 minutes, press Cancel and add the fresh basil. 6. Pour the sauce over the fish. Garnish with fresh basil or a lemon wedge, if desired.
Per Serving:
calories: 221 | fat: 11g | protein: 27g | carbs: 1g | net carbs: 1g | fiber: 0g

Coconut Milk-Braised Squid

Prep time: 10 minutes | Cook time: 20 minutes | Serves 3

1 pound (454 g) squid, sliced
1 teaspoon sugar-free tomato paste
1 cup coconut milk
1 teaspoon cayenne pepper
½ teaspoon salt

1. Put all ingredients from the list above in the instant pot. 2. Close and seal the lid and cook the squid on Manual (High Pressure) for 20 minutes. 3. When the cooking time is finished, do the quick pressure release. 4. Serve the squid with coconut milk gravy.
Per Serving:
calories: 326 | fat: 21g | protein: 25g | carbs: 10g | net carbs: 8g | fiber: 2g

Shrimp Zoodle Alfredo

Prep time: 10 minutes | Cook time: 10 minutes | Serves 4

10 ounces (283 g) salmon fillet (2 fillets)
4 ounces (113 g) Mozzarella, sliced
4 cherry tomatoes, sliced
1 teaspoon erythritol
1 teaspoon dried basil
½ teaspoon ground black pepper
1 tablespoon apple cider vinegar
1 tablespoon butter
1 cup water, for cooking

1. Melt the butter on Sauté mode and add shrimp. 2. Sprinkle them with seafood seasoning and sauté then for 2 minutes. 3. After this, spiralizer the zucchini with the help of the spiralizer and add in the shrimp. 4. Add coconut cream and close the lid. Cook the meal on Sauté mode for 8 minutes.
Per Serving:
calories: 213 | fat: 16g | protein: 12g | carbs: 7g | net carbs: 5g | fiber: 2g

Salmon Fillets and Bok Choy

Prep time: 5 minutes | Cook time: 8 minutes | Serves 4

1½ cups water
2 tablespoons unsalted butter
4 (1-inch thick) salmon fillets
½ teaspoon cayenne pepper
Sea salt and freshly ground pepper, to taste
2 cups Bok choy, sliced
1 cup chicken broth
3 cloves garlic, minced
1 teaspoon grated lemon zest
½ teaspoon dried dill weed

1. Pour the water into your Instant Pot and insert a trivet. 2. Brush the salmon with the melted butter and season with the cayenne pepper, salt, and black pepper on all sides. 3. Lock the lid. Select the Manual mode and set the cooking time for 3 minutes at Low Pressure. 4. When the timer beeps, perform a quick pressure release. Carefully remove the lid. 5. Add the remaining ingredients. 6. Lock the lid. Select the Manual mode and set the cooking time for 5 minutes at High Pressure. 7. When the timer beeps, perform a quick pressure release. Carefully remove the lid. 8. Serve the poached salmon with the veggies on the side.
Per Serving:
calories: 209 | fat: 11.3g | protein: 23.9g | carbs: 2.1g | net carbs: 1.6g | fiber: 0.5g

Mediterranean Salmon with Whole-Wheat Couscous

Prep time: 5 minutes | Cook time: 30 minutes | Serves 4

Couscous
1 cup whole-wheat couscous
1 cup water
1 tablespoon extra-virgin olive
oil
1 teaspoon dried basil
¼ teaspoon fine sea salt
1 pint cherry or grape tomatoes,

halved
8 ounces zucchini, halved lengthwise, then sliced crosswise ¼ inch thick
Salmon
1 pound skinless salmon fillet
2 teaspoons extra-virgin olive oil

1 tablespoon fresh lemon juice
1 garlic clove, minced
¼ teaspoon dried oregano
¼ teaspoon fine sea salt
¼ teaspoon freshly ground black pepper
1 tablespoon capers, drained
Lemon wedges for serving

1. Pour 1 cup water into the Instant Pot. Have ready two-tier stackable stainless-steel containers. 2. To make the couscous: In one of the containers, stir together the couscous, water, oil, basil, and salt. Sprinkle the tomatoes and zucchini over the top. 3. To make the salmon: Place the salmon fillet in the second container. In a small bowl, whisk together the oil, lemon juice, garlic, oregano, salt, pepper, and capers. Spoon the oil mixture over the top of the salmon. 4. Place the container with the couscous and vegetables on the bottom and the salmon container on top. Cover the top container with its lid and then latch the containers together. Grasping the handle, lower the containers into the Instant Pot. 5. Secure the lid and set the Pressure Release to Sealing. Select the Pressure Cook or Manual setting and set the cooking time for 20 minutes at high pressure. (The pot will take about 10 minutes to come up to pressure before the cooking program begins.) 6. When the cooking program ends, let the pressure release naturally for 5 minutes, then move the Pressure Release to Venting to release any remaining steam. Open the pot and, wearing heat-resistant mitts, lift out the stacked containers. Unlatch, unstack, and open the containers, taking care not to get burned by the steam. 7. Using a fork, fluff the couscous and mix in the vegetables. Spoon the couscous onto plates, then use a spatula to cut the salmon into four pieces and place a piece on top of each couscous serving. Serve right away, with lemon wedges on the side.

Per Serving:
calories: 427 | fat: 18g | protein: 28g | carbs: 36g | sugars: 2g | fiber: 6g | sodium: 404mg

Steamed Halibut with Lemon

Prep time: 10 minutes | Cook time: 9 minutes | Serves 3

3 halibut fillet
½ lemon, sliced
½ teaspoon white pepper

½ teaspoon ground coriander
1 tablespoon avocado oil
1 cup water, for cooking

1. Pour water and insert the steamer rack in the instant pot. 2. Rub the fish fillets with white pepper, ground coriander, and avocado oil. 3. Place the fillets in the steamer rack. 4. Then top the halibut with sliced lemon. Close and seal the lid. 5. Cook the meal on High Pressure for 9 minutes. Make a quick pressure release.

Per Serving:
calories: 328 | fat: 7g | protein: 60g | carbs: 1g | net carbs: 1g | fiber: 0g

Asian Cod with Brown Rice, Asparagus, and Mushrooms

Prep time: 5 minutes | Cook time: 25 minutes | Serves 2

¾ cup Minute brand brown rice
½ cup water
Two 5-ounce skinless cod fillets

1 tablespoon soy sauce or tamari
1 tablespoon fresh lemon juice
½ teaspoon peeled and grated

fresh ginger
1 tablespoon extra-virgin olive oil or 1 tablespoon unsalted butter, cut into 8 pieces
2 green onions, white and green parts, thinly sliced
12 ounces asparagus, trimmed

4 ounces shiitake mushrooms, stems removed and sliced
⅛ teaspoon fine sea salt
⅛ teaspoon freshly ground black pepper
Lemon wedges for serving

1. Pour 1 cup water into the Instant Pot. Have ready two-tier stackable stainless-steel containers. 2. In one of the containers, combine the rice and ½ cup water, then gently shake the container to spread the rice into an even layer, making sure all of the grains are submerged. Place the fish fillets on top of the rice. In a small bowl, stir together the soy sauce, lemon juice, and ginger. Pour the soy sauce mixture over the fillets. Drizzle 1 teaspoon olive oil on each fillet (or top with two pieces of the butter), and sprinkle the green onions on and around the fish. 3. In the second container, arrange the asparagus in the center in as even a layer as possible. Place the mushrooms on either side of the asparagus. Drizzle with the remaining 2 teaspoons olive oil (or put the remaining six pieces butter on top of the asparagus, spacing them evenly). Sprinkle the salt and pepper evenly over the vegetables. 4. Place the container with the rice and fish on the bottom and the vegetable container on top. Cover the top container with its lid and then latch the containers together. Grasping the handle, lower the containers into the Instant Pot. 5. Secure the lid and set the Pressure Release to Sealing. Select the Pressure Cook or Manual setting and set the cooking time for 15 minutes at high pressure. (The pot will take about 10 minutes to come up to pressure before the cooking program begins.) 6. When the cooking program ends, let the pressure release naturally for 5 minutes, then move the Pressure Release to Venting to release any remaining steam. Open the pot and, wearing heat-resistant mitts, lift out the stacked containers. Unlatch, unstack, and open the containers, taking care not to get burned by the steam. 7. Transfer the vegetables, rice, and fish to plates and serve right away, with the lemon wedges on the side.

Per Serving:
calories: 344 | fat: 11g | protein: 27g | carbs: 46g | sugars: 6g | fiber: 7g | sodium: 637mg

Foil-Packet Salmon

Prep time: 2 minutes | Cook time: 7 minutes | Serves 2

2 (3-ounce / 85-g) salmon fillets
¼ teaspoon garlic powder
1 teaspoon salt

¼ teaspoon pepper
¼ teaspoon dried dill
½ lemon
1 cup water

1. Place each filet of salmon on a square of foil, skin-side down. 2. Season with garlic powder, salt, and pepper and squeeze the lemon juice over the fish. 3. Cut the lemon into four slices and place two on each filet. Close the foil packets by folding over edges. 4. Add the water to the Instant Pot and insert a trivet. Place the foil packets on the trivet. 5. Secure the lid. Select the Steam mode and set the cooking time for 7 minutes at Low Pressure. 6. Once cooking is complete, do a quick pressure release. Carefully open the lid. 7. Check the internal temperature with a meat thermometer to ensure the thickest part of the filets reached at least 145°F (63°C). Salmon should easily flake when fully cooked. Serve immediately.

Per Serving:
calories: 128 | fat: 4.9g | protein: 19.1g | carbs: 0.3g | net carbs: 0.2g | fiber: 0.1g

Braised Striped Bass with Zucchini and Tomatoes

Prep time: 20 minutes | Cook time: 16 minutes | Serves 4

2 tablespoons extra-virgin olive oil, divided, plus extra for drizzling
3 zucchini (8 ounces / 227 g each), halved lengthwise and sliced ¼ inch thick
1 onion, chopped
¾ teaspoon table salt, divided
3 garlic cloves, minced
1 teaspoon minced fresh oregano or ¼ teaspoon dried
¼ teaspoon red pepper flakes

1 (28-ounce / 794-g) can whole peeled tomatoes, drained with juice reserved, halved
1½ pounds (680 g) skinless striped bass, 1½ inches thick, cut into 2-inch pieces
¼ teaspoon pepper
2 tablespoons chopped pitted kalamata olives
2 tablespoons shredded fresh mint

1. Using highest sauté function, heat 1 tablespoon oil in Instant Pot for 5 minutes (or until just smoking). Add zucchini and cook until tender, about 5 minutes; transfer to bowl and set aside. 2. Add remaining 1 tablespoon oil, onion, and ¼ teaspoon salt to now-empty pot and cook, using highest sauté function, until onion is softened, about 5 minutes. Stir in garlic, oregano, and pepper flakes and cook until fragrant, about 30 seconds. Stir in tomatoes and reserved juice. 3. Sprinkle bass with remaining ½ teaspoon salt and pepper. Nestle bass into tomato mixture and spoon some of cooking liquid on top of pieces. Lock lid in place and close pressure release valve. Select high pressure cook function and set cook time for 0 minutes. Once Instant Pot has reached pressure, immediately turn off pot and quick-release pressure. Carefully remove lid, allowing steam to escape away from you. 4. Transfer bass to plate, tent with aluminum foil, and let rest while finishing vegetables. Stir zucchini into pot and let sit until heated through, about 5 minutes. Stir in olives and season with salt and pepper to taste. Serve bass with vegetables, sprinkling individual portions with mint and drizzling with extra oil.

Per Serving:
calories: 302 | fat: 12g | protein: 34g | carbs: 15g | fiber: 6g | sodium: 618mg

Garlic Tuna Casserole

Prep time: 7 minutes | Cook time: 9 minutes | Serves 4

1 cup grated Parmesan or shredded Cheddar cheese, plus more for topping
1 (8-ounce / 227-g) package cream cheese (1 cup), softened
½ cup chicken broth
1 tablespoon unsalted butter
½ small head cauliflower, cut into 1-inch pieces
1 cup diced onions

2 cloves garlic, minced, or more to taste
2 (4-ounce / 113-g) cans chunk tuna packed in water, drained
1½ cups cold water
For Garnish:
Chopped fresh flat-leaf parsley
Sliced green onions
Cherry tomatoes, halved
Ground black pepper

1. In a blender, add the Parmesan cheese, cream cheese, and broth and blitz until smooth. Set aside. 2. Set your Instant Pot to Sauté. Add and melt the butter. Add the cauliflower and onions and sauté for 4 minutes, or until the onions are softened. Fold in the garlic and sauté for an additional 1 minute. 3. Place the cheese sauce and tuna

in a large bowl. Mix in the veggies and stir well. Transfer the mixture to a casserole dish. 4. Place a trivet in the bottom of your Instant Pot and add the cold water. Use a foil sling, lower the casserole dish onto the trivet. Tuck in the sides of the sling. 5. Lock the lid. Select the Manual mode and set the cooking time for 5 minutes for al dente cauliflower or 8 minutes for softer cauliflower at High Pressure. 6. Once cooking is complete, do a quick pressure release. Carefully open the lid. 7. Serve topped with the cheese and garnished with the parsley, green onions, cherry tomatoes, and freshly ground pepper.

Per Serving:
calories: 378 | fat: 26.8g | protein: 23.8g | carbs: 10.5g | net carbs: 9.3g | fiber: 1.2g

Lemon Shrimp Skewers

Prep time: 10 minutes | Cook time: 2 minutes | Serves 4

1 tablespoon lemon juice
1 teaspoon coconut aminos
12 ounces (340 g) shrimp,

peeled
1 teaspoon olive oil
1 cup water

1. Put the shrimp in the mixing bowl. 2. Add lemon juice, coconut aminos, and olive oil. 3. Then string the shrimp on the skewers. 4. Pour water in the instant pot. 5. Then insert the trivet. 6. Put the shrimp skewers on the trivet. 7. Close the lid and cook the seafood on Manual mode (High Pressure) for 2 minutes. 8. When the time is finished, make a quick pressure release.

Per Serving:
calories: 113 | fat: 3g | protein: 19g | carbs: 2g | net carbs: 2g | fiber: 0g

Rosemary Baked Haddock

Prep time: 7 minutes | Cook time: 10 minutes | Serves 2

2 eggs, beaten
12 ounces (340 g) haddock fillet, chopped
1 tablespoon cream cheese

¾ teaspoon dried rosemary
2 ounces (57 g) Parmesan, grated
1 teaspoon butter

1. Whisk the beaten eggs until homogenous. Add the cream cheese, dried rosemary, and dill. 2. Grease the springform with the butter and place the haddock inside. 3. Pour the egg mixture over the fish and add sprinkle with Parmesan. 4. Set the Manual mode (High Pressure) and cook for 5 minutes. Then make a natural release pressure for 5 minutes.

Per Serving:
calories: 380 | fat: 16g | protein: 56g | carbs: 18g | net carbs: 18g | fiber: 0g

Cod Fillet with Olives

Prep time: 15 minutes | Cook time: 10 minutes | Serves 2

8 ounces (227 g) cod fillet
¼ cup sliced olives
1 teaspoon olive oil

¼ teaspoon salt
1 cup water, for cooking

1. Pour water and insert the steamer rack in the instant pot. 2. Then cut the cod fillet into 2 servings and sprinkle with salt and olive oil. 3. Then place the fish on the foil and top with the sliced olives. Wrap

the fish and transfer it in the steamer rack. 4. Close and seal the lid. Cook the fish on Manual mode (High Pressure) for 10 minutes. 5. Allow the natural pressure release for 5 minutes.

Per Serving:
calories: 130 | fat: 5g | protein: 20g | carbs: 1g | net carbs: 1g | fiber: 0g

Lemon Pepper Tilapia with Broccoli and Carrots

Prep time: 0 minutes | Cook time: 15 minutes | Serves 4

1 pound tilapia fillets
1 teaspoon lemon pepper seasoning
¼ teaspoon fine sea salt
2 tablespoons extra-virgin olive oil
2 garlic cloves, minced
1 small yellow onion, sliced
½ cup low-sodium vegetable broth
2 tablespoons fresh lemon juice
1 pound broccoli crowns, cut into bite-size florets
8 ounces carrots, cut into ¼-inch thick rounds

1. Sprinkle the tilapia fillets all over with the lemon pepper seasoning and salt. 2. Select the Sauté setting on the Instant Pot and heat the oil and garlic for 2 minutes, until the garlic is bubbling but not browned. Add the onion and sauté for about 3 minutes more, until it begins to soften. 3. Pour in the broth and lemon juice, then use a wooden spoon to nudge any browned bits from the bottom of the pot. Using tongs, add the fish fillets to the pot in a single layer; it's fine if they overlap slightly. Place the broccoli and carrots on top. 4. Secure the lid and set the Pressure Release to Sealing. Press the Cancel button to reset the cooking program, then select the Pressure Cook or Manual setting and set the cooking time for 1 minute at low pressure. (The pot will take about 10 minutes to come up to pressure before the cooking program begins.) 5. When the cooking program ends, let the pressure release naturally for 10 minutes (don't open the pot before the 10 minutes are up, even if the float valve has gone down), then move the Pressure Release to Venting to release any remaining steam. Open the pot. Use a fish spatula to transfer the vegetables and fillets to plates. Serve right away.

Per Serving:
calories: 243 | fat: 9g | protein: 28g | carbs: 15g | sugars: 4g | fiber: 5g | sodium: 348mg

Haddock and Veggie Foil Packets

Prep time: 5 minutes | Cook time: 10 minutes | Serves 4

1½ cups water
1 lemon, sliced
2 bell peppers, sliced
1 brown onion, sliced into rings
4 sprigs parsley
2 sprigs thyme
2 sprigs rosemary
4 haddock fillets
Sea salt, to taste
⅓ teaspoon ground black pepper, or more to taste
2 tablespoons extra-virgin olive oil

1. Pour the water and lemon into your Instant Pot and insert a steamer basket. 2. Assemble the packets with large sheets of heavy-duty foil. 3. Place the peppers, onion rings, parsley, thyme, and rosemary in the center of each foil. Place the fish fillets on top of the veggies. 4. Sprinkle with the salt and black pepper and drizzle the olive oil over the fillets. Place the packets in the steamer basket. 5. Lock the lid. Select the Manual mode and set the cooking time for 10 minutes at

Low Pressure. 6. When the timer beeps, perform a quick pressure release. Carefully remove the lid. 7. Serve warm.

Per Serving:
calories: 218 | fat: 7.7g | protein: 32.3g | carbs: 4.8g | net carbs: 4.0g | fiber: 0.8g

Lemony Fish and Asparagus

Prep time: 5 minutes | Cook time: 3 minutes | Serves 4

2 lemons
2 cups cold water
2 tablespoons extra-virgin olive oil
4 (4-ounce / 113-g) white fish fillets, such as cod or haddock
1 teaspoon fine sea salt
1 teaspoon ground black pepper
1 bundle asparagus, ends trimmed
2 tablespoons lemon juice
Fresh dill, for garnish

1. Grate the zest off the lemons until you have about 1 tablespoon and set the zest aside. Slice the lemons into ⅛-inch slices. 2. Pour the water into the Instant Pot. Add 1 tablespoon of the olive oil to each of two stackable steamer pans. 3. Sprinkle the fish on all sides with the lemon zest, salt, and pepper. 4. Arrange two fillets in each steamer pan and top each with the lemon slices and then the asparagus. Sprinkle the asparagus with the salt and drizzle the lemon juice over the top. 5. Stack the steamer pans in the Instant Pot. Cover the top steamer pan with its lid. 6. Lock the lid. Select the Manual mode and set the cooking time for 3 minutes at High Pressure. 7. Once cooking is complete, do a natural pressure release for 7 minutes, then release any remaining pressure. Carefully open the lid. 8. Lift the steamer pans out of the Instant Pot. 9. Transfer the fish and asparagus to a serving plate. Garnish with the lemon slices and dill. 10. Serve immediately.

Per Serving:
calories: 163 | fat: 5.8g | protein: 23.7g | carbs: 7.1g | net carbs: 4.1g | fiber: 3.0g

Ahi Tuna and Cherry Tomato Salad

Prep time: 5 minutes | Cook time: 4 minutes | Serves 4

1 cup water
2 sprigs thyme
2 sprigs rosemary
2 sprigs parsley
1 lemon, sliced
1 pound (454 g) ahi tuna
⅓ teaspoon ground black pepper
1 head lettuce
1 cup cherry tomatoes, halved
1 red bell pepper, julienned
2 tablespoons extra-virgin olive oil
1 teaspoon Dijon mustard
Sea salt, to taste

1. Pour the water into your Instant Pot. Add the thyme, rosemary, parsley, and lemon and insert a trivet. 2. Lay the fish on the trivet and season with the ground black pepper. 3. Lock the lid. Select the Manual mode and set the cooking time for 4 minutes at High Pressure. 4. When the timer beeps, perform a quick pressure release. Carefully remove the lid. 5. In a salad bowl, place the remaining ingredients and toss well. Add the flaked tuna and toss again. 6. Serve chilled.

Per Serving:
calories: 253 | fat: 13.5g | protein: 28.3g | carbs: 4.9g | net carbs: 3.6g | fiber: 1.3g

Salmon with Dill Butter

Prep time: 7 minutes | Cook time: 8 minutes | Serves 2

1 teaspoon salt
2 tablespoons chopped fresh dill

10 ounces (283 g) salmon fillet
¼ cup butter
½ cup water

1. Put butter and salt in the baking pan. 2. Add salmon fillet and dill. Cover the pan with foil. 3. Pour water in the instant pot and insert the baking pan with fish inside. 4. Set the Steam mode and cook the salmon for 8 minutes. 5. Unwrap the cooked salmon and serve!
Per Serving:
calories: 399 | fat: 32g | protein: 28g | carbs: 2g | net carbs: 2g | fiber: 0g

Turmeric Salmon

Prep time: 10 minutes | Cook time: 4 minutes | Serves 3

1 pound (454 g) salmon fillet
1 teaspoon ground black pepper
½ teaspoon salt

1 teaspoon ground turmeric
1 teaspoon lemon juice
1 cup water

1. In the shallow bowl, mix up salt, ground black pepper, and ground turmeric. 2. Sprinkle the salmon fillet with lemon juice and rub with the spice mixture. 3. Then pour water in the instant pot and insert the steamer rack. 4. Wrap the salmon fillet in the foil and place it on the rack. 5. Close and seal the lid. 6. Cook the fish on Manual mode (High Pressure) for 4 minutes. 7. Make a quick pressure release and cut the fish on servings.
Per Serving:
calories: 205 | fat: 9g | protein: 30g | carbs: 1g | net carbs: 1g | fiber: 0g

Ginger Cod

Prep time: 10 minutes | Cook time: 20 minutes | Serves 2

1 teaspoon ginger paste
8 ounces (227 g) cod fillet, chopped

1 tablespoon coconut oil
¼ cup coconut milk

1. Melt the coconut oil in the instant pot on Sauté mode. 2. Then add ginger paste and coconut milk and bring the mixture to boil. 3. Add chopped cod and sauté the meal for 12 minutes. Stir the fish cubes with the help of the spatula from time to time.
Per Serving:
calories: 222 | fat: 15g | protein: 21g | carbs: 2g | net carbs: 1g | fiber: 1g

Mussels with Fennel and Leeks

Prep time: 20 minutes | Cook time: 6 minutes | Serves 4

1 tablespoon extra-virgin olive oil, plus extra for drizzling
1 fennel bulb, 1 tablespoon fronds minced, stalks discarded, bulb halved, cored, and sliced thin

1 leek, ends trimmed, leek halved lengthwise, sliced 1 inch thick, and washed thoroughly
4 garlic cloves, minced
3 sprigs fresh thyme

¼ teaspoon red pepper flakes
½ cup dry white wine

3 pounds (1.4 kg) mussels, scrubbed and debearded

1. Using highest sauté function, heat oil in Instant Pot until shimmering. Add fennel and leek and cook until softened, about 5 minutes. Stir in garlic, thyme sprigs, and pepper flakes and cook until fragrant, about 30 seconds. Stir in wine, then add mussels. 2. Lock lid in place and close pressure release valve. Select high pressure cook function and set cook time for 0 minutes. Once Instant Pot has reached pressure, immediately turn off pot and quick-release pressure. Carefully remove lid, allowing steam to escape away from you. 3. Discard thyme sprigs and any mussels that have not opened. Transfer mussels to individual serving bowls, sprinkle with fennel fronds, and drizzle with extra oil. Serve.
Per Serving:
calories: 384 | fat: 11g | protein: 42g | carbs: 23g | fiber: 2g | sodium: 778mg

Rainbow Trout with Mixed Greens

Prep time: 5 minutes | Cook time: 12 minutes | Serves 4

1 cup water
1½ (680 g) pounds rainbow trout fillets
4 tablespoons melted butter, divided
Sea salt and ground black pepper, to taste

1 pound (454 g) mixed greens, trimmed and torn into pieces
1 bunch of scallions
½ cup chicken broth
1 tablespoon apple cider vinegar
1 teaspoon cayenne pepper

1. Pour the water into your Instant Pot and insert a steamer basket. 2. Add the fish to the basket. Drizzle with 1 tablespoon of the melted butter and season with the salt and black pepper. 3. Lock the lid. Select the Manual mode and set the cooking time for 12 minutes at Low pressure. 4. When the timer beeps, perform a quick pressure release. Carefully remove the lid. 5. Wipe down the Instant Pot with a damp cloth. 6. Add and warm the remaining 3 tablespoons of butter. Once hot, add the greens, scallions, broth, vinegar, and cayenne pepper and cook until the greens are wilted, stirring occasionally. 7. Serve the prepared trout fillets with the greens on the side.
Per Serving:
calories: 349 | fat: 18.1g | protein: 38.9g | carbs: 7.7g | net carbs: 3.3g | fiber: 4.4g

Salmon Steaks with Garlicky Yogurt

Prep time: 2 minutes | Cook time: 4 minutes | Serves 4

1 cup water
2 tablespoons olive oil
4 salmon steaks
Coarse sea salt and ground black pepper, to taste
Garlicky Yogurt:

1 (8-ounce / 227-g) container full-fat Greek yogurt
2 cloves garlic, minced
2 tablespoons mayonnaise
⅓ teaspoon Dijon mustard

1. Pour the water into the Instant Pot and insert a trivet. 2. Rub the olive oil into the fish and sprinkle with the salt and black pepper on all sides. Put the fish on the trivet. 3. Lock the lid. Select the Manual mode and set the cooking time for 4 minutes at High Pressure. 4. When the timer beeps, perform a quick pressure release. Carefully remove the lid. 5. Meanwhile, stir together all the ingredients for the garlicky yogurt in a bowl. 6. Serve the salmon steaks alongside the

garlicky yogurt.
Per Serving:
calories: 128 | fat: 11.2g | protein: 2.5g | carbs:4.9g | net carbs: 4.7g | fiber: 0.2g

Salmon with Wild Rice and Orange Salad

Prep time: 20 minutes | Cook time: 18 minutes | Serves 4

1 cup wild rice, picked over and rinsed	1 teaspoon ground dried Aleppo pepper
3 tablespoons extra-virgin olive oil, divided	½ teaspoon table salt
1½ teaspoon table salt, for cooking rice	1 small shallot, minced
2 oranges, plus ⅛ teaspoon grated orange zest	1 tablespoon red wine vinegar
	2 teaspoons Dijon mustard
4 (6-ounce / 170-g) skinless salmon fillets, 1½ inches thick	1 teaspoon honey
	2 carrots, peeled and shredded
	¼ cup chopped fresh mint

1. Combine 6 cups water, rice, 1 tablespoon oil, and 1½ teaspoons salt in Instant Pot. Lock lid in place and close pressure release valve. Select high pressure cook function and cook for 15 minutes. Turn off Instant Pot and let pressure release naturally for 15 minutes. Quick-release any remaining pressure, then carefully remove lid, allowing steam to escape away from you. Drain rice and set aside to cool slightly. Wipe pot clean with paper towels. 2. Add ½ cup water to now-empty Instant Pot. Fold sheet of aluminum foil into 16 by 6-inch sling. Slice 1 orange ¼ inch thick and shingle widthwise in 3 rows across center of sling. Sprinkle flesh side of salmon with Aleppo pepper and ½ teaspoon salt, then arrange skinned side down on top of orange slices. Using sling, lower salmon into Instant Pot; allow narrow edges of sling to rest along sides of insert. Lock lid in place and close pressure release valve. Select high pressure cook function and cook for 3 minutes. 3. Meanwhile, cut away peel and pith from remaining 1 orange. Quarter orange, then slice crosswise into ¼-inch pieces. Whisk remaining 2 tablespoons oil, shallot, vinegar, mustard, honey, and orange zest together in large bowl. Add rice, orange pieces, carrots, and mint, and gently toss to combine. Season with salt and pepper to taste. 4. Turn off Instant Pot and quick-release pressure. Carefully remove lid, allowing steam to escape away from you. Using sling, transfer salmon to large plate. Gently lift and tilt fillets with spatula to remove orange slices. Serve salmon with salad.
Per Serving:
calories: 690 | fat: 34g | protein: 43g | carbs: 51g | fiber: 5g | sodium: 770mg

Lemon Butter Mahi Mahi

Prep time: 10 minutes | Cook time: 9 minutes | Serves 4

1 pound (454 g) mahi-mahi fillet	1 tablespoon butter, softened
1 teaspoon grated lemon zest	½ teaspoon salt
1 tablespoon lemon juice	1 cup water, for cooking

1. Cut the fish on 4 servings and sprinkle with lemon zest, lemon juice, salt, and rub with softened butter. 2. Then put the fish in the baking pan in one layer. 3. Pour water and insert the steamer rack in the instant pot. 4. Put the mold with fish on the rack. Close and seal the lid. 5. Cook the Mahi Mahi on Manual mode (High Pressure) for

9 minutes. Make a quick pressure release.
Per Serving:
calories: 128 | fat: 4g | protein: 21g | carbs: 0g | net carbs: 0g | fiber: 0g

Fish Tagine

Prep time: 25 minutes | Cook time: 12 minutes | Serves 4

2 tablespoons extra-virgin olive oil, plus extra for drizzling	¼ teaspoon red pepper flakes
	¼ teaspoon saffron threads, crumbled
1 large onion, halved and sliced ¼ inch thick	1 (8-ounce / 227-g) bottle clam juice
1 pound (454 g) carrots, peeled, halved lengthwise, and sliced ¼ inch thick	1½ pounds (680 g) skinless halibut fillets, 1½ inches thick, cut into 2-inch pieces
2 (2-inch) strips orange zest, plus 1 teaspoon grated zest	¼ cup pitted oil-cured black olives, quartered
¾ teaspoon table salt, divided	2 tablespoons chopped fresh parsley
2 tablespoons tomato paste	1 teaspoon sherry vinegar
4 garlic cloves, minced, divided	
1¼ teaspoons paprika	
1 teaspoon ground cumin	

1. Using highest sauté function, heat oil in Instant Pot until shimmering. Add onion, carrots, orange zest strips, and ¼ teaspoon salt, and cook until vegetables are softened and lightly browned, 10 to 12 minutes. Stir in tomato paste, three-quarters of garlic, paprika, cumin, pepper flakes, and saffron and cook until fragrant, about 30 seconds. Stir in clam juice, scraping up any browned bits. 2. Sprinkle halibut with remaining ½ teaspoon salt. Nestle halibut into onion mixture and spoon some of cooking liquid on top of pieces. Lock lid in place and close pressure release valve. Select high pressure cook function and set cook time for 0 minutes. Once Instant Pot has reached pressure, immediately turn off pot and quick-release pressure. 3. Discard orange zest. Gently stir in olives, parsley, vinegar, grated orange zest, and remaining garlic. Season with salt and pepper to taste. Drizzle extra oil over individual portions before serving.
Per Serving:
calories: 310 | fat: 15g | protein: 34g | carbs: 18g | fiber: 4g | sodium: 820mg

Dill Salmon Cakes

Prep time: 15 minutes | Cook time: 10 minutes | Serves 4

1 pound (454 g) salmon fillet, chopped	2 eggs, beaten
	½ cup almond flour
1 tablespoon chopped dill	1 tablespoon coconut oil

1. Put the chopped salmon, dill, eggs, and almond flour in the food processor. 2. Blend the mixture until it is smooth. 3. Then make the small balls (cakes) from the salmon mixture. 4. After this, heat up the coconut oil on Sauté mode for 3 minutes. 5. Put the salmon cakes in the instant pot in one layer and cook them on Sauté mode for 2 minutes from each side or until they are light brown.
Per Serving:
calories: 297 | fat: 19g | protein: 28g | carbs: 4g | net carbs: 2g | fiber: 2g

Cod with Warm Tabbouleh Salad

Prep time: 10 minutes | Cook time: 6 minutes | Serves 4

1 cup medium-grind bulgur, rinsed

1 teaspoon table salt, divided

1 lemon, sliced ¼ inch thick, plus 2 tablespoons juice

4 (6-ounce / 170-g) skinless cod fillets, 1½ inches thick

3 tablespoons extra-virgin olive oil, divided, plus extra for drizzling

¼ teaspoon pepper

1 small shallot, minced

10 ounces (283 g) cherry tomatoes, halved

1 cup chopped fresh parsley

½ cup chopped fresh mint

1. Arrange trivet included with Instant Pot in base of insert and add ½ cup water. Fold sheet of aluminum foil into 16 by 6-inch sling, then rest 1½-quart round soufflé dish in center of sling. Combine 1 cup water, bulgur, and ½ teaspoon salt in dish. Using sling, lower soufflé dish into pot and onto trivet; allow narrow edges of sling to rest along sides of insert. 2. Lock lid in place and close pressure release valve. Select high pressure cook function and cook for 3 minutes. Turn off Instant Pot and quick-release pressure. Carefully remove lid, allowing steam to escape away from you. Using sling, transfer soufflé dish to wire rack; set aside to cool. Remove trivet; do not discard sling or water in pot. 3. Arrange lemon slices widthwise in 2 rows across center of sling. Brush cod with 1 tablespoon oil and sprinkle with remaining ½ teaspoon salt and pepper. Arrange cod skinned side down in even layer on top of lemon slices. Using sling, lower cod into Instant Pot; allow narrow edges of sling to rest along sides of insert. Lock lid in place and close pressure release valve. Select high pressure cook function and cook for 3 minutes. 4. Meanwhile, whisk remaining 2 tablespoons oil, lemon juice, and shallot together in large bowl. Add bulgur, tomatoes, parsley, and mint, and gently toss to combine. Season with salt and pepper to taste. 5. Turn off Instant Pot and quick-release pressure. Carefully remove lid, allowing steam to escape away from you. Using sling, transfer cod to large plate. Gently lift and tilt fillets with spatula to remove lemon slices. Serve cod with salad, drizzling individual portions with extra oil.

Per Serving:

calories: 380 | fat: 12g | protein: 36g | carbs: 32g | fiber: 6g | sodium: 690mg

Shrimp Louie Salad with Thousand Island Dressing

Prep time: 5 minutes | Cook time: 20 minutes | Serves 4

2 cups water

1½ teaspoons fine sea salt

1 pound medium shrimp, peeled and deveined

4 large eggs

Thousand island Dressing

¼ cup no-sugar-added ketchup

¼ cup mayonnaise

1 tablespoon fresh lemon juice

1 teaspoon Worcestershire sauce

⅛ teaspoon cayenne pepper

Freshly ground black pepper

2 green onions, white and green parts, sliced thinly

2 hearts romaine lettuce or 1 head iceberg lettuce, shredded

1 English cucumber, sliced

8 radishes, sliced

1 cup cherry tomatoes, sliced

1 large avocado, pitted, peeled, and sliced

1. Combine the water and salt in the Instant Pot and stir to dissolve the salt. 2. Secure the lid and set the Pressure Release to Sealing. Select the Steam setting and set the cooking time for 0 (zero) minutes at low pressure. (The pot will take about 10 minutes to come up to pressure before the cooking program begins.) 3. Meanwhile, prepare an ice bath. 4. When the cooking program ends, perform a quick release by moving the Pressure Release to Venting. Open the pot and stir in the shrimp, using a wooden spoon to nudge them all down into the water. Cover the pot and leave the shrimp for 2 minutes on the Keep Warm setting. The shrimp will gently poach and cook through. Uncover the pot and, wearing heat-resistant mitts, lift out the inner pot and drain the shrimp in a colander. Transfer them to the ice bath to cool for 5 minutes, then drain them in the colander and set aside in the refrigerator. 5. Rinse out the inner pot and return it to the housing. Pour in 1 cup water and place the wire metal steam rack into the pot. Place the eggs on top of the steam rack. 6. Secure the lid and set the Pressure Release to Sealing. Press the Cancel button to reset the cooking program, then select the Egg, Pressure Cook, or Manual setting and set the cooking time for 5 minutes at high pressure. (The pot will take about 5 minutes to come up to pressure before the cooking program begins.) 7. While the eggs are cooking, prepare another ice bath. 8. When the cooking program ends, let the pressure release naturally for 5 minutes, then move the Pressure Release to Venting to release any remaining steam. Using tongs, transfer the eggs to the ice bath and let cool for 5 minutes. 9. To make the dressing: In a small bowl, stir together the ketchup, mayonnaise, lemon juice, Worcestershire sauce, cayenne, ¼ teaspoon black pepper, and green onions. 10. Arrange the lettuce, cucumber, radishes, tomatoes, and avocado on individual plates or in large, shallow individual bowls. Mound the cooked shrimp in the center of each salad. Peel the eggs, quarter them lengthwise, and place the quarters around the shrimp. 11. Spoon the dressing over the salads and top with additional black pepper. Serve right away.

Per Serving:

calories: 407 | fat: 23g | protein: 35g | carbs: 16g | sugars: 10g | fiber: 6g | sodium: 1099mg

Salade Niçoise with Oil-Packed Tuna

Prep time: 5 minutes | Cook time: 20 minutes | Serves 4

8 ounces small red potatoes, quartered

8 ounces green beans, trimmed

4 large eggs

french vinaigrette

2 tablespoons extra-virgin olive oil

2 tablespoons cold-pressed avocado oil

2 tablespoons white wine vinegar

1 tablespoon water

1 teaspoon Dijon mustard

½ teaspoon dried oregano

¼ teaspoon fine sea salt

1 tablespoon minced shallot

2 hearts romaine lettuce, leaves separated and torn into bite-size pieces

½ cup grape tomatoes, halved

¼ cup pitted Niçoise or Greek olives

One 7-ounce can oil-packed tuna, drained and flaked

Freshly ground black pepper

1 tablespoon chopped fresh flat-leaf parsley

1. Pour 1 cup water into the Instant Pot and place a steamer basket into the pot. Add the potatoes, green beans, and eggs to the basket. 2. Secure the lid and set the Pressure Release to Sealing. Select the Steam setting and set the cooking time for 3 minutes at high pressure. (The pot will take about 15 minutes to come up to pressure before the cooking program begins.) 3. To make the vinaigrette: While the vegetables and eggs are steaming, in a small jar or other small container with a tight-fitting lid, combine the olive oil, avocado oil, vinegar, water, mustard, oregano, salt, and shallot and

shake vigorously to emulsify. Set aside. 4. Prepare an ice bath. 5. When the cooking program ends, perform a quick release by moving the Pressure Release to Venting. Open the pot and, wearing heat-resistant mitts, lift out the steamer basket. Using tongs, transfer the eggs and green beans to the ice bath, leaving the potatoes in the steamer basket. 6. While the eggs and green beans are cooling, divide the lettuce, tomatoes, olives, and tuna among four shallow individual bowls. Drain the eggs and green beans. Peel and halve the eggs lengthwise, then arrange them on the salads along with the green beans and potatoes. 7. Spoon the vinaigrette over the salads and sprinkle with the pepper and parsley. Serve right away.

Per Serving:

calories: 367 | fat: 23g | protein: 20g | carbs: 23g | sugars: 7g | fiber: 4g | sodium: 268mg

Mascarpone Tilapia with Nutmeg

Prep time: 10 minutes | Cook time: 20 minutes | Serves 2

10 ounces (283 g) tilapia	1 teaspoon ground nutmeg
½ cup mascarpone	1 tablespoon olive oil
1 garlic clove, diced	½ teaspoon salt

1. Pour olive oil in the instant pot. 2. Add diced garlic and sauté it for 4 minutes. 3. Add tilapia and sprinkle it with ground nutmeg. Sauté the fish for 3 minutes per side. 4. Add mascarpone and close the lid. 5. Sauté tilapia for 10 minutes.

Per Serving:

calories: 293 | fat: 17g | protein: 33g | carbs: 3g | net carbs: 2g | fiber: 1g

Mackerel and Broccoli Casserole

Prep time: 15 minutes | Cook time: 15 minutes | Serves 5

1 cup shredded broccoli	cheese
10 ounces (283 g) mackerel, chopped	1 cup coconut milk
	1 teaspoon ground cumin
½ cup shredded Cheddar	1 teaspoon salt

1. Sprinkle the chopped mackerel with ground cumin and salt and transfer in the instant pot. 2. Top the fish with shredded broccoli and Cheddar cheese, 3. Then add coconut milk. Close and seal the lid. 4. Cook the casserole on Manual mode (High Pressure) for 15 minutes. 5. Allow the natural pressure release for 10 minutes and open the lid.

Per Serving:

calories: 312 | fat: 25g | protein: 18g | carbs: 4g | net carbs: 2g | fiber: 2g

Salmon with Garlicky Broccoli Rabe and White Beans

Prep time: 20 minutes | Cook time: 10 minutes | Serves 4

2 tablespoons extra-virgin olive oil, plus extra for drizzling	broth
	¼ teaspoon red pepper flakes
4 garlic cloves, sliced thin	1 lemon, sliced ¼ inch thick, plus lemon wedges for serving
½ cup chicken or vegetable	
4 (6-ounce / 170-g) skinless salmon fillets, 1½ inches thick	trimmed and cut into 1-inch pieces
½ teaspoon table salt	1 (15-ounce / 425-g) can cannellini beans, rinsed
¼ teaspoon pepper	
1 pound (454 g) broccoli rabe,	

1. Using highest sauté function, cook oil and garlic in Instant Pot until garlic is fragrant and light golden brown, about 3 minutes. Using slotted spoon, transfer garlic to paper towel–lined plate and season with salt to taste; set aside for serving. Turn off Instant Pot, then stir in broth and pepper flakes. 2. Fold sheet of aluminum foil into 16 by 6-inch sling. Arrange lemon slices widthwise in 2 rows across center of sling. Sprinkle flesh side of salmon with salt and pepper, then arrange skinned side down on top of lemon slices. Using sling, lower salmon into Instant Pot; allow narrow edges of sling to rest along sides of insert. Lock lid in place and close pressure release valve. Select high pressure cook function and cook for 3 minutes. 3. Turn off Instant Pot and quick-release pressure. Carefully remove lid, allowing steam to escape away from you. Using sling, transfer salmon to large plate. Tent with foil and let rest while preparing broccoli rabe mixture. 4. Stir broccoli rabe and beans into cooking liquid, partially cover, and cook, using highest sauté function, until broccoli rabe is tender, about 5 minutes. Season with salt and pepper to taste. Gently lift and tilt salmon fillets with spatula to remove lemon slices. Serve salmon with broccoli rabe mixture and lemon wedges, sprinkling individual portions with garlic chips and drizzling with extra oil.

Per Serving:

calories: 510 | fat: 30g | protein: 43g | carbs: 15g | fiber: 6g | sodium: 650mg

Fish Packets with Pesto and Cheese

Prep time: 8 minutes | Cook time: 6 minutes | Serves 4

1½ cups cold water.	1 (4-ounce / 113-g) jar pesto
4 (4-ounce / 113-g) white fish fillets, such as cod or haddock	½ cup shredded Parmesan cheese (about 2 ounces / 57 g)
1 teaspoon fine sea salt	Halved cherry tomatoes, for garnish
½ teaspoon ground black pepper	

1. Pour the water into your Instant Pot and insert a steamer basket. 2. Sprinkle the fish on all sides with the salt and pepper. Take four sheets of parchment paper and place a fillet in the center of each sheet. 3. Dollop 2 tablespoons of the pesto on top of each fillet and sprinkle with 2 tablespoons of the Parmesan cheese. 4. Wrap the fish in the parchment by folding in the edges and folding down the top like an envelope to close tightly. 5. Stack the packets in the steamer basket, seam-side down. 6. Lock the lid. Select the Manual mode and set the cooking time for 6 minutes at Low Pressure. 7. Once cooking is complete, do a natural pressure release for 10 minutes, then release any remaining pressure. Carefully open the lid. 8. Remove the fish packets from the pot. Transfer to a serving plate and garnish with the cherry tomatoes. 9. Serve immediately.

Per Serving:

calories: 257 | fat: 17.8g | protein: 23.7g | carbs: 2.3g | net carbs: 1.3g | fiber: 1.0g

Italian Salmon

Prep time: 10 minutes | Cook time: 4 minutes | Serves 2

10 ounces (283 g) salmon fillet
1 teaspoon Italian seasoning
1 cup water

1. Pour water and insert the trivet in the instant pot. 2. Then rub the salmon fillet with Italian seasoning and wrap in the foil. 3. Place the wrapped fish on the trivet and close the lid. 4. Cook the meal on Manual mode (High Pressure) for 4 minutes. 5. Make a quick pressure release and remove the fish from the foil. 6. Cut it into servings.
Per Serving:
calories: 195 | fat: 10g | protein: 27g | carbs: 0g | net carbs: 0g | fiber: 0g

Tuna Salad with Tomatoes and Peppers

Prep time: 10 minutes | Cook time: 4 minutes | Serves 4

1½ cups water	2 tablespoons Kalamata olives,
1 pound (454 g) tuna steaks	pitted and halved
1 green bell pepper, sliced	2 tablespoons extra-virgin olive
1 red bell pepper, sliced	oil
2 Roma tomatoes, sliced	2 tablespoons balsamic vinegar
1 head lettuce	½ teaspoon chili flakes
1 red onion, chopped	Sea salt, to taste

1. Add the water to the Instant Pot and insert a steamer basket. 2. Arrange the tuna steaks in the basket. Put the bell peppers and tomato slices on top. 3. Lock the lid. Select the Manual mode and set the cooking time for 4 minutes at High Pressure. 4. When the timer beeps, perform a quick pressure release. Carefully remove the lid. 5. Flake the fish with a fork. 6. Divide the lettuce leaves among 4 serving plates to make a bed for your salad. Add the onion and olives. Drizzle with the olive oil and balsamic vinegar. 7. Season with the chili flakes and salt. Place the prepared fish, tomatoes, and bell peppers on top. 8. Serve immediately.
Per Serving:
calories: 170 | fat: 4.8g | protein: 23.9g | carbs: 7.6g | net carbs: 6.0g | fiber: 1.6g

Greek Shrimp with Tomatoes and Feta

Prep time: 10 minutes | Cook time: 2 minutes | Serves 6

3 tablespoons unsalted butter	1 teaspoon dried oregano
1 tablespoon garlic	1 teaspoon salt
½ teaspoon red pepper flakes,	1 pound (454 g) frozen shrimp,
or more as needed	peeled
1½ cups chopped onion	1 cup crumbled feta cheese
1 (14½-ounce / 411-g) can	½ cup sliced black olives
diced tomatoes, undrained	¼ cup chopped parsley

1. Preheat the Instant Pot by selecting Sauté and adjusting to high heat. When the inner cooking pot is hot, add the butter and heat until it foams. Add the garlic and red pepper flakes, and cook just until fragrant, about 1 minute. 2. Add the onion, tomatoes, oregano, and salt, and stir to combine. 3. Add the frozen shrimp. 4. Lock the lid into place. Select Manual and adjust the pressure to Low. Cook for

1 minute. When the cooking is complete, quick-release the pressure. Unlock the lid. 5. Mix the shrimp in with the lovely tomato broth. 6. Allow the mixture to cool slightly. Right before serving, sprinkle with the feta cheese, olives, and parsley. This dish makes a soupy broth, so it's great over mashed cauliflower.
Per Serving:
calories: 361 | fat: 22g | protein: 30g | carbs: 13g | net carbs: 11g | fiber: 2g

Tuna Stuffed Poblano Peppers

Prep time: 15 minutes | Cook time: 12 minutes | Serves 4

7 ounces (198 g) canned tuna,	2 ounces (57 g) Provolone
shredded	cheese, grated
1 teaspoon cream cheese	4 poblano pepper
¼ teaspoon minced garlic	1 cup water, for cooking

1. Remove the seeds from poblano peppers. 2. In the mixing bowl, mix up shredded tuna, cream cheese, minced garlic, and grated cheese. 3. Then fill the peppers with tuna mixture and put it in the baking pan. 4. Pour water and insert the baking pan in the instant pot. 5. Cook the meal on Manual mode (High Pressure) for 12 minutes. Then make a quick pressure release.
Per Serving:
calories: 153 | fat: 8g | protein: 17g | carbs: 2g | net carbs: 1g | fiber: 1g

Perch Fillets with Red Curry

Prep time: 5 minutes | Cook time: 6 minutes | Serves 4

1 cup water	Sea salt and ground black
2 sprigs rosemary	pepper, to taste
1 large-sized lemon, sliced	1 tablespoon red curry paste
1 pound (454 g) perch fillets	1 tablespoons butter
1 teaspoon cayenne pepper	

1. Add the water, rosemary, and lemon slices to the Instant Pot and insert a trivet. 2. Season the perch fillets with the cayenne pepper, salt, and black pepper. Spread the red curry paste and butter over the fillets. 3. Arrange the fish fillets on the trivet. 4. Lock the lid. Select the Manual mode and set the cooking time for 6 minutes at Low Pressure. 5. When the timer beeps, perform a quick pressure release. Carefully remove the lid. Serve with your favorite keto sides.
Per Serving:
calories: 142 | fat: 4.3g | protein: 22.5g | carbs: 3.2g | net carbs: 1.6g | fiber: 1.6g

Steamed Lobster Tails with Thyme

Prep time: 10 minutes | Cook time: 4 minutes | Serves 4

4 lobster tails	1 teaspoon dried thyme
1 tablespoon butter, softened	1 cup water

1. Pour water and insert the steamer rack in the instant pot. 2. Put the lobster tails on the rack and close the lid. 3. Cook the meal on Manual mode (High Pressure) for 4 minutes. Make a quick pressure release. 4. After this, mix up butter and dried thyme. Peel the lobsters and rub them with thyme butter.

Per Serving:
calories: 126 | fat: 3g | protein: 24g | carbs: 0g | net carbs: 0g | fiber: 0g

Cod with Warm Beet and Arugula Salad

Prep time: 15 minutes | Cook time: 8 minutes | Serves 4

¼ cup extra-virgin olive oil, divided, plus extra for drizzling
1 shallot, sliced thin
2 garlic cloves, minced
1½ pounds (680 g) small beets, scrubbed, trimmed, and cut into ½-inch wedges
½ cup chicken or vegetable

broth
1 tablespoon dukkah, plus extra for sprinkling
¼ teaspoon table salt
4 (6-ounce / 170-g) skinless cod fillets, 1½ inches thick
1 tablespoon lemon juice
2 ounces (57 g) baby arugula

1. Using highest sauté function, heat 1 tablespoon oil in Instant Pot until shimmering. Add shallot and cook until softened, about 2 minutes. Stir in garlic and cook until fragrant, about 30 seconds. Stir in beets and broth. Lock lid in place and close pressure release valve. Select high pressure cook function and cook for 3 minutes. Turn off Instant Pot and quick-release pressure. Carefully remove lid, allowing steam to escape away from you. 2. Fold sheet of aluminum foil into 16 by 6-inch sling. Combine 2 tablespoons oil, dukkah, and salt in bowl, then brush cod with oil mixture. Arrange cod skinned side down in center of sling. Using sling, lower cod into Instant Pot; allow narrow edges of sling to rest along sides of insert. Lock lid in place and close pressure release valve. Select high pressure cook function and cook for 2 minutes. 3. Turn off Instant Pot and quick-release pressure. Carefully remove lid, allowing steam to escape away from you. Using sling, transfer cod to large plate. Tent with foil and let rest while finishing beet salad. 4. Combine lemon juice and remaining 1 tablespoon oil in large bowl. Using slotted spoon, transfer beets to bowl with oil mixture. Add arugula and gently toss to combine. Season with salt and pepper to taste. 5 Serve cod with salad, sprinkling individual portions with extra dukkah and drizzling with extra oil.
Per Serving:
calories: 340 | fat: 16g | protein: 33g | carbs: 14g | fiber: 4g | sodium: 460mg

Foil-Pack Haddock with Spinach

Prep time: 15 minutes | Cook time: 15 minutes | Serves 4

12 ounces (340 g) haddock fillet
1 cup spinach
1 tablespoon avocado oil

1 teaspoon minced garlic
½ teaspoon ground coriander
1 cup water, for cooking

1. Blend the spinach until smooth and mix up with avocado oil, ground coriander, and minced garlic. 2. Then cut the haddock into 4 fillets and place on the foil. 3. Top the fish fillets with spinach mixture and place them on the rack. 4. Pour water and insert the rack in the instant pot. 5. Close and seal the lid and cook the haddock on Manual (High Pressure) for 15 minutes. 6. Do a quick pressure release.
Per Serving:
calories: 103 | fat: 1g | protein: 21g | carbs: 1g | net carbs: 1g | fiber: 0g

Almond Milk Curried Fish

Prep time: 10 minutes | Cook time: 3 minutes | Serves 2

8 ounces (227 g) cod fillet, chopped

1 teaspoon curry paste
1 cup organic almond milk

1. Mix up curry paste and almond milk and pour the liquid in the instant pot. 2. Add chopped cod fillet and close the lid. 3. Cook the fish curry on Manual mode (High Pressure) for 3 minutes. 4. Then make the quick pressure release for 5 minutes.
Per Serving:
calories: 138 | fat: 4g | protein: 21g | carbs: 5g | net carbs: 5g | fiber: 0g

Fish Bake with Veggies

Prep time: 10 minutes | Cook time: 5 minutes | Serves 4

1½ cups water
Cooking spray
2 ripe tomatoes, sliced
2 cloves garlic, minced
1 teaspoon dried oregano
1 teaspoon dried basil
½ teaspoon dried rosemary
1 red onion, sliced
1 head cauliflower, cut into

florets
1 pound (454 g) tilapia fillets, sliced
Sea salt, to taste
1 tablespoon olive oil
1 cup crumbled feta cheese
⅓ cup Kalamata olives, pitted and halved

1. Pour the water into your Instant Pot and insert a trivet. 2. Spritz a casserole dish with cooking spray. Add the tomato slices to the dish. Scatter the top with the garlic, oregano, basil, and rosemary. 3. Mix in the onion and cauliflower. Arrange the fish fillets on top. Sprinkle with the salt and drizzle with the olive oil. 4. Place the feta cheese and Kalamata olives on top. Lower the dish onto the trivet. 5. Lock the lid. Select the Manual mode and set the cooking time for 5 minutes at High Pressure. 6. When the timer beeps, perform a quick pressure release. Carefully remove the lid. 7. Allow to cool for 5 minutes before serving.
Per Serving:
calories: 302 | fat: 15.0g | protein: 30.5g | carbs: 11.3g | net carbs: 8.2g | fiber: 3.1g

Tuna Spinach Cakes

Prep time: 15 minutes | Cook time: 8 minutes | Serves 4

10 ounces (283 g) tuna, shredded
1 cup spinach
1 egg, beaten

1 teaspoon ground coriander
2 tablespoon coconut flakes
1 tablespoon avocado oil

1. Blend the spinach in the blender until smooth. 2. Then transfer it in the mixing bowl and add tuna, egg, and ground coriander. 3. Add coconut flakes and stir the mass with the help of the spoon. 4. Heat up avocado oil in the instant pot on Sauté mode for 2 minutes. 5. Then make the medium size cakes from the tuna mixture and place them in the hot oil. 6. Cook the tuna cakes on Sauté mode for 3 minutes. Then flip the on another side and cook for 3 minutes more or until they are light brown.
Per Serving:
calories: 163 | fat: 8g | protein:20g | carbs: 1g | net carbs: 0g | fiber: 1g

Clam Chowder with Bacon and Celery

Prep time: 10 minutes | Cook time: 4 minutes | Serves 2

5 ounces (142 g) clams
1 ounce (28 g) bacon, chopped
3 ounces (85 g) celery, chopped
½ cup water
½ cup heavy cream

1. Cook the bacon on Sauté mode for 1 minute. 2. Then add clams, celery, water, and heavy cream. 3. Close and seal the lid. 4. Cook the seafood on steam mode (High Pressure) for 3 minutes. Make a quick pressure release. 5. Ladle the clams with the heavy cream mixture in the bowls.
Per Serving:
calories: 221 | fat: 17g | protein: 7g | carbs: 10g | net carbs: 9g | fiber: 1g

Louisiana Shrimp Gumbo

Prep time: 10 minutes | Cook time: 4 minutes | Serves 6

1 pound (454 g) shrimp
¼ cup chopped celery stalk
1 chili pepper, chopped
¼ cup chopped okra
1 tablespoon coconut oil
2 cups chicken broth
1 teaspoon sugar-free tomato paste

1. Put all ingredients in the instant pot and stir until you get a light red color. 2. Then close and seal the lid. 3. Cook the meal on Manual mode (High Pressure) for 4 minutes. 4. When the time is finished, allow the natural pressure release for 10 minutes.
Per Serving:
calories: 126 | fat: 4g | protein: 19g | carbs: 2g | net carbs: 2g | fiber: 0g

Garam Masala Fish

Prep time: 10 minutes | Cook time: 10 minutes | Serves 4

2 tablespoons sesame oil
½ teaspoon cumin seeds
½ cup chopped leeks
1 teaspoon ginger-garlic paste
1 pound (454 g) cod fillets, boneless and sliced
2 ripe tomatoes, chopped
1½ tablespoons fresh lemon juice
½ teaspoon garam masala
½ teaspoon turmeric powder
1 tablespoon chopped fresh dill leaves
1 tablespoon chopped fresh curry leaves
1 tablespoon chopped fresh parsley leaves
Coarse sea salt, to taste
½ teaspoon smoked cayenne pepper
¼ teaspoon ground black pepper, or more to taste

1. Set the Instant Pot to Sauté. Add and heat the sesame oil until hot. Sauté the cumin seeds for 30 seconds. 2. Add the leeks and cook for another 2 minutes until translucent. Add the ginger-garlic paste and cook for an additional 40 seconds. 3. Stir in the remaining ingredients. 4. Lock the lid. Select the Manual mode and set the cooking time for 6 minutes at Low Pressure. 5. When the timer beeps, perform a quick pressure release. Carefully remove the lid. 6. Serve immediately.
Per Serving:
calories: 166 | fat: 7.8g | protein: 18.4g | carbs: 5.9g | net carbs: 3.9g | fiber: 2.0g

Salmon with Lemon-Garlic Mashed Cauliflower

Prep time: 15 minutes | Cook time: 10 minutes | Serves 4

2 tablespoons extra-virgin olive oil
4 garlic cloves, peeled and smashed
½ cup chicken or vegetable broth
¾ teaspoon table salt, divided
1 large head cauliflower (3 pounds / 1.4 kg), cored and cut
into 2-inch florets
4 (6-ounce / 170-g) skinless salmon fillets, 1½ inches thick
½ teaspoon ras el hanout
½ teaspoon grated lemon zest
3 scallions, sliced thin
1 tablespoon sesame seeds, toasted

1. Using highest sauté function, cook oil and garlic in Instant Pot until garlic is fragrant and light golden brown, about 3 minutes. Turn off Instant Pot, then stir in broth and ¼ teaspoon salt. Arrange cauliflower in pot in even layer. 2. Fold sheet of aluminum foil into 16 by 6-inch sling. Sprinkle flesh side of salmon with ras el hanout and remaining ½ teaspoon salt, then arrange skinned side down in center of sling. Using sling, lower salmon into Instant Pot on top of cauliflower; allow narrow edges of sling to rest along sides of insert. Lock lid in place and close pressure release valve. Select high pressure cook function and cook for 2 minutes. 3. Turn off Instant Pot and quick-release pressure. Carefully remove lid, allowing steam to escape away from you. Using sling, transfer salmon to large plate. Tent with foil and let rest while finishing cauliflower. 4. Using potato masher, mash cauliflower mixture until no large chunks remain. Using highest sauté function, cook cauliflower, stirring often, until slightly thickened, about 3 minutes. Stir in lemon zest and season with salt and pepper to taste. Serve salmon with cauliflower, sprinkling individual portions with scallions and sesame seeds.
Per Serving:
calories: 480 | fat: 31g | protein: 38g | carbs: 9g | fiber: 3g | sodium: 650mg

Trout Casserole

Prep time: 5 minutes | Cook time: 10 minutes | Serves 3

1½ cups water
1½ tablespoons olive oil
3 plum tomatoes, sliced
½ teaspoon dried oregano
1 teaspoon dried basil
3 trout fillets
½ teaspoon cayenne pepper, or
more to taste
⅓ teaspoon black pepper
Salt, to taste
1 bay leaf
1 cup shredded Pepper Jack cheese

1. Pour the water into your Instant Pot and insert a trivet. 2. Grease a baking dish with the olive oil. Add the tomatoes slices to the baking dish and sprinkle with the oregano and basil. 3. Add the fish fillets and season with the cayenne pepper, black pepper, and salt. Add the bay leaf. Lower the baking dish onto the trivet. 4. Lock the lid. Select the Manual mode and set the cooking time for 10 minutes at High Pressure. 5. When the timer beeps, perform a quick pressure release. Carefully remove the lid. 6. Scatter the Pepper Jack cheese on top, lock the lid, and allow the cheese to melt. 7. Serve warm.
Per Serving:
calories: 361 | fat: 23.5g | protein: 25.2g | carbs: 12.1g | net carbs:

11.3g | fiber: 0.8g

Tuna Fillets with Lemon Butter

Prep time: 5 minutes | Cook time: 3 minutes | Serves 4

1 cup water
⅓ cup lemon juice
2 sprigs fresh thyme
2 sprigs fresh parsley
2 sprigs fresh rosemary
1 pound (454 g) tuna fillets

4 cloves garlic, pressed
Sea salt, to taste
¼ teaspoon black pepper, or more to taste
2 tablespoons butter, melted
1 lemon, sliced

1. Pour the water into your Instant Pot. Add the lemon juice, thyme, parsley, and rosemary and insert a steamer basket. 2. Put the tuna fillets in the basket. Top with the garlic and season with the salt and black pepper. 3. Drizzle the melted butter over the fish fillets and place the lemon slices on top. 4. Lock the lid. Select the Manual mode and set the cooking time for 3 minutes at Low Pressure. 5. When the timer beeps, perform a quick pressure release. Carefully remove the lid. Serve immediately.
Per Serving:
calories: 178 | fat: 7.0g | protein: 25.4g | carbs: 3.5g | net carbs: 3.2g | fiber: 0.3g

Chili and Turmeric Haddock

Prep time: 10 minutes | Cook time: 5 minutes | Serves 4

1 chili pepper, minced
1 pound (454 g) haddock, chopped
½ teaspoon ground turmeric

½ cup fish stock
1 cup water

1. In the mixing bowl mix up chili pepper, ground turmeric, and fish stock. 2. Then add chopped haddock and transfer the mixture in the baking mold. 3. Pour water in the instant pot and insert the trivet. 4. Place the baking mold with fish on the trivet and close the lid. 5. Cook the meal on Manual (High Pressure) for 5 minutes. Make a quick pressure release.
Per Serving:
calories: 130 | fat: 1g | protein: 28g | carbs: 0g | net carbs: 0g | fiber: 0g

Coconut Shrimp Curry

Prep time: 10 minutes | Cook time: 4 minutes | Serves 5

15 ounces (425 g) shrimp, peeled
1 teaspoon chili powder
1 teaspoon garam masala

1 cup coconut milk
1 teaspoon olive oil
½ teaspoon minced garlic

1. Heat up the instant pot on Sauté mode for 2 minutes. 2. Then add olive oil. Cook the ingredients for 1 minute. 3. Add shrimp and sprinkle them with chili powder, garam masala, minced garlic, and coconut milk. 4. Carefully stir the ingredients and close the lid. 5. Cook the shrimp curry on Manual mode for 1 minute. Make a quick pressure release.
Per Serving:
calories: 222 | fat: 14g | protein: 21g | carbs: 4g | net carbs: 3g | fiber: 1

Chapter 5 | Poultry

Chicken and Bacon Ranch Casserole

Prep time: 5 minutes | Cook time: 30 minutes | Serves 4

4 slices bacon	1 tablespoon coconut oil
4 (6-ounce / 170-g) boneless, skinless chicken breasts, cut into 1-inch cubes	½ cup chicken broth
	½ cup ranch dressing
	½ cup shredded Cheddar cheese
½ teaspoon salt	
¼ teaspoon pepper	2 ounces (57 g) cream cheese

1. Press the Sauté button to heat your Instant Pot. 2. Add the bacon slices and cook for about 7 minutes until crisp, flipping occasionally. 3. Remove from the pot and place on a paper towel to drain. Set aside. 4. Season the chicken cubes with salt and pepper. 5. Set your Instant Pot to Sauté and melt the coconut oil. 6. Add the chicken cubes and brown for 3 to 4 minutes until golden brown. 7. Stir in the broth and ranch dressing. 8. Secure the lid. Select the Manual mode and set the cooking time for 20 minutes at High Pressure. 9. Once cooking is complete, do a quick pressure release. Carefully open the lid. 10. Stir in the Cheddar and cream cheese. Crumble the cooked bacon and scatter on top. Serve immediately.
Per Serving:
calories: 467 | fat: 25.8g | protein: 46.2g | carbs: 1.3g | net carbs: 1.2g | fiber: 0.1g

Ann's Chicken Cacciatore

Prep time: 25 minutes | Cook time: 3 to 9 minutes | Serves 8

1 large onion, thinly sliced	¼ teaspoons pepper
3 pound chicken, cut up, skin removed, trimmed of fat	1–2 garlic cloves, minced
	1–2 teaspoons dried oregano
2 6-ounce cans tomato paste	½ teaspoon dried basil
4-ounce can sliced mushrooms, drained	½ teaspoon celery seed, optional
1 teaspoon salt	1 bay leaf
¼ cup dry white wine	

1. In the inner pot of the Instant Pot, place the onion and chicken. 2. Combine remaining ingredients and pour over the chicken. 3. Secure the lid and make sure vent is at sealing. Cook on Slow Cook mode, low 7–9 hours, or high 3–4 hours.
Per Serving:
calories: 161 | fat: 4g | protein: 19g | carbs: 12g | sugars: 3g | fiber: 3g | sodium: 405mg

Chicken Tagine

Prep time: 15 minutes | Cook time: 11 minutes | Serves 4

2 (15-ounce / 425-g) cans chickpeas, rinsed, divided	¼ teaspoon cayenne pepper
	1 fennel bulb, 1 tablespoon fronds minced, stalks discarded, bulb halved and cut lengthwise into ½-inch-thick wedges
1 tablespoon extra-virgin olive oil	
5 garlic cloves, minced	
1½ teaspoons paprika	
½ teaspoon ground turmeric	1 cup chicken broth
½ teaspoon ground cumin	3 (2-inch) strips lemon zest, plus lemon wedges for serving
¼ teaspoon ground ginger	

4 (5- to 7-ounce / 142- to 198-g) bone-in chicken thighs, skin removed, trimmed	green or black olives, halved
	⅓ cup raisins
½ teaspoon table salt	2 tablespoons chopped fresh parsley
½ cup pitted large brine-cured	

1. Using potato masher, mash ½ cup chickpeas in bowl to paste. Using highest sauté function, cook oil, garlic, paprika, turmeric, cumin, ginger, and cayenne in Instant Pot until fragrant, about 1 minute. Turn off Instant Pot, then stir in remaining whole chickpeas, mashed chickpeas, fennel wedges, broth, and zest. 2. Sprinkle chicken with salt. Nestle chicken skinned side up into pot and spoon some of cooking liquid over top. Lock lid in place and close pressure release valve. Select high pressure cook function and cook for 10 minutes. 3. Turn off Instant Pot and quick-release pressure. Carefully remove lid, allowing steam to escape away from you. Discard lemon zest. Stir in olives, raisins, parsley, and fennel fronds. Season with salt and pepper to taste. Serve with lemon wedges.
Per Serving:
calories: 489 | fat: 16g | protein: 41g | carbs: 48g | fiber: 13g | sodium: 717mg

Marjoram Chicken Wings with Cream Cheese

Prep time: 7 minutes | Cook time: 10 minutes | Serves 2

1 teaspoon marjoram	pepper
1 teaspoon cream cheese	14 ounces (397 g) chicken wings
½ green pepper	
½ teaspoon salt	¾ cup water
½ teaspoon ground black	1 teaspoon coconut oil

1. Rub the chicken wings with the marjoram, salt, and ground black pepper. 2. Blend the green pepper until you get a purée. 3. Rub the chicken wings in the green pepper purée. 4. Then toss the coconut oil in the instant pot bowl and preheat it on the Sauté mode. 5. Add the chicken wings and cook them for 3 minutes from each side or until light brown. 6. Then add cream cheese and water. 7. Cook the meal on Manual mode for 4 minutes at High Pressure. 8. When the time is over, make a quick pressure release. 9. Let the cooked chicken wings chill for 1 to 2 minutes and serve them!
Per Serving:
calories: 411 | fat: 18g | protein: 58g | carbs: 2g | net carbs: 1g | fiber: 1g

Tomato Chicken Legs

Prep time: 10 minutes | Cook time: 35 minutes | Serves 2

2 chicken legs	1 cup chicken stock
2 tomatoes, chopped	1 teaspoon peppercorns

1. Put all ingredients in the instant pot. 2. Close and seal the lid. Set Manual mode (High Pressure). 3. Cook the chicken legs for 35 minutes. 4. Make a quick pressure release. 5. Transfer the cooked chicken legs in the serving bowls and add 1 ladle of the chicken stock.
Per Serving:
calories: 294 | fat: 16g | protein: 31g | carbs: 6g | net carbs: 4g | fiber: 2g

hredded Chicken

Prep time: 5 minutes | Cook time: 14 minutes | Serves 4

½ teaspoon salt
½ teaspoon pepper
½ teaspoon dried oregano
½ teaspoon dried basil
½ teaspoon garlic powder

2 (6-ounce / 170-g) boneless, skinless chicken breasts
1 tablespoon coconut oil
1 cup water

1. In a small bowl, combine the salt, pepper, oregano, basil, and garlic powder. Rub this mix over both sides of the chicken. 2. Set your Instant Pot to Sauté and heat the coconut oil until sizzling. 3. Add the chicken and sear for 3 to 4 minutes until golden on both sides. 4. Remove the chicken and set aside. 5. Pour the water into the Instant Pot and use a wooden spoon or rubber spatula to make sure no seasoning is stuck to bottom of pot. 6. Add the trivet to the Instant Pot and place the chicken on top. 7. Secure the lid. Select the Manual mode and set the cooking time for 10 minutes at High Pressure. 8. Once cooking is complete, do a natural pressure release for 5 minutes, then release any remaining pressure. Carefully open the lid. 9. Remove the chicken and shred, then serve.

Per Serving:
calories: 135 | fat: 5g | protein: 20g | carbs: 0g | net carbs: 0g | fiber: 0g

Classic Chicken Salad

Prep time: 5 minutes | Cook time: 12 minutes | Serves 8

2 pounds (907 g) chicken breasts
1 cup vegetable broth
2 sprigs fresh thyme
1 teaspoon granulated garlic
1 teaspoon onion powder
1 bay leaf
½ teaspoon ground black

pepper
1 cup mayonnaise
2 stalks celery, chopped
2 tablespoons chopped fresh chives
1 teaspoon fresh lemon juice
1 teaspoon Dijon mustard
½ teaspoon coarse sea salt

1. Combine the chicken, broth, thyme, garlic, onion powder, bay leaf, and black pepper in the Instant Pot. 2. Lock the lid. Select the Poultry mode and set the cooking time for 12 minutes at High Pressure. 3. When the timer beeps, perform a natural pressure release for 10 minutes, then release any remaining pressure. Carefully remove the lid. 4. Remove the chicken from the Instant Pot and let rest for a few minutes until cooled slightly. 5. Slice the chicken breasts into strips and place in a salad bowl. Add the remaining ingredients and gently stir until well combined. Serve immediately.

Per Serving:
calories: 348 | fat: 26.7g | protein: 25.1g | carbs: 1.5g | net carbs: 1.1g | fiber: 0.4g

Cheesy Stuffed Cabbage

Prep time: 30 minutes | Cook time: 18 minutes | Serves 6 to 8

1–2 heads savoy cabbage
1 pound ground turkey
1 egg
1 cup reduced-fat shredded cheddar cheese

2 tablespoons evaporated skim milk
¼ cup reduced-fat shredded Parmesan cheese
¼ cup reduced-fat shredded

mozzarella cheese
¼ cup finely diced onion
¼ cup finely diced bell pepper
¼ cup finely diced mushrooms
1 teaspoon salt
½ teaspoon black pepper
1 teaspoon garlic powder

6 basil leaves, fresh and cut chiffonade
1 tablespoon fresh parsley, chopped
1 quart of your favorite pasta sauce

1. Remove the core from the cabbages. 2. Boil pot of water and place 1 head at a time into the water for approximately 10 minutes. 3. Allow cabbage to cool slightly. Once cooled, remove the leaves carefully and set aside. You'll need about 15 or 16. 4. Mix together the meat and all remaining ingredients except the pasta sauce. 5. One leaf at a time, put a heaping tablespoon of meat mixture in the center. 6. Tuck the sides in and then roll tightly. 7. Add ½ cup sauce to the bottom of the inner pot of the Instant Pot. 8. Place the rolls, fold-side down, into the pot and layer them, putting a touch of sauce between each layer and finally on top. (You may want to cook the rolls in two batches.) 9. Lock lid and make sure vent is at sealing. Set timer on 18 minutes on Manual at high pressure, then manually release the pressure when cook time is over.

Per Serving:
calories: 199| fat: 8g | protein: 2mg | carbs: 14g | sugars: 7g | fiber: 3g | sodium: 678mg

BBQ Turkey Meat Loaf

Prep time: 5 minutes | Cook time: 40 minutes | Serves 6

1 pound 93 percent lean ground turkey
⅓ cup low-sugar or unsweetened barbecue sauce, plus 2 tablespoons
⅓ cup gluten-free panko (Japanese bread crumbs)
1 large egg

½ small yellow onion, finely diced
1 garlic clove, minced
½ teaspoon fine sea salt
½ teaspoon freshly ground black pepper
Cooked cauliflower "rice" or brown rice for serving

1. Pour 1 cup water into the Instant Pot. Lightly grease a 7 by 3-inch round cake pan or a 5½ by 3-inch loaf pan with olive oil or coat with nonstick cooking spray. 2. In a medium bowl, combine the turkey, ⅓ cup barbecue sauce, panko, egg, onion, garlic, salt, and pepper and mix well with your hands until all of the ingredients are evenly distributed. Transfer the mixture to the prepared pan, pressing it into an even layer. Cover the pan tightly with aluminum foil. Place the pan on a long-handled silicone steam rack, then, holding the handles of the steam rack, lower it into the pot. (If you don't have the long-handled rack, use the wire metal steam rack and a homemade sling) 3. Secure the lid and set the Pressure Release to Sealing. Select the Pressure Cook or Manual setting and set the cooking time for 25 minutes at high pressure if using a 7-inch round cake pan, or for 35 minutes at high pressure if using a 5½ by 3-inch loaf pan. (The pot will take about 10 minutes to come up to pressure before the cooking program begins.) 4. Preheat a toaster oven or position an oven rack 4 to 6 inches below the heat source and preheat the broiler. 5. When the cooking program ends, perform a quick pressure release by moving the Pressure Release to Venting. Open the pot and, wearing heat-resistant mitts, grasp the handles of the steam rack and lift it out of the pot. Uncover the pan, taking care not to get burned by the steam or to drip condensation onto the meat loaf. Brush the remaining 2 tablespoons barbecue sauce on top of the meat loaf. 6. Broil the meat loaf for a few minutes, just until the glaze becomes bubbly

and browned. Cut the meat loaf into slices and serve hot, with the cauliflower "rice" alongside.

Per Serving:

calories: 236 | fat: 11g | protein: 25g | carbs: 10g | sugars: 2g | fiber: 3g | sodium: 800mg

Chicken and Scallions Stuffed Peppers

Prep time: 5 minutes | Cook time: 20 minutes | Serves 5

1 tablespoon butter, at room temperature	⅓ teaspoon ground cumin
½ cup scallions, chopped	¼ teaspoon shallot powder
1 pound (454 g) ground chicken	6 ounces (170 g) goat cheese, crumbled
½ teaspoon sea salt	1½ cups water
½ teaspoon chili powder	5 bell peppers, tops, membrane, and seeds removed
⅓ teaspoon paprika	½ cup sour cream

1. Set your Instant Pot to Sauté and melt the butter. 2. Add the scallions and chicken and sauté for 2 to 3 minutes. 3. Stir in the sea salt, chili powder, paprika, cumin, and shallot powder. Add the crumbled goat cheese, stir, and reserve the mixture in a bowl. 4. Clean your Instant Pot. Pour the water into the Instant Pot and insert the trivet. 5. Stuff the bell peppers with enough of the chicken mixture, and don't pack the peppers too tightly. Put the peppers on the trivet. 6. Lock the lid. Select the Poultry mode and set the cooking time for 15 minutes at High Pressure. 7. When the timer beeps, perform a natural pressure release for 10 minutes, then release any remaining pressure. Carefully remove the lid. 8. Remove from the Instant Pot and serve with the sour cream.

Per Serving:

calories: 338 | fat: 19.8g | protein: 30.3g | carbs: 8.6g | net carbs: 7.4g | fiber: 1.2g

Unstuffed Peppers with Ground Turkey and Quinoa

Prep time: 0 minutes | Cook time: 35 minutes | Serves 8

2 tablespoons extra-virgin olive oil	1 cup low-sodium chicken broth
1 yellow onion, diced	One 14½-ounce can fire-roasted diced tomatoes and their liquid
2 celery stalks, diced	
2 garlic cloves, chopped	
2 pounds 93 percent lean ground turkey	3 red, orange, and/or yellow bell peppers, seeded and cut into 1-inch squares
2 teaspoons Cajun seasoning blend (plus 1 teaspoon fine sea salt if using a salt-free blend)	1 green onion, white and green parts, thinly sliced
½ teaspoon freshly ground black pepper	1½ tablespoons chopped fresh flat-leaf parsley
¼ teaspoon cayenne pepper	Hot sauce (such as Crystal or Frank's RedHot) for serving
1 cup quinoa, rinsed	

1. Select the Sauté setting on the Instant Pot and heat the oil for 2 minutes. Add the onion, celery, and garlic and sauté for about 4 minutes, until the onion begins to soften. Add the turkey, Cajun seasoning, black pepper, and cayenne and sauté, using a wooden spoon or spatula to break up the meat as it cooks, for about 6 minutes, until cooked through and no streaks of pink remain. 2. Sprinkle the quinoa over the turkey in an even layer. Pour the broth and the diced tomatoes and their liquid over the quinoa, spreading the tomatoes on top. Sprinkle the bell peppers over the top in an even layer. 3. Secure the lid and set the Pressure Release to Sealing. Press the Cancel button to reset the cooking program, then select the Pressure Cook or Manual setting and set the cooking time for 8 minutes at high pressure. (The pot will take about 15 minutes to come up to pressure before the cooking program begins.) 4. When the cooking program ends, let the pressure release naturally for at least 15 minutes, then move the Pressure Release to Venting to release any remaining steam. Open the pot and sprinkle the green onion and parsley over the top in an even layer. 5. Spoon the unstuffed peppers into bowls, making sure to dig down to the bottom of the pot so each person gets an equal amount of peppers, quinoa, and meat. Serve hot, with hot sauce on the side.

Per Serving:

calories: 320 | fat: 14g | protein: 27g | carbs: 23g | sugars: 3g | fiber: 3g | sodium: 739mg

Chicken Tacos with Fried Cheese Shells

Prep time: 5 minutes | Cook time: 25 minutes | Serves 6

Chicken:	1 tablespoon chili powder
4 (6-ounce / 170-g) boneless, skinless chicken breasts	2 teaspoons garlic powder
	2 teaspoons cumin
1 cup chicken broth	Cheese Shells:
1 teaspoon salt	1½ cups shredded whole-milk Mozzarella cheese
¼ teaspoon pepper	

1. Combine all ingredients for the chicken in the Instant Pot. 2. Secure the lid. Select the Manual mode and set the cooking time for 20 minutes at High Pressure. 3. Once cooking is complete, do a quick pressure release. Carefully open the lid. 4. Shred the chicken and serve in bowls or cheese shells. 5. Make the cheese shells: Heat a nonstick skillet over medium heat. 6. Sprinkle ¼ cup of Mozzarella cheese in the skillet and fry until golden. Flip and turn off the heat. Allow the cheese to get brown. Fill with chicken and fold. The cheese will harden as it cools. Repeat with the remaining cheese and filling. 7. Serve warm.

Per Serving:

calories: 233 | fat: 8.2g | protein: 32.4g | carbs: 2.4g | net carbs: 1.7g | fiber: 1.7g

Dijon Turkey

Prep time: 15 minutes | Cook time: 14 minutes | Serves 4

14 ounces (397 g) ground turkey	1 teaspoon onion powder
	1 teaspoon salt
1 tablespoon Dijon mustard	½ cup chicken broth
½ cup coconut flour	1 tablespoon avocado oil

1. In the mixing bowl, mix up ground turkey, Dijon mustard, coconut flour, onion powder, and salt. 2. Make the meatballs with the help of the fingertips. 3. Then pour avocado oil in the instant pot and heat it up for1 minute. 4. Add the meatballs and cook them for 2 minutes from each side. 5. Then add chicken broth. Close and seal the lid. 6. Cook the meatballs for 10 minutes. Make a quick pressure release.

Per Serving:

calories: 268 | fat: 13g | protein: 30g | carbs: 11g | net carbs: 5g | fiber: 6g

Mushroom Chicken Alfredo

Prep time: 15 minutes | Cook time: 10 minutes | Serves 4

½ cup sliced cremini mushrooms	1 cup heavy cream
¼ cup chopped leek	1 pound (454 g) chicken fillet, chopped
1 tablespoon sesame oil	1 teaspoon Italian seasoning
1 teaspoon chili flakes	1 tablespoon cream cheese

1. Brush the instant pot boil with sesame oil from inside. 2. Put the chicken in the instant pot in one layer. 3. Then top it with mushrooms and leek. 4. Sprinkle the ingredients with chili flakes, heavy cream, Italian seasoning, and cream cheese. 5. Close and seal the lid. 6. Cook the meal on Manual mode (High Pressure) for 10 minutes. 7. When the time is finished, allow the natural pressure release for 10 minutes.

Per Serving:

calories: 367 | fat: 24g | protein: 34g | carbs: 2g | net carbs: 2g | fiber: 0g

African Chicken Peanut Stew

Prep time: 10 minutes | Cook time: 10 minutes | Serves 6

1 cup chopped onion	1 tablespoon sugar-free tomato paste
2 tablespoons minced garlic	
1 tablespoon minced fresh ginger	1 pound (454 g) boneless, skinless chicken breasts or thighs, cut into large chunks
1 teaspoon salt	
½ teaspoon ground cumin	3 to 4 cups chopped Swiss chard
½ teaspoon ground coriander	
½ teaspoon freshly ground black pepper	1 cup cubed raw pumpkin
½ teaspoon ground cinnamon	½ cup water
⅛ teaspoon ground cloves	1 cup chunky peanut butter

1. In the inner cooking pot of the Instant Pot, stir together the onion, garlic, ginger, salt, cumin, coriander, pepper, cinnamon, cloves, and tomato paste. Add the chicken, chard, pumpkin, and water. 2. Lock the lid into place. Select Manual and adjust the pressure to High. Cook for 10 minutes. When the cooking is complete, let the pressure release naturally. Unlock the lid. 3. Mix in the peanut butter a little at a time. Taste with each addition, as your reward for cooking. The final sauce should be thick enough to coat the back of a spoon in a thin layer. 4. Serve over mashed cauliflower, cooked zucchini noodles, steamed vegetables, or with a side salad.

Per Serving:

calories: 411 | fat: 27g | protein: 31g | carbs: 15g | net carbs: 10g | fiber: 5g

Authentic Chicken Shawarma

Prep time: 15 minutes | Cook time: 17 minutes | Serves 4

1 pound (454 g) chicken fillet	1 tablespoon tahini sauce
½ teaspoon ground coriander	1 teaspoon lemon juice
½ teaspoon smoked paprika	1 teaspoon heavy cream
½ teaspoon dried thyme	1 cup water, for cooking

1. Rub the chicken fillet with ground coriander, smoked paprika, thyme, and wrap in the foil. 2. Then pour water and insert the steamer rack in the instant pot. 3. Place the wrapped chicken in the steamer; close and seal the lid. 4. Cook the chicken on Manual mode (High Pressure) for 17 minutes. Make a quick pressure release. 5. Make the sauce: Mix up heavy cream, lemon juice, and tahini paste. 6. Slice the chicken and sprinkle it with sauce.

Per Serving:

calories: 234 | fat: 10g | protein: 33g | carbs: 1g | net carbs: 1g | fiber: 0g

Chicken in Wine

Prep time: 10 minutes | Cook time: 12 minutes | Serves 6

2 pounds chicken breasts, trimmed of skin and fat	10¾-ounce can French onion soup
10¾-ounce can 98% fat-free, reduced-sodium cream of mushroom soup	1 cup dry white wine or chicken broth

1. Place the chicken into the Instant Pot. 2. Combine soups and wine. Pour over chicken. 3. Secure the lid and make sure vent is set to sealing. Cook on Manual mode for 12 minutes. 4. When cook time is up, let the pressure release naturally for 5 minutes and then release the rest manually.

Per Serving:

calories: 225 | fat: 5g | protein: 35g | carbs: 7g | sugars: 3g | fiber: 1g | sodium: 645mg

BLT Chicken Salad

Prep time: 15 minutes | Cook time: 17 minutes | Serves 4

4 slices bacon	1 cup water
2 (6-ounce / 170-g) chicken breasts	2 cups chopped romaine lettuce
	Sauce:
1 teaspoon salt	⅓ cup mayonnaise
½ teaspoon garlic powder	1 ounce (28 g) chopped pecans
¼ teaspoon dried parsley	½ cup diced Roma tomatoes
¼ teaspoon pepper	½ avocado, diced
¼ teaspoon dried thyme	1 tablespoon lemon juice

1. Press the Sauté button to heat your Instant Pot. 2. Add the bacon and cook for about 7 minutes, flipping occasionally, until crisp. Remove and place on a paper towel to drain. When cool enough to handle, crumble the bacon and set aside. 3. Sprinkle the chicken with salt, garlic powder, parsley, pepper, and thyme. 4. Pour the water into the Instant Pot. Use a wooden spoon to ensure nothing is stuck to the bottom of the pot. Add the trivet to the pot and place the chicken on top of the trivet. 5. Secure the lid. Select the Manual mode and set the cooking time for 10 minutes at High Pressure. 6. Meanwhile, whisk together all the ingredients for the sauce in a large salad bowl. 7. Once cooking is complete, do a quick pressure release. Carefully open the lid. 8. Remove the chicken and let sit for 10 minutes. Cut the chicken into cubes and transfer to the salad bowl, along with the cooked bacon. Gently stir until the chicken is thoroughly coated. Mix in the lettuce right before serving.

Per Serving:

calories: 431 | fat: 32.6g | protein: 24.3g | carbs: 5.1g | net carbs: 2.4g | fiber: 2.7g

Greek Chicken

Prep time: 25 minutes | Cook time: 20 minutes | Serves 6

4 potatoes, unpeeled, quartered
2 pounds chicken pieces, trimmed of skin and fat
2 large onions, quartered
1 whole bulb garlic, cloves minced

3 teaspoons dried oregano
¾ teaspoons salt
½ teaspoons pepper
1 tablespoon olive oil
1 cup water

1. Place potatoes, chicken, onions, and garlic into the inner pot of the Instant Pot, then sprinkle with seasonings. Top with oil and water. 2. Secure the lid and make sure vent is set to sealing. Cook on Manual mode for 20 minutes. 3. When cook time is over, let the pressure release naturally for 5 minutes, then release the rest manually.
Per Serving:
calorie: 278 | fat: 6g | protein: 27g | carbs: 29g | sugars: 9g | fiber: 4g | sodium: 358mg

Barbecue Shredded Chicken

Prep time: 5 minutes | Cook time: 25 minutes | Serves 4

1 (5-pound / 2.2-kg) whole chicken
3 teaspoons salt
1 teaspoon pepper
1 teaspoon dried parsley
1 teaspoon garlic powder

½ medium onion, cut into 3 to 4 large pieces
1 cup water
½ cup sugar-free barbecue sauce, divided

1. Scatter the chicken with salt, pepper, parsley, and garlic powder. Put the onion pieces inside the chicken cavity. 2. Pour the water into the Instant Pot and insert the trivet. Place seasoned chicken on the trivet. Brush with half of the barbecue sauce. 3. Lock the lid. Select the Manual mode and set the cooking time for 25 minutes at High Pressure. 4. When the timer beeps, perform a natural pressure release for 10 minutes, then release any remaining pressure. Carefully remove the lid. 5. Using a clean brush, add the remaining half of the sauce to chicken. For crispy skin or thicker sauce, you can broil in the oven for 5 minutes until lightly browned. 6. Slice or shred the chicken and serve warm.
Per Serving:
calories: 1054 | fat: 73.1g | protein: 70.8g | carbs: 6.6g | net carbs: 5.5g | fiber: 1.1g

Stuffed Chicken with Spinach and Feta

Prep time: 10 minutes | Cook time: 25 minutes | Serves 4

½ cup frozen spinach
⅓ cup crumbled feta cheese
1¼ teaspoons salt, divided
4 (6-ounce / 170-g) boneless, skinless chicken breasts, butterflied

¼ teaspoon pepper
¼ teaspoon dried oregano
¼ teaspoon dried parsley
¼ teaspoon garlic powder
2 tablespoons coconut oil
1 cup water

1. Combine the spinach, feta cheese, and ¼ teaspoon of salt in a medium bowl. Divide the mixture evenly and spoon onto the chicken breasts. 2. Close the chicken breasts and secure with toothpicks or butcher's string. Sprinkle the chicken with the remaining 1 teaspoon of salt, pepper, oregano, parsley, and garlic powder. 3. Set your Instant Pot to Sauté and heat the coconut oil. 4. Sear each chicken breast until golden brown, about 4 to 5 minutes per side. 5. Remove the chicken breasts and set aside. 6. Pour the water into the Instant Pot and scrape the bottom to remove any chicken or seasoning that is stuck on. Add the trivet to the Instant Pot and place the chicken on the trivet. 7. Secure the lid. Select the Manual mode and set the cooking time for 15 minutes at High Pressure. 8. Once cooking is complete, do a natural pressure release for 15 minutes, then release any remaining pressure. Carefully open the lid. Serve warm.
Per Serving:
calories: 303 | fat: 12.1g | protein: 40.9g | carbs: 1.3g | net carbs: 0.6g | fiber: 0.7g

Chicken Casserole

Prep time: 15 minutes | Cook time: 15 minutes | Serves 4

1 cup broccoli florets
1½ cups Alfredo sauce
½ cup chopped fresh spinach
¼ cup whole-milk ricotta cheese
½ teaspoon salt

¼ teaspoon pepper
1 pound (454 g) thin-sliced deli chicken
1 cup shredded whole-milk Mozzarella cheese
1 cup water

1. Put the broccoli florets in a large bowl. Add the Alfredo sauce, spinach, ricotta, salt, and pepper to the bowl and stir to mix well. Using a spoon, separate the veggie mix into three sections. 2. Layer the chicken into the bottom of a 7-cup glass bowl. Place one section of the veggie mix on top in an even layer and top with a layer of shredded Mozzarella cheese. Repeat until all veggie mix has been used and finish with a layer of Mozzarella cheese. Cover the dish with aluminum foil. 3. Pour the water into the Instant Pot and insert the trivet. Place the dish on the trivet. 4. Secure the lid. Select the Manual mode and set the cooking time for 15 minutes at High Pressure. 5. Once cooking is complete, do a quick pressure release. Carefully open the lid. 6. If desired, broil in oven for 3 to 5 minutes until golden. Serve warm.
Per Serving:
calories: 284 | fat: 13g | protein: 29g | carbs: 10g | net carbs: 9g | fiber: 1g

Cajun Chicken

Prep time: 15 minutes | Cook time: 25 minutes | Serves 4

1 teaspoon Cajun seasoning
¼ cup apple cider vinegar
1 pound (454 g) chicken fillet

1 tablespoon sesame oil
¼ cup water

1. Put all ingredients in the instant pot. Close and seal the lid. 2. Cook the chicken fillets on Manual mode (High Pressure) for 25 minutes. 3. Allow the natural pressure release for 10 minutes.
Per Serving:
calories: 249 | fat: 12g | protein: 33g | carbs: 0g | net carbs: 0g | fiber: 0g

Spicy Chicken with Bacon and Peppers

Prep time: 5 minutes | Cook time: 13 minutes | Serves 6

2 slices bacon, chopped
1½ pounds (680 g) ground chicken
2 garlic cloves, minced
½ cup green onions, chopped
1 green bell pepper, seeded and chopped
1 red bell pepper, seeded and chopped
1 serrano pepper, chopped
1 tomato, chopped
1 cup water
⅓ cup chicken broth
1 teaspoon paprika
1 teaspoon onion powder
¼ teaspoon ground allspice
2 bay leaves
Sea salt and ground black pepper, to taste

1. Press the Sauté button to heat your Instant Pot. 2. Add the bacon and cook for about 3 minutes until crisp. Reserve the bacon in a bowl. 3. Add the ground chicken to the bacon grease of the pot and brown for 2 to 3 minutes, crumbling it with a spatula. Reserve it in the bowl of bacon. 4. Add the garlic, green onions, and peppers and sauté for 3 minutes until tender. Add the remaining ingredients to the Instant Pot, along with the cooked bacon and chicken. Stir to mix well. 5. Lock the lid. Select the Poultry mode and set the cooking time for 5 minutes at High Pressure. 6. When the timer beeps, perform a natural pressure release for 10 minutes, then release any remaining pressure. Carefully remove the lid. Serve warm.
Per Serving:
calories: 236 | fat: 13.8g | protein: 24.9g | carbs: 3.0g | net carbs: 2.0g | fiber: 1.0g

Simple Chicken Masala

Prep time: 10 minutes | Cook time: 17 minutes | Serves 3

12 ounces (340 g) chicken fillet
1 tablespoon masala spices
1 tablespoon avocado oil
3 tablespoons organic almond milk

1. Heat up avocado oil in the instant pot on Sauté mode for 2 minutes. 2. Meanwhile, chop the chicken fillet roughly and mix it up with masala spices. 3. Add almond milk and transfer the chicken in the instant pot. 4. Cook the chicken bites on Sauté mode for 15 minutes. Stir the meal occasionally.
Per Serving:
calories: 211 | fat: 9g | protein: 25g | carbs: 6g | net carbs: 6g | fiber: 0g

Tangy Meatballs

Prep time: 10 minutes | Cook time: 10 minutes | Makes 20 meatballs

1 pound (454 g) ground chicken
1 egg, lightly beaten
½ medium onion, diced
1 teaspoon garlic powder
1 teaspoon pepper
1 teaspoon salt
1 cup water
Sauce:
2 teaspoons erythritol
1 teaspoon rice vinegar
½ teaspoon sriracha

1. Stir together the ground chicken, beaten egg, onion, garlic powder, salt, and pepper in a large bowl. Shape into bite-sized balls with your hands. 2. Pour the water into Instant Pot and insert a steamer basket. Put the meatballs in the basket. 3. Secure the lid. Select the Manual mode and set the cooking time for 10 minutes at High Pressure. 4. Meanwhile, whisk together all ingredients for the sauce in a separate bowl. 5. Once cooking is complete, do a quick pressure release. Carefully open the lid. 6. Toss the meatballs in the prepared sauce and serve.
Per Serving:
calories: 151 | fat: 7.7g | protein: 17.5g | carbs: 3.2g | net carbs: 2.7g | fiber: 0.5g

Tuscan Chicken Drumsticks

Prep time: 15 minutes | Cook time: 12 minutes | Serves 4

4 chicken drumsticks
1 cup chopped spinach
1 teaspoon minced garlic
1 teaspoon ground paprika
1 cup heavy cream
1 teaspoon cayenne pepper
1 ounce (28 g) sun-dried tomatoes, chopped

1. Put all ingredients in the instant pot. 2. Close and seal the lid. 3. Cook the meal on Manual mode (High Pressure) for 12 minutes. 4. Then allow the natural pressure release for 10 minutes. 5. Serve the chicken with hot sauce from the instant pot.
Per Serving:
calories: 188 | fat: 14g | protein: 14g | carbs: 2g | net carbs: 1g | fiber: 1g

Sesame Chicken with Broccoli

Prep time: 15 minutes | Cook time: 12 minutes | Serves 2

½ teaspoon five spices
½ teaspoon sesame seeds
½ cup chopped broccoli
6 ounces (170 g) chicken fillet,
sliced
½ cup chicken broth
1 teaspoon coconut aminos
1 tablespoon avocado oil

1. In the mixing bowl, mix up avocado oil, coconut aminos, and sesame seeds. 2. Add five spices. 3. After this, mix up sliced chicken fillet and coconut aminos mixture. 4. Put the chicken in the instant pot. Add chicken broth and broccoli. 5. Close and seal the lid. 6. Cook the meal on Manual mode (High Pressure) for 12 minutes. Make a quick pressure release.
Per Serving:
calories: 195 | fat: 8g | protein: 27g | carbs: 3g | net carbs: 2g | fiber: 1g

Kung Pao Chicken

Prep time: 5 minutes | Cook time: 17 minutes | Serves 5

2 tablespoons coconut oil
1 pound (454 g) boneless, skinless chicken breasts, cubed
1 cup cashews, chopped
6 tablespoons hot sauce
½ teaspoon chili powder
½ teaspoon finely grated ginger
½ teaspoon kosher salt
½ teaspoon freshly ground black pepper

1. Set the Instant Pot to Sauté and melt the coconut oil. 2. Add the remaining ingredients to the Instant Pot and mix well. 3. Secure the lid. Select the Manual mode and set the cooking time for 17 minutes

at High Pressure. 4. Once cooking is complete, do a quick pressure release. Carefully open the lid. 5. Serve warm.

Per Serving:
calories: 381 | fat: 25.0g | protein: 30.5g | carbs: 9.6g | net carbs: 8.6g | fiber: 1.0g

Orange Chicken Thighs with Bell Peppers

Prep time: 15 to 20 minutes | Cook time: 7 minutes | Serves 4 to 6

6 boneless skinless chicken thighs, cut into bite-sized pieces
2 packets crystallized True Orange flavoring
½ teaspoon True Orange Orange Ginger seasoning
½ teaspoon coconut aminos
¼ teaspoon Worcestershire sauce
Olive oil or cooking spray
2 cups bell pepper strips, any color combination (I used red)
1 onion, chopped
1 tablespoon green onion, chopped fine

3 cloves garlic, minced or chopped
½ teaspoon pink salt
½ teaspoon black pepper
1 teaspoon garlic powder
1 teaspoon ground ginger
¼–½ teaspoon red pepper flakes
2 tablespoons tomato paste
½ cup chicken bone broth or water
1 tablespoon brown sugar substitute (I use Sukrin Gold)
½ cup Seville orange spread (I use Crofter's brand)

1. Combine the chicken with the 2 packets of crystallized orange flavor, the orange ginger seasoning, the coconut aminos, and the Worcestershire sauce. Set aside. 2. Turn the Instant Pot to Sauté and add a touch of olive oil or cooking spray to the inner pot. Add in the orange ginger marinated chicken thighs. 3. Sauté until lightly browned. Add in the peppers, onion, green onion, garlic, and seasonings. Mix well. 4. Add the remaining ingredients; mix to combine. 5. Lock the lid, set the vent to sealing, set to 7 minutes. 6. Let the pressure release naturally for 2 minutes, then manually release the rest when cook time is up.

Per Serving:
calories: 120| fat: 2g | protein: 12g | carbs: 8g | sugars: 10g | fiber: 1.6g | sodium: 315mg

Chicken Casablanca

Prep time: 20 minutes | Cook time: 12 minutes | Serves 8

2 large onions, sliced
1 teaspoon ground ginger
3 garlic cloves, minced
2 tablespoons canola oil, divided
3 pounds skinless chicken pieces
3 large carrots, diced
2 large potatoes, unpeeled, diced
½ teaspoon ground cumin

½ teaspoon salt
½ teaspoon pepper
¼ teaspoon cinnamon
2 tablespoons raisins
14½-ounce can chopped tomatoes
3 small zucchini, sliced
15-ounce can garbanzo beans, drained
2 tablespoons chopped parsley

1. Using the Sauté function of the Instant Pot, cook the onions, ginger, and garlic in 1 tablespoon of the oil for 5 minutes, stirring constantly. Remove onions, ginger, and garlic from pot and set aside. 2. Brown the chicken pieces with the remaining oil, then add the cooked onions, ginger and garlic back in as well as all of the remaining ingredients, except the parsley. 3. Secure the lid and make sure vent is in the sealing position. Cook on Manual mode for 12 minutes. 4. When cook time is up, let the pressure release naturally for 5 minutes and then release the rest of the pressure manually.

Per Serving:
calories: 395 | fat: 10g | protein: 36g | carbs: 40g | sugars: 10g | fiber: 8g | sodium: 390mg

Creamy Nutmeg Chicken

Prep time: 20 minutes | Cook time: 10 minutes | Serves 6

1 tablespoon canola oil
6 boneless chicken breast halves, skin and visible fat removed
¼ cup chopped onion
¼ cup minced parsley
2 (10¾-ounce) cans 98% fat-free, reduced-sodium cream of

mushroom soup
½ cup fat-free sour cream
½ cup fat-free milk
1 tablespoon ground nutmeg
¼ teaspoon sage
¼ teaspoon dried thyme
¼ teaspoon crushed rosemary

1. Press the Sauté button on the Instant Pot and then add the canola oil. Place the chicken in the oil and brown chicken on both sides. Remove the chicken to a plate. 2. Sauté the onion and parsley in the remaining oil in the Instant Pot until the onions are tender. Press Cancel on the Instant Pot, then place the chicken back inside. 3. Mix together the remaining ingredients in a bowl then pour over the chicken. 4. Secure the lid and set the vent to sealing. Set on Manual mode for 10 minutes. 5. When cooking time is up, let the pressure release naturally.

Per Serving:
calories: 264 | fat: 8g | protein: 31g | carbs: 15g | sugars: 5g | fiber: 1g | sodium: 495mg

Chicken Escabèche

Prep time: 5 minutes | Cook time: 15 minutes | Serves 4

1 cup filtered water
1 pound (454 g) chicken, mixed pieces
3 garlic cloves, smashed
2 bay leaves
1 onion, chopped
½ cup red wine vinegar

½ teaspoon coriander
½ teaspoon ground cumin
½ teaspoon mint, finely chopped
½ teaspoon kosher salt
½ teaspoon freshly ground black pepper

1. Pour the water into the Instant Pot and insert the trivet. 2. Thoroughly combine the chicken, garlic, bay leaves, onion, vinegar, coriander, cumin, mint, salt, and black pepper in a large bowl. 3. Put the bowl on the trivet and cover loosely with aluminum foil. 4. Secure the lid. Select the Manual mode and set the cooking time for 15 minutes at High Pressure. 5. Once cooking is complete, do a natural pressure release for 10 minutes, then release any remaining pressure. Carefully open the lid. 6. Remove the dish from the Instant Pot and cool for 5 to 10 minutes before serving.

Per Serving:
calories: 196 | fat: 3.7g | protein: 33.5g | carbs: 4.0g | net carbs: 3.3g | fiber: 0.7g

Baked Cheesy Mushroom Chicken

Prep time: 5 minutes | Cook time: 15 minutes | Serves 4

1 tablespoon butter
2 cloves garlic, smashed
½ cup chopped yellow onion
1 pound (454 g) chicken breasts, cubed
10 ounces (283 g) button mushrooms, thinly sliced
1 cup chicken broth
½ teaspoon shallot powder
½ teaspoon turmeric powder
½ teaspoon dried basil
½ teaspoon dried sage
½ teaspoon cayenne pepper
⅓ teaspoon ground black pepper
Kosher salt, to taste
½ cup heavy cream
1 cup shredded Colby cheese

1. Set your Instant Pot to Sauté and melt the butter. 2. Add the garlic, onion, chicken, and mushrooms and sauté for about 4 minutes, or until the vegetables are softened. 3. Add the remaining ingredients except the heavy cream and cheese to the Instant Pot and stir to incorporate. 4. Lock the lid. Select the Meat/Stew mode and set the cooking time for 6 minutes at High Pressure. 5. When the timer beeps, perform a natural pressure release for 10 minutes, then release any remaining pressure. Carefully remove the lid. 6. Stir in the heavy cream until heated through. Pour the mixture into a baking dish and scatter the cheese on top. 7. Bake in the preheated oven at 400ºF (205ºC) until the cheese bubbles. 8. Allow to cool for 5 minutes and serve.

Per Serving:
calories: 439 | fat: 29g | protein: 34g | carbs: 10g | net carbs: 8g | fiber: 2g

Bacon-Wrapped Chicken Tenders

Prep time: 15 minutes | Cook time: 15 minutes | Serves 2

4 ounces (113 g) chicken fillet
2 bacon slices
½ teaspoon ground paprika
¼ teaspoon salt
1 teaspoon olive oil
1 cup water, for cooking

1. Cut the chicken fillet on 2 tenders and sprinkle them with salt, ground paprika, and olive oil. 2. Wrap the chicken tenders in the bacon and transfer in the steamer rack, 3. Pour water and insert the steamer rack with the chicken tenders in the instant pot. 4. Close and seal the lid and cook the meal on Manual mode (High Pressure) for 15 minutes. 5. When the time is finished, allow the natural pressure release for 10 minutes.

Per Serving:
calories: 232 | fat: 14g | protein: 23g | carbs: 1g | net carbs: 1g | fiber: 0g

Braised Chicken with Mushrooms and Tomatoes

Prep time: 20 minutes | Cook time: 25 minutes | Serves 4

1 tablespoon extra-virgin olive oil
1 pound (454 g) portobello mushroom caps, gills removed, caps halved and sliced ½ inch
thick
1 onion, chopped fine
¾ teaspoon salt, divided
4 garlic cloves, minced
1 tablespoon tomato paste
1 tablespoon all-purpose flour
2 teaspoons minced fresh sage
½ cup dry red wine
1 (14½-ounce / 411-g) can diced tomatoes, drained
4 (5- to 7-ounce / 142- to 198-
g) bone-in chicken thighs, skin removed, trimmed
¼ teaspoon pepper
2 tablespoons chopped fresh parsley
Shaved Parmesan cheese

1. Using highest sauté function, heat oil in Instant Pot until shimmering. Add mushrooms, onion, and ¼ teaspoon salt. Partially cover and cook until mushrooms are softened and have released their liquid, about 5 minutes. Stir in garlic, tomato paste, flour, and sage and cook until fragrant, about 1 minute. Stir in wine, scraping up any browned bits, then stir in tomatoes. 2. Sprinkle chicken with remaining ½ teaspoon salt and pepper. Nestle chicken skinned side up into pot and spoon some of sauce on top. Lock lid in place and close pressure release valve. Select high pressure cook function and cook for 15 minutes. 3. Turn off Instant Pot and quick-release pressure. Carefully remove lid, allowing steam to escape away from you. Transfer chicken to serving dish, tent with aluminum foil, and let rest while finishing sauce. 4. Using highest sauté function, bring sauce to simmer and cook until thickened slightly, about 5 minutes. Season sauce with salt and pepper to taste. Spoon sauce over chicken and sprinkle with parsley and Parmesan. Serve.

Per Serving:
calories: 230 | fat: 7g | protein: 21g | carbs: 15g | fiber:2g | sodium: 730mg

Chicken with Lentils and Butternut Squash

Prep time: 15 minutes | Cook time: 28 minutes | Serves 4

2 large shallots, halved and sliced thin, divided
5 teaspoons extra-virgin olive oil, divided
½ teaspoon grated lemon zest plus 2 teaspoons juice
1 teaspoon table salt, divided
4 (5- to 7-ounce / 142- to 198-g) bone-in chicken thighs, trimmed
¼ teaspoon pepper
2 garlic cloves, minced
1½ teaspoons caraway seeds
1 teaspoon ground coriander
1 teaspoon ground cumin
½ teaspoon paprika
⅛ teaspoon cayenne pepper
2 cups chicken broth
1 cup French green lentils, picked over and rinsed
2 pounds (907 g) butternut squash, peeled, seeded, and cut into 1½-inch pieces
1 cup fresh parsley or cilantro leaves

1. Combine half of shallots, 1 tablespoon oil, lemon zest and juice, and ¼ teaspoon salt in bowl; set aside. Pat chicken dry with paper towels and sprinkle with ½ teaspoon salt and pepper. Using highest sauté function, heat remaining 2 teaspoons oil in Instant Pot for 5 minutes (or until just smoking). Place chicken skin side down in pot and cook until well browned on first side, about 5 minutes; transfer to plate. 2. Add remaining shallot and remaining ¼ teaspoon salt to fat left in pot and cook, using highest sauté function, until shallot is softened, about 2 minutes. Stir in garlic, caraway, coriander, cumin, paprika, and cayenne and cook until fragrant, about 30 seconds. Stir in broth, scraping up any browned bits, then stir in lentils. 3. Nestle chicken skin side up into lentils and add any accumulated juices. Arrange squash on top. Lock lid in place and close pressure release valve. Select high pressure cook function and cook for 15 minutes. 4. Turn off Instant Pot and quick-release pressure. Carefully remove lid, allowing steam to escape away from you. Transfer chicken to

plate and discard skin, if desired. Season lentil mixture with salt and pepper to taste. Add parsley to shallot mixture and toss to combine. Serve chicken with lentil mixture, topping individual portions with shallot-parsley salad.

Per Serving:
calories: 513 | fat: 14g | protein: 42g | carbs: 60g | fiber: 17g | sodium: 773mg

Chicken and Kale Sandwiches

Prep time: 10 minutes | Cook time: 10 minutes | Serves 2

4 ounces (113 g) kale leaves
8 ounces (227 g) chicken fillet
1 tablespoon butter
1 ounce (28 g) lemon
¼ cup water

1. Dice the chicken fillet. 2. Squeeze the lemon juice over the poultry. 3. Transfer the poultry into the instant pot; add water and butter. 4. Close the lid and cook the chicken on the Poultry mode for 10 minutes. 5. When the chicken is cooked, place it on the kale leaves to make the medium sandwiches.

Per Serving:
calories: 298 | fat: 14g | protein: 35g | carbs: 7g | net carbs: 6g | fiber: 1g

Mexican Chicken with Red Salsa

Prep time: 10 minutes | Cook time: 20 minutes | Serves 8

2 pounds (907 g) boneless, skinless chicken thighs, cut into bite-size pieces
1½ tablespoons ground cumin
1½ tablespoons chili powder
1 tablespoon salt
2 tablespoons vegetable oil
1 (14½-ounce / 411-g) can
diced tomatoes, undrained
1 (5-ounce / 142-g) can sugar-free tomato paste
1 small onion, chopped
3 garlic cloves, minced
2 ounces (57 g) pickled jalapeños from a can, with juice
½ cup sour cream

1. Preheat the Instant Pot by selecting Sauté and adjusting to high heat. 2. In a medium bowl, coat the chicken with the cumin, chili powder, and salt. 3. Put the oil in the inner cooking pot. When it is shimmering, add the coated chicken pieces. (This step lets the spices bloom a bit to get their full flavor.) Cook the chicken for 4 to 5 minutes. 4. Add the tomatoes, tomato paste, onion, garlic, and jalapeños. 5. Lock the lid into place. Select Manual and adjust the pressure to High. Cook for 15 minutes. When the cooking is complete, let the pressure release naturally for 10 minutes, then quick-release any remaining pressure. Unlock and remove the lid. 6. Use two forks to shred the chicken. Serve topped with the sour cream. This dish is good with mashed cauliflower, steamed vegetables, or a salad.

Per Serving:
calories: 329 | fat: 24g | protein: 21g | carbs: 8g | net carbs: 6g | fiber: 2g

Ground Turkey Tetrazzini

Prep time: 5 minutes | Cook time: 20 minutes | Serves 6

1 tablespoon extra-virgin olive oil
2 garlic cloves, minced
1 yellow onion, diced

8 ounces cremini or button mushrooms, sliced
½ teaspoon fine sea salt
¼ teaspoon freshly ground black pepper
1 pound 93 percent lean ground turkey
1 teaspoon poultry seasoning
6 ounces whole-grain extra-broad egg-white pasta (such as No Yolks brand) or whole-wheat elbow pasta
2 cups low-sodium chicken
broth
1½ cups frozen green peas, thawed
3 cups baby spinach
Three ¾-ounce wedges Laughing Cow creamy light Swiss cheese, or 2 tablespoons Neufchâtel cheese, at room temperature
⅓ cup grated Parmesan cheese
1 tablespoon chopped fresh flat-leaf parsley

1. Select the Sauté setting on the Instant Pot and heat the oil and garlic for 2 minutes, until the garlic is bubbling but not browned. Add the onion, mushrooms, salt, and pepper and sauté for about 5 minutes, until the mushrooms have wilted and begun to give up their liquid. Add the turkey and poultry seasoning and sauté, using a wooden spoon or spatula to break up the meat as it cooks, for about 4 minutes more, until cooked through and no streaks of pink remain. 2. Stir in the pasta. Pour in the broth and use the spoon or spatula to nudge the pasta into the liquid as much as possible. It's fine if some pieces are not completely submerged. 3. Secure the lid and set the Pressure Release to Sealing. Press the Cancel button to reset the cooking program, then select the Pressure Cook or Manual setting and set the cooking time for 5 minutes at high pressure. (The pot will take about 5 minutes to come up to pressure before the cooking program begins.) 4. When the cooking program ends, let the pressure release naturally for 5 minutes, then move the Pressure Release to Venting to release any remaining steam. Open the pot and stir in the peas, spinach, Laughing Cow cheese, and Parmesan. Let stand for 2 minutes, then stir the mixture once more. 5. Ladle into bowls or onto plates and sprinkle with the parsley. Serve right away.

Per Serving:
calories: 321 | fat: 11g | protein: 26g | carbs: 35g | sugars: 4g | fiber: 5g | sodium: 488mg

Instant Pot Crack Chicken

Prep time: 15 minutes | Cook time: 20 minutes | Serves 4

1 cup chicken broth
1 teaspoon dried dill
1 teaspoon dried oregano
½ teaspoon onion powder
1 pound (454 g) skinless, boneless chicken breast
½ teaspoon salt
2 tablespoons mascarpone cheese
2 ounces (57 g) Cheddar cheese, shredded

1. Pour the chicken broth in the instant pot. 2. Add dried ill, oregano, onion powder, chicken breast, and salt. 3. Close and seal the lid. 4. Cook the chicken breast on Manual mode (High Pressure) for 15 minutes. 5. Then make a quick pressure release and transfer the cooked chicken in the bowl. 6. Blend the chicken broth mixture with the help of the immersion blender. 7. Add mascarpone cheese and Cheddar cheese. Sauté the liquid for 2 minutes on Sauté mode. 8. Meanwhile, shred the chicken. 9. Add it in the mascarpone mixture and mix it up. Sauté the meal for 3 minutes more.

Per Serving:
calories: 212 | fat: 9g | protein: 30g | carbs: 1g | net carbs: 1g | fiber: 0g

Chicken in Mushroom Gravy

Prep time: 10 minutes | Cook time: 10 minutes | Serves 6

6 (5 ounces each) boneless, skinless chicken-breast halves
Salt and pepper to taste
¼ cup dry white wine or low-sodium chicken broth

10¾-ounce can 98% fat-free, reduced-sodium cream of mushroom soup
4 ounces sliced mushrooms

1. Place chicken in the inner pot of the Instant Pot. Season with salt and pepper. 2. Combine wine and soup in a bowl, then pour over the chicken. Top with the mushrooms. 3. Secure the lid and make sure the vent is set to sealing. Set on Manual mode for 10 minutes. 4. When cooking time is up, let the pressure release naturally.
Per Serving:
calories: 204 | fat: 4g | protein: 34g | carbs: 6g | sugars: 1g | fiber: 1g | sodium: 320mg

Bruschetta and Cheese Stuffed Chicken

Prep time: 10 minutes | Cook time: 10 minutes | Serves 4

6 ounces (170 g) diced Roma tomatoes
2 tablespoons avocado oil
1 tablespoon thinly sliced fresh basil, plus more for garnish
1½ teaspoons balsamic vinegar
Pinch of salt
Pinch of black pepper

4 boneless, skinless chicken breasts (about 2 pounds / 907 g)
12 ounces (340 g) goat cheese, divided
2 teaspoons Italian seasoning, divided
1 cup water

1. Prepare the bruschetta by mixing the tomatoes, avocado oil, basil, vinegar, salt, and pepper in a small bowl. Let it marinate until the chicken is done. 2. Pat the chicken dry with a paper towel. Butterfly the breast open but do not cut all the way through. Stuff each breast with 3 ounces (85 g) of the goat cheese. Use toothpicks to close the edges. 3. Sprinkle ½ teaspoon of the Italian seasoning on top of each breast. 4. Pour the water into the pot. Place the trivet inside. Lay a piece of aluminum foil on top of the trivet and place the chicken breasts on top. It is okay if they overlap. 5. Close the lid and seal the vent. Cook on High Pressure for 10 minutes. Quick release the steam. 6. Remove the toothpicks and top each breast with one-fourth of the bruschetta.
Per Serving:
calories: 581 | fat: 34g | protein: 64g | carbs: 5g | net carbs: 4g | fiber: 1g

Chicken Thighs with Feta

Prep time: 7 minutes | Cook time: 15 minutes | Serves 2

4 lemon slices
2 chicken thighs
1 tablespoon Greek seasoning

4 ounces (113 g) feta, crumbled
1 teaspoon butter
½ cup water

1. Rub the chicken thighs with Greek seasoning. 2. Then spread the chicken with butter. 3. Pour water in the instant pot and place the trivet. 4. Place the chicken on the foil and top with the lemon slices. Top it with feta. 5. Wrap the chicken in the foil and transfer on the

trivet. 6. Cook on the Sauté mode for 10 minutes. Then make a quick pressure release for 5 minutes. 7. Discard the foil from the chicken thighs and serve!
Per Serving:
calories: 341 | fat: 24g | protein: 27g | carbs: 6g | net carbs: 6g | fiber: 0g

Crack Chicken Breasts

Prep time: 5 minutes | Cook time: 15 minutes | Serves 2

½ pound (227 g) boneless, skinless chicken breasts
2 ounces (57 g) cream cheese, softened
½ cup grass-fed bone broth
¼ cup tablespoons keto-

friendly ranch dressing
½ cup shredded full-fat Cheddar cheese
3 slices bacon, cooked and chopped into small pieces

1. Combine all the ingredients except the Cheddar cheese and bacon in the Instant Pot. 2. Secure the lid. Select the Manual mode and set the cooking time for 15 minutes at High Pressure. 3. Once cooking is complete, do a quick pressure release. Carefully open the lid. 4. Add the Cheddar cheese and bacon and stir well, then serve.
Per Serving:
calories: 549 | fat: 45.7g | protein: 32.4g | carbs: 2.4g | net carbs: 2.4g | fiber: 0g

Broccoli Chicken Divan

Prep time: 15 minutes | Cook time: 10 minutes | Serves 4

1 cup chopped broccoli
2 tablespoons cream cheese
½ cup heavy cream
1 tablespoon curry powder

¼ cup chicken broth
½ cup grated Cheddar cheese
6 ounces (170 g) chicken fillet, cooked and chopped

1. Mix up broccoli and curry powder and put the mixture in the instant pot. 2. Add heavy cream and cream cheese. 3. Then add chicken and mix up the ingredients. 4. Then add chicken broth and heavy cream. 5. Top the mixture with Cheddar cheese. Close and seal the lid. 6. Cook the meal on Manual mode (High Pressure) for 10 minutes. Allow the natural pressure release for 5 minutes, open the lid and cool the meal for 10 minutes.
Per Serving:
calories: 222 | fat: 15g | protein: 18g | carbs: 3g | net carbs: 2g | fiber: 1g

Sage Chicken Thighs

Prep time: 10 minutes | Cook time: 16 minutes | Serves 4

1 teaspoon dried sage
1 teaspoon ground turmeric
2 teaspoons avocado oil

4 skinless chicken thighs
1 cup water
1 teaspoon sesame oil

1. Rub the chicken thighs with dried sage, ground turmeric, sesame oil, and avocado oil. 2. Then pour water in the instant pot and insert the steamer rack. 3. Place the chicken thighs on the rack and close the lid. 4. Cook the meal on Manual (High Pressure) for 16 minutes. 5. Then make a quick pressure release and open the lid. 6. Let the

cooked chicken thighs cool for 10 minutes before serving.
Per Serving:
calories: 293 | fat: 12g | protein: 42g | carbs: 1g | net carbs: 1g | fiber: 0g

Chicken Meatballs with Green Cabbage

Prep time: 15 minutes | Cook time: 4 minutes | Serves 4

1 pound (454 g) ground chicken	black pepper, divided
¼ cup heavy (whipping) cream	¼ teaspoon ground allspice
2 teaspoons salt, divided	4 to 6 cups thickly chopped green cabbage
½ teaspoon ground caraway seeds	½ cup coconut milk
1½ teaspoons freshly ground	2 tablespoons unsalted butter

1. To make the meatballs, put the chicken in a bowl. Add the cream, 1 teaspoon of salt, the caraway, ½ teaspoon of pepper, and the allspice. Mix thoroughly. Refrigerate the mixture for 30 minutes. Once the mixture has cooled, it is easier to form the meatballs. 2. Using a small scoop, form the chicken mixture into small-to medium-size meatballs. Place half the meatballs in the inner cooking pot of your Instant Pot and cover them with half the cabbage. Place the remaining meatballs on top of the cabbage, then cover them with the rest of the cabbage. 3. Pour in the milk, place pats of the butter here and there, and sprinkle with the remaining 1 teaspoon of salt and 1 teaspoon of pepper. 4. Lock the lid into place. Select Manual and adjust the pressure to High. Cook for 4 minutes. When the cooking is complete, quick-release the pressure. Unlock the lid. Serve the meatballs on top of the cabbage.
Per Serving:
calories: 338 | fat: 23g | protein: 23g | carbs: 7g | net carbs: 4g | fiber: 3g

Poblano Chicken

Prep time: 10 minutes | Cook time: 29 minutes | Serves 4

2 Poblano peppers, sliced	½ cup coconut cream
16 ounces (454 g) chicken fillet	1 tablespoon butter
½ teaspoon salt	½ teaspoon chili powder

1. Heat up the butter on Sauté mode for 3 minutes. 2. Add Poblano and cook them for 3 minutes. 3. Meanwhile, cut the chicken fillet into the strips and sprinkle with salt and chili powder. 4. Add the chicken strips to the instant pot. 5. Then add coconut cream and close the lid. Cook the meal on Sauté mode for 20 minutes.
Per Serving:
calories: 320 | fat: 18g | protein: 34g | carbs: 4g | net carbs: 3g | fiber: 1g

Cheese Stuffed Chicken

Prep time: 15 minutes | Cook time: 20 minutes | Serves 4

12 ounces (340 g) chicken fillet	½ teaspoon dried cilantro
4 ounces (113 g) provolone cheese, sliced	½ teaspoon smoked paprika
1 tablespoon cream cheese	1 cup water, for cooking

1. Beat the chicken fillet well and rub it with dried cilantro and smoked paprika. 2. Then spread it with cream cheese and top with Provolone cheese. 3. Roll the chicken fillet into the roll and wrap in the foil. 4. Pour water and insert the rack in the instant pot. 5. Place the chicken roll on the rack. Close and seal the lid. 6. Cook it on Manual mode (High Pressure) for 20 minutes. 7. Make a quick pressure release and slice the chicken roll into the servings.
Per Serving:
calories: 271 | fat: 15g | protein: 32g | carbs: 1g | net carbs: 1g | fiber: 0g

Paprika Chicken Wings

Prep time: 10 minutes | Cook time: 13 minutes | Serves 4

1 pound (454 g) boneless chicken wings	1 teaspoon avocado oil
1 teaspoon ground paprika	¼ teaspoon minced garlic
	¾ cup beef broth

1. Pour the avocado oil in the instant pot. 2. Rub the chicken wings with ground paprika and minced garlic and put them in the instant pot. 3. Cook the chicken on Sauté mode for 4 minutes from each side. 4. Then add beef broth and close the lid. 5. Sauté the meal for 5 minutes more.
Per Serving:
calories: 226 | fat: 9g | protein: 34g | carbs: 1g | net carbs: 1g | fiber: 0g

Chicken Alfredo with Bacon

Prep time: 10 minutes | Cook time: 27 minutes | Serves 4

2 (6-ounce / 170-g) boneless, skinless chicken breasts, butterflied	2 tablespoons coconut oil
½ teaspoon garlic powder	1 cup water
¼ teaspoon dried parsley	1 stick butter
¼ teaspoon dried thyme	2 cloves garlic, finely minced
¼ teaspoon salt	¼ cup heavy cream
⅛ teaspoon pepper	½ cup grated Parmesan cheese
	¼ cup cooked crumbled bacon

1. Sprinkle the chicken breasts with the garlic powder, parsley, thyme, salt, and pepper. 2. Set your Instant Pot to Sauté and melt the coconut oil. 3. Add the chicken and sear for 3 to 5 minutes until golden brown on both sides. 4. Remove the chicken with tongs and set aside. 5. Pour the water into the Instant Pot and insert the trivet. Place the chicken on the trivet. 6. Secure the lid. Select the Manual mode and set the cooking time for 20 minutes at High Pressure. 7. Once cooking is complete, do a quick pressure release. Carefully open the lid. 8. Remove the chicken from the pot to a platter and set aside. 9. Pour the water out of the Instant Pot, reserving ½ cup; set aside. 10. Set your Instant Pot to Sauté again and melt the butter. 11. Add the garlic, heavy cream, cheese, and reserved water to the Instant Pot. Cook for 3 to 4 minutes until the sauce starts to thicken, stirring frequently. 12. Stir in the crumbled bacon and pour the mixture over the chicken. Serve immediately.
Per Serving:
calories: 526| fat: 42g | protein: 28g | carbs: 3g | net carbs: 3g | fiber: 0g

Pecorino Chicken

Prep time: 10 minutes | Cook time: 15 minutes | Serves 3

2 ounces (57 g) Pecorino cheese, grated
10 ounces (283 g) chicken breast, skinless, boneless

1 tablespoon butter
¾ cup heavy cream
½ teaspoon salt
½ teaspoon red hot pepper

1. Chop the chicken breast into the cubes. 2. Toss butter in the instant pot and preheat it on the Sauté mode. 3. Add the chicken cubes. 4. Sprinkle the poultry with the salt and red hot pepper. 5. Add cream and mix up together all the ingredients. 6. Close the lid of the instant pot and seal it. 7. Set Poultry mode and put a timer on 15 minutes. 8. When the time is over, let the chicken rest for 5 minutes more. 9. Transfer the meal on the plates and sprinkle with the grated cheese. The cheese shouldn't melt immediately.

Per Serving:
calories: 340 | fat: 25g | protein: 28g | carbs: 1g | net carbs: 1g | fiber: 0g

Chicken Fajitas with Bell Peppers

Prep time: 10 minutes | Cook time: 5 minutes | Serves 4

1½ pounds (680 g) boneless, skinless chicken breasts
¼ cup avocado oil
2 tablespoons water
1 tablespoon Mexican hot sauce
2 cloves garlic, minced
1 teaspoon lime juice
1 teaspoon ground cumin
1 teaspoon salt

1 teaspoon erythritol
¼ teaspoon chili powder
¼ teaspoon smoked paprika
5 ounces (142 g) sliced yellow bell pepper strips
5 ounces (142 g) sliced red bell pepper strips
5 ounces (142 g) sliced green bell pepper strips

1. Slice the chicken into very thin strips lengthwise. Cut each strip in half again. Imagine the thickness of restaurant fajitas when cutting. 2. In a measuring cup, whisk together the avocado oil, water, hot sauce, garlic, lime juice, cumin, salt, erythritol, chili powder, and paprika to form a marinade. Add to the pot, along with the chicken and peppers. 3. Close the lid and seal the vent. Cook on High Pressure for 5 minutes. Quick release the steam.

Per Serving:
calories: 319 | fat: 18g | protein: 34g | carbs: 6g | net carbs: 4g | fiber: 2g

Cider Chicken with Pecans

Prep time: 10 minutes | Cook time: 15 minutes | Serves 2

6 ounces (170 g) chicken fillet, cubed
2 pecans, chopped
1 teaspoon coconut aminos

½ bell pepper, chopped
1 tablespoon coconut oil
¼ cup apple cider vinegar
¼ cup chicken broth

1. Melt coconut oil on Sauté mode and add chicken cubes. 2. Add bell pepper, and pecans. 3. Sauté the ingredients for 10 minutes and add apple cider vinegar, chicken broth, and coconut aminos. 4. Sauté the chicken for 5 minutes more.

Per Serving:
calories: 341 | fat: 23g | protein: 27g | carbs: 5g | net carbs: 3g | fiber: 2g

Chicken Carnitas

Prep time: 5 minutes | Cook time: 15 minutes | Serves 8

3 pounds (1.4 kg) whole chicken, cut into pieces
⅓ cup vegetable broth
3 cloves garlic, pressed
1 tablespoon avocado oil
1 guajillo chili, minced
Sea salt, to taste

½ teaspoon paprika
⅓ teaspoon cayenne pepper
½ teaspoon ground bay leaf
⅓ teaspoon black pepper
2 tablespoons chopped fresh coriander, for garnish
1 cup crème fraiche, for serving

1. Combine all the ingredients except the coriander and crème fraiche in the Instant Pot. 2. Lock the lid. Select the Poultry mode and set the cooking time for 15 minutes at High Pressure. 3. When the timer beeps, perform a quick pressure release. Carefully remove the lid. 4. Shred the chicken with two forks and discard the bones. Garnish with the coriander and serve with a dollop of crème fraiche.

Per Serving:
calories: 298 | fat: 15.9g | protein: 35.6g | carbs: 2.4g | net carbs: 2.1g | fiber: 0.3g

Chicken with Spiced Sesame Sauce

Prep time: 20 minutes | Cook time: 8 minutes | Serves 5

2 tablespoons tahini (sesame sauce)
¼ cup water
1 tablespoon low-sodium soy sauce
¼ cup chopped onion

1 teaspoon red wine vinegar
2 teaspoons minced garlic
1 teaspoon shredded ginger root (Microplane works best)
2 pounds chicken breast, chopped into 8 portions

1. Place first seven ingredients in bottom of the inner pot of the Instant Pot. 2. Add coarsely chopped chicken on top. 3. Secure the lid and make sure vent is at sealing. Set for 8 minutes using Manual setting. When cook time is up, let the pressure release naturally for 10 minutes, then perform a quick release. 4. Remove ingredients and shred chicken with fork. Combine with other ingredients in pot for a tasty sandwich filling or sauce.

Per Serving:
calorie: 215 | fat: 7g | protein: 35g | carbs: 2g | sugars: 0g | fiber: 0g | sodium: 178mg

Chicken Enchilada Bowl

Prep time: 10 minutes | Cook time: 35 minutes | Serves 4

2 (6-ounce / 170-g) boneless, skinless chicken breasts
2 teaspoons chili powder
½ teaspoon garlic powder
½ teaspoon salt
¼ teaspoon pepper
2 tablespoons coconut oil
¾ cup red enchilada sauce

¼ cup chicken broth
1 (4-ounce / 113-g) can green chilies
¼ cup diced onion
2 cups cooked cauliflower rice
1 avocado, diced
½ cup sour cream
1 cup shredded Cheddar cheese

1. Sprinkle the chili powder, garlic powder, salt, and pepper on chicken breasts. 2. Set your Instant Pot to Sauté and melt the coconut oil. Add the chicken breasts and sear each side for about 5 minutes until golden brown. 3. Pour the enchilada sauce and broth over the chicken. Using a wooden spoon or rubber spatula, scrape the bottom of pot to make sure nothing is sticking. Stir in the chilies and onion. 4. Secure the lid. Select the Manual mode and set the cooking time for 25 minutes at High Pressure. 5. Once cooking is complete, do a quick pressure release. Carefully open the lid. 6. Remove the chicken and shred with two forks. Serve the chicken over the cauliflower rice and place the avocado, sour cream, and Cheddar cheese on top.

Per Serving:
calories: 434 | fat: 26.1g | protein: 29.3g | carbs: 11.8g | net carbs: 7.0g | fiber: 4.8g

Chicken with Tomatoes and Spinach

Prep time: 5 minutes | Cook time: 18 minutes | Serves 4

4 boneless, skinless chicken breasts (about 2 pounds / 907 g)
2½ ounces (71 g) sun-dried tomatoes, coarsely chopped (about 2 tablespoons)
¼ cup chicken broth
2 tablespoons creamy, no-sugar-added balsamic vinegar dressing
1 tablespoon whole-grain mustard
2 cloves garlic, minced
1 teaspoon salt
8 ounces (227 g) fresh spinach
¼ cup sour cream
1 ounce (28 g) cream cheese, softened

1. Place the chicken breasts in the Instant Pot. Add the tomatoes, broth, and dressing. 2. Close the lid and seal the vent. Cook on High Pressure for 10 minutes. Quick release the steam. Press Cancel. 3. Remove the chicken from the pot and place on a plate. Cover with aluminum foil to keep warm while you make the sauce. 4. Turn the pot to Sauté mode. Whisk in the mustard, garlic, and salt and then add the spinach. Stir the spinach continuously until it is completely cooked down, 2 to 3 minutes. The spinach will absorb the sauce but will release it again as it continues to cook down. 5. Once the spinach is completely wilted, add the sour cream and cream cheese. Whisk until completed incorporated. 6. Let the sauce simmer to thicken and reduce by about one-third, about 5 minutes. Stir occasionally to prevent burning. Press Cancel. 7. Pour the sauce over the chicken. Serve.

Per Serving:
calories: 357 | fat: 13g | protein: 52g | carbs: 7g | net carbs: 5g | fiber: 2g

Thai Yellow Curry with Chicken Meatballs

Prep time: 5 minutes | Cook time: 30 minutes | Serves 4

1 pound 95 percent lean ground chicken
⅓ cup gluten-free panko (Japanese bread crumbs)
1 egg white
1 tablespoon coconut oil
1 yellow onion, cut into 1-inch pieces
One 14-ounce can light coconut milk
3 tablespoons yellow curry paste
¾ cup water
8 ounces carrots, halved lengthwise, then cut crosswise
into 1-inch lengths (or quartered if very large)
8 ounces zucchini, quartered lengthwise, then cut crosswise into 1-inch lengths (or cut into halves, then thirds if large)
8 ounces cremini mushrooms, quartered
Fresh Thai basil leaves for serving (optional)
Fresno or jalapeño chile, thinly sliced, for serving (optional)
1 lime, cut into wedges
Cooked cauliflower "rice" for serving

1. In a medium bowl, combine the chicken, panko, and egg white and mix until evenly combined. Set aside. 2. Select the Sauté setting on the Instant Pot and heat the oil for 2 minutes. Add the onion and sauté for 5 minutes, until it begins to soften and brown. Add ½ cup of the coconut milk and the curry paste and sauté for 1 minute more, until bubbling and fragrant. Press the Cancel button to turn off the pot, then stir in the water. 3. Using a 1½-tablespoon cookie scoop, shape and drop meatballs into the pot in a single layer. 4. Secure the lid and set the Pressure Release to Sealing. Select the Pressure Cook or Manual setting and set the cooking time for 5 minutes at high pressure. (The pot will take about 5 minutes to come up to pressure before the cooking program begins.) 5. When the cooking program ends, perform a quick pressure release by moving the Pressure Release to Venting, or let the pressure release naturally. Open the pot and stir in the carrots, zucchini, mushrooms, and remaining 1¼ cups coconut milk. 6. Press the Cancel button to reset the cooking program, then select the Sauté setting. Bring the curry to a simmer (this will take about 2 minutes), then let cook, uncovered, for about 8 minutes, until the carrots are fork-tender. Press the Cancel button to turn off the pot. 7. Ladle the curry into bowls. Serve piping hot, topped with basil leaves and chile slices, if desired, and the lime wedges and cauliflower "rice" on the side.

Per Serving:
calories: 349 | fat: 15g | protein: 30g | carbs: 34g | sugars: 8g | fiber: 5g | sodium: 529mg

Chapter 6   Stews and Soups

Easy Southern Brunswick Stew

2 pounds pork butt, visible fat removed

17-ounce can white corn

1¼ cups ketchup

2 cups diced, cooked potatoes

10-ounce package frozen peas

2 10¾-ounce cans reduced-sodium tomato soup

Hot sauce to taste, optional

1. Place pork in the Instant Pot and secure the lid. 2. Press the Slow Cook setting and cook on low 6–8 hours. 3. When cook time is over, remove the meat from the bone and shred, removing and discarding all visible fat. 4. Combine all the meat and remaining ingredients (except the hot sauce) in the inner pot of the Instant Pot. 5. Secure the lid once more and cook in Slow Cook mode on low for 30 minutes more. Add hot sauce if you wish.

Per Serving:
calories: 213 | fat: 7g | protein: 13g | carbs: 27g | sugars: 9g | fiber: 3g | sodium: 584mg

Green Chile Corn Chowder

Prep time: 20 minutes | Cook time: 7 to 8 hours | Serves 8

16-ounce can cream-style corn

3 potatoes, peeled and diced

2 tablespoons chopped fresh chives

4-ounce can diced green chilies, drained

2-ounce jar chopped pimentos, drained

½ cup chopped cooked ham

2 10½-ounce cans 100% fat-free lower-sodium chicken broth

Pepper to taste

Tabasco sauce to taste

1 cup fat-free milk

1. Combine all ingredients, except milk, in the inner pot of the Instant Pot. 2. Secure the lid and cook using the Slow Cook function on low 7–8 hours or until potatoes are tender. 3. When cook time is up, remove the lid and stir in the milk. Cover and let simmer another 20 minutes.

Per Serving:
calories: 124 | fat: 2g | protein: 6g | carbs: 21g | sugars: 7g | fiber: 2g | sodium: 563mg

Southwestern Bean Soup with Corn Dumplings

Prep time: 50 minutes | Cook time: 4 to 12 hours | Serves 8

15½-ounce can red kidney beans, rinsed and drained

15½-ounce can black beans, pinto beans, or great northern beans, rinsed and drained

3 cups water

14½-ounce can Mexican-style stewed tomatoes

10-ounce package frozen whole-kernel corn, thawed

1 cup sliced carrots

1 cup chopped onions

4-ounce can chopped green chilies

3 teaspoons sodium-free instant bouillon powder (any flavor)

1–2 teaspoons chili powder

2 cloves garlic, minced

Sauce:

⅓ cup flour

¼ cup yellow cornmeal

1 teaspoon baking powder

Dash of pepper

1 egg white, beaten

2 tablespoons milk

1 tablespoon oil

1. Combine the 11 soup ingredients in inner pot of the Instant Pot. 2. Secure the lid and cook on the Low Slow Cook setting for 10–12 hours or high for 4–5 hours. 3. Make dumplings by mixing together flour, cornmeal, baking powder, and pepper. 4. Combine egg white, milk, and oil. Add to flour mixture. Stir with fork until just combined. 5. At the end of the soup's cooking time, turn the Instant Pot to Slow Cook function high if you don't already have it there. Remove the lid and drop dumpling mixture by rounded teaspoonfuls to make 8 mounds atop the soup. 6. Secure the lid once more and cook for an additional 30 minutes.

Per Serving:
calories: 197 | fat: 1g | protein: 9g | carbs: 39g | sugars: 6g | fiber: 8g | sodium: 367mg

Chicken Vegetable Soup

Prep time: 12 to 25 minutes | Cook time: 4 minutes | Serves 6

1–2 raw chicken breasts, cubed

½ medium onion, chopped

4 cloves garlic, minced

½ sweet potato, small cubes

1 large carrot, peeled and cubed

4 stalks celery, chopped, leaves included

½ cup frozen corn

¼ cup frozen peas

¼ cup frozen lima beans

1 cup frozen green beans (bite-sized)

¼–½ cup chopped savoy cabbage

14½-ounce can low-sodium petite diced tomatoes

3 cups low-sodium chicken bone broth

½ teaspoon black pepper

1 teaspoon garlic powder

¼ cup chopped fresh parsley

¼–½ teaspoon red pepper flakes

1. Add all of the ingredients, in the order listed, to the inner pot of the Instant Pot. 2. Lock the lid in place, set the vent to sealing, press Manual, and cook at high pressure for 4 minutes. 3. Release the pressure manually as soon as cooking time is finished.

Per Serving:
calories: 176 | fat: 3g | protein: 21g | carbs: 18g | sugars: 7g | fiber: 4g | sodium: 169mg

Cabbage and Pork Soup

Prep time: 10 minutes | Cook time: 12 minutes | Serves 3

1 teaspoon butter

½ cup shredded white cabbage

½ teaspoon ground coriander

½ teaspoon salt

½ teaspoon chili flakes

2 cups chicken broth

½ cup ground pork

1. Melt the butter in the Instant Pot on Sauté mode. 2. Add cabbage and sprinkle with ground coriander, salt, and chili flakes. 3. Fold in the chicken broth and ground pork. 4. Close the lid and select Manual mode. Set cooking time for 12 minutes on High Pressure. 5. When timer beeps, use a quick pressure release. Open the lid. 6. Ladle the soup and serve warm.

Per Serving:
calories: 350 | fat: 23.9g | protein: 30.2g | carbs: 1.3g | net carbs: 1.0g | fiber: 0.3g

Creamy Carrot Soup with Warm Spices

Prep time: 15 minutes | Cook time: 10 minutes | Serves 6 to 8

2 tablespoons extra-virgin olive oil
2 onions, chopped
1 teaspoon table salt
1 tablespoon grated fresh ginger
1 tablespoon ground coriander
1 tablespoon ground fennel
1 teaspoon ground cinnamon
4 cups vegetable or chicken broth
2 cups water

2 pounds (907 g) carrots, peeled and cut into 2-inch pieces
½ teaspoon baking soda
2 tablespoons pomegranate molasses
½ cup plain Greek yogurt
½ cup hazelnuts, toasted, skinned, and chopped
½ cup chopped fresh cilantro or mint

1. Using highest sauté function, heat oil in Instant Pot until shimmering. Add onions and salt and cook until onions are softened, about 5 minutes. Stir in ginger, coriander, fennel, and cinnamon and cook until fragrant, about 30 seconds. Stir in broth, water, carrots, and baking soda. 2. Lock lid in place and close pressure release valve. Select high pressure cook function and cook for 3 minutes. Turn off Instant Pot and quick-release pressure. Carefully remove lid, allowing steam to escape away from you. 3. Working in batches, process soup in blender until smooth, 1 to 2 minutes. Return processed soup to Instant Pot and bring to simmer using highest sauté function. Season with salt and pepper to taste. Drizzle individual portions with pomegranate molasses and top with yogurt, hazelnuts, and cilantro before serving.

Per Serving:
calories: 190 | fat: 11g | protein: 4g | carbs: 20g | fiber: 5g | sodium: 820mg

Buttercup Squash Soup

Prep time: 15 minutes | Cook time: 10 minutes | Serves 6

2 tablespoons extra-virgin olive oil
1 medium onion, chopped
4 to 5 cups Vegetable Broth or Chicken Bone Broth
1½ pounds buttercup squash,

peeled, seeded, and cut into 1-inch chunks
½ teaspoon kosher salt
¼ teaspoon ground white pepper
Whole nutmeg, for grating

. Set the electric pressure cooker to the Sauté setting. When the pot is hot, pour in the olive oil. 2. Add the onion and sauté for 3 to 5 minutes, until it begins to soften. Hit Cancel. 3. Add the broth, squash, salt, and pepper to the pot and stir. (If you want a thicker soup, use 4 cups of broth. If you want a thinner, drinkable soup, use 5 cups.) 4. Close and lock the lid of the pressure cooker. Set the valve to sealing. 5. Cook on high pressure for 10 minutes. 6. When the cooking is complete, hit Cancel and allow the pressure to release naturally. 7. Once the pin drops, unlock and remove the lid. 8. Use an immersion blender to purée the soup right in the pot. If you don't have an immersion blender, transfer the soup to a blender or food processor and purée. (Follow the instructions that came with your machine for blending hot foods.) 9. Pour the soup into serving bowls and grate nutmeg on top.

Per Serving:
calories: 320 | fat: 15.86g | protein: 36.2g | carbs: 7g | sugars: 3.37g |

fiber: 1.6g | sodium: 856mg

Chicken and Mushroom Soup

Prep time: 5 minutes | Cook time: 15 minutes | Serves 4

1 onion, cut into thin slices
3 garlic cloves, minced
2 cups chopped mushrooms
1 yellow summer squash, chopped
1 pound (454 g) boneless, skinless chicken breast, cut into large chunks

2½ cups chicken broth
1 teaspoon salt
1 teaspoon freshly ground black pepper
1 teaspoon Italian seasoning or poultry seasoning
1 cup heavy (whipping) cream

1. Put the onion, garlic, mushrooms, squash, chicken, chicken broth, salt, pepper, and Italian seasoning in the inner cooking pot of the Instant Pot. 2. Lock the lid into place. Select Manual and adjust the pressure to High. Cook for 15 minutes. When the cooking is complete, let the pressure release naturally for 10 minutes, then quick-release any remaining pressure. Unlock the lid. 3. Using tongs, transfer the chicken pieces to a bowl and set aside. 4. Tilt the pot slightly. Using an immersion blender, roughly purée the vegetables, leaving a few intact for texture and visual appeal. 5. Shred the chicken and stir it back in to the soup. 6. Add the cream and stir well. Serve.

Per Serving:
calories: 427 | fat: 28g | protein: 31g | carbs: 13g | net carbs: 11g | fiber: 2g

Chicken and Kale Soup

Prep time: 5 minutes | Cook time: 5 minutes | Serves 4

2 cups chopped cooked chicken breast
12 ounces (340 g) frozen kale
1 onion, chopped
2 cups water
1 tablespoon powdered chicken broth base

½ teaspoon ground cinnamon
Pinch ground cloves
2 teaspoons minced garlic
1 teaspoon freshly ground black pepper
1 teaspoon salt
2 cups full-fat coconut milk

1. Put the chicken, kale, onion, water, chicken broth base, cinnamon, cloves, garlic, pepper, and salt in the inner cooking pot of the Instant Pot. 2. Lock the lid into place. Select Manual and adjust the pressure to High. Cook for 5 minutes. When the cooking is complete, let the pressure release naturally for 10 minutes, then quick-release any remaining pressure. Unlock the lid. 3. Stir in the coconut milk. Taste and adjust any seasonings as needed before serving.

Per Serving:
calories: 387 | fat: 27g | protein: 26g | carbs: 10g | net carbs: 8g | fiber: 2g

Cabbage Roll Soup

Prep time: 10 minutes | Cook time: 8 minutes | Serves 4

½ pound (227 g) 84% lean ground pork
½ pound (227 g) 85% lean ground beef
½ medium onion, diced
½ medium head cabbage,

thinly sliced
2 tablespoons sugar-free tomato paste
½ cup diced tomatoes
2 cups chicken broth
1 teaspoon salt

½ teaspoon thyme   ¼ teaspoon pepper
½ teaspoon garlic powder

1. Press the Sauté button and add beef and pork to Instant Pot. Brown meat until no pink remains. Add onion and continue cooking until onions are fragrant and soft. Press the Cancel button. 2. Add remaining ingredients to Instant Pot. Press the Manual button and adjust time for 8 minutes. 3. When timer beeps, allow a 15-minute natural release and then quick-release the remaining pressure. Serve warm.

Per Serving:
calories: 304 | fat: 16g | protein: 24g | carbs: 12g | net carbs: 8g | fiber: 4g

Ham and Potato Chowder

Prep time: 25 minutes | Cook time: 8 hour s | Serves 5

5-ounce package scalloped potatoes	bouillon powder
Sauce mix from potato package	4 cups water
1 cup extra-lean, reduced-sodium, cooked ham, cut into narrow strips	1 cup chopped celery
	⅓ cup chopped onions
	Pepper to taste
4 teaspoons sodium-free	2 cups fat-free half-and-half
	⅓ cup flour

1. Combine potatoes, sauce mix, ham, bouillon powder, water, celery, onions, and pepper in the inner pot of the Instant Pot. 2. Secure the lid and cook using the Slow Cook function on low for 7 hours. 3. Combine half-and-half and flour. Remove the lid and gradually add to the inner pot, blending well. 4. Secure the lid once more and cook on the low Slow Cook function for up to 1 hour more, stirring occasionally until thickened.

Per Serving:
calories: 241 | fat: 3g | protein: 11g | carbs: 41g | sugars: 8g | fiber: 3g | sodium: 836mg

Beef Stew with Eggplant and Potatoes

Prep time: 15 minutes | Cook time: 50 minutes | Serves 6 to 8

2 pounds (907 g) boneless short ribs, trimmed and cut into 1-inch pieces	1 teaspoon ground cardamom
	¾ teaspoon ground cinnamon
1½ teaspoons table salt, divided	4 cups chicken broth
2 tablespoons extra-virgin olive oil	1 cup water
	1 pound (454 g) eggplant, cut into 1-inch pieces
1 onion, chopped fine	1 pound (454 g) Yukon Gold potatoes, unpeeled, cut into 1-inch pieces
3 tablespoons tomato paste	
¼ cup all-purpose flour	
3 garlic cloves, minced	½ cup chopped fresh mint or parsley
1 tablespoon ground cumin	
1 teaspoon ground turmeric	

1. Pat beef dry with paper towels and sprinkle with 1 teaspoon salt. Using highest sauté function, heat oil in Instant Pot for 5 minutes (or until just smoking). Brown half of beef on all sides, 7 to 9 minutes; transfer to bowl. Set aside remaining uncooked beef. 2. Add onion to fat left in pot and cook, using highest sauté function, until softened, about 5 minutes. Stir in tomato paste, flour, garlic, cumin, turmeric, cardamom, cinnamon, and remaining ½ teaspoon salt. Cook until fragrant, about 1 minute. Slowly whisk in broth and water, scraping up any browned bits. Stir in eggplant and potatoes. Nestle remaining uncooked beef into pot along with browned beef, and add any accumulated juices. 3. Lock lid in place and close pressure release valve. Select high pressure cook function and cook for 30 minutes. Turn off Instant Pot and quick-release pressure. Carefully remove lid, allowing steam to escape away from you. 4. Using wide, shallow spoon, skim excess fat from surface of stew. Stir in mint and season with salt and pepper to taste. Serve.

Per Serving:
calories: 330 | fat: 15g | protein: 26g | carbs: 22g | fiber: 4g | sodium: 790mg

Broccoli and Red Feta Soup

Prep time: 10 minutes | Cook time: 25 minutes | Serves 4

1 cup broccoli, chopped	4 cups beef broth
½ cup coconut cream	1 teaspoon chili flakes
1 teaspoon unsweetened tomato purée	6 ounces (170 g) feta, crumbled

1. Put broccoli, coconut cream, tomato purée, and beef broth in the Instant Pot. Sprinkle with chili flakes and stir to mix well. 2. Close the lid and select Manual mode. Set cooking time for 8 minutes on High Pressure. 3. When timer beeps, make a quick pressure release and open the lid. 4. Add the feta cheese and stir the soup on Sauté mode for 5 minutes or until the cheese melt. 5. Serve immediately.

Per Serving:
calories: 229 | fat: 17.7g | protein: 12.3g | carbs: 6.1g | net carbs: 4.8g | fiber: 1.3g

Chicken Poblano Pepper Soup

Prep time: 10 minutes | Cook time: 20 minutes | Serves 8

1 cup diced onion	1 teaspoon ground coriander
3 poblano peppers, chopped	1 teaspoon ground cumin
5 garlic cloves	1 to 2 teaspoons salt
2 cups diced cauliflower	2 cups water
1½ pounds (680 g) chicken breast, cut into large chunks	2 ounces (57 g) cream cheese, cut into small chunks
¼ cup chopped fresh cilantro	1 cup sour cream

1. To the inner cooking pot of the Instant Pot, add the onion, poblanos, garlic, cauliflower, chicken, cilantro, coriander, cumin, salt, and water. 2. Lock the lid into place. Select Manual and adjust the pressure to High. Cook for 15 minutes. When the cooking is complete, let the pressure release naturally for 10 minutes, then quick-release any remaining pressure. Unlock the lid. 3. Remove the chicken with tongs and place in a bowl. 4. Tilting the pot, use an immersion blender to roughly purée the vegetable mixture. It should still be slightly chunky. 5. Turn the Instant Pot to Sauté and adjust to high heat. When the broth is hot and bubbling, add the cream cheese and stir until it melts. Use a whisk to blend in the cream cheese if needed. 6. Shred the chicken and stir it back into the pot. Once it is heated through, serve, topped with sour cream, and enjoy.

Per Serving:
calories: 202 | fat: 10g | protein: 20g | carbs: 8g | net carbs: 5g | fiber: 3g

Gigante Bean Soup with Celery and Olives

Prep time: 30 minutes | Cook time: 12 minutes | Serves 6 to 8

1½ tablespoons table salt, for brining
1 pound (454 g) dried gigante beans, picked over and rinsed
2 tablespoons extra-virgin olive oil, plus extra for drizzling
5 celery ribs, cut into ½-inch pieces, plus ½ cup leaves, minced
1 onion, chopped
½ teaspoon table salt

4 garlic cloves, minced
4 cups vegetable or chicken broth
4 cups water
2 bay leaves
½ cup pitted kalamata olives, chopped
2 tablespoons minced fresh marjoram or oregano
Lemon wedges

1. Dissolve 1½ tablespoons salt in 2 quarts cold water in large container. Add beans and soak at room temperature for at least 8 hours or up to 24 hours. Drain and rinse well. 2. Using highest sauté function, heat oil in Instant Pot until shimmering. Add celery pieces, onion, and ½ teaspoon salt and cook until vegetables are softened, about 5 minutes. Stir in garlic and cook until fragrant, about 30 seconds. Stir in broth, water, beans, and bay leaves. 3. Lock lid in place and close pressure release valve. Select high pressure cook function and cook for 6 minutes. Turn off Instant Pot and let pressure release naturally for 15 minutes. Quick-release any remaining pressure, then carefully remove lid, allowing steam to escape away from you. 4. Combine celery leaves, olives, and marjoram in bowl. Discard bay leaves. Season soup with salt and pepper to taste. Top individual portions with celery-olive mixture and drizzle with extra oil. Serve with lemon wedges.
Per Serving:
calories: 250 | fat: 5g | protein: 13g | carbs: 40g | fiber: 11g | sodium: 660mg

Chicken Zucchini Soup

Prep time: 8 minutes | Cook time: 14 minutes | Serves 6

¼ cup coconut oil or unsalted butter
1 cup chopped celery
¼ cup chopped onions
2 cloves garlic, minced
1 pound (454 g) boneless, skinless chicken breasts, cut into 1-inch cubes

6 cups chicken broth
1 tablespoon dried parsley
1 teaspoon fine sea salt
½ teaspoon dried marjoram
½ teaspoon ground black pepper
1 bay leaf
2 cups zucchini noodles

1. Place the coconut oil in the Instant Pot and press Sauté. Once melted, add the celery, onions, and garlic and cook, stirring occasionally, for 4 minutes, or until the onions are soft. Press Cancel to stop the Sauté. 2. Add the cubed chicken, broth, parsley, salt, marjoram, pepper, and bay leaf. Seal the lid, press Manual, and set the timer for 10 minutes. Once finished, let the pressure release naturally. 3. Remove the lid and stir well. Place the noodles in bowls, using ⅓ cup per bowl. Ladle the soup over the noodles and serve immediately; if it sits too long, the noodles will get too soft.
Per Serving:
calories: 253 | fat: 15g | protein: 21g | carbs: 11g | net carbs: 10g | fiber: 1g

Beef and Eggplant Tagine

Prep time: 15 minutes | Cook time: 25 minutes | Serves 6

1 pound (454 g) beef fillet, chopped
1 eggplant, chopped
6 ounces (170 g) scallions, chopped

4 cups beef broth
1 teaspoon ground allspices
1 teaspoon erythritol
1 teaspoon coconut oil

1. Put all ingredients in the Instant Pot. Stir to mix well. 2. Close the lid. Select Manual mode and set cooking time for 25 minutes on High Pressure. 3. When timer beeps, use a natural pressure release for 15 minutes, then release any remaining pressure. Open the lid. 4. Serve warm.
Per Serving:
calories: 158 | fat: 5.3g | protein: 21.1g | carbs: 8.2g | net carbs: 4.7g | fiber: 3.5g

Chicken Noodle Soup

Prep time: 15 minutes | Cook time: 20 minutes | Serves 12

2 tablespoons avocado oil
1 medium onion, chopped
3 celery stalks, chopped
1 teaspoon kosher salt
¼ teaspoon freshly ground black pepper
2 teaspoons minced garlic
5 large carrots, peeled and cut into ¼-inch-thick rounds

3 pounds bone-in chicken breasts (about 3)
4 cups Chicken Bone Broth or low-sodium store-bought chicken broth
4 cups water
2 tablespoons soy sauce
6 ounces whole grain wide egg noodles

1. Set the electric pressure cooker to the Sauté setting. When the pot is hot, pour in the avocado oil. 2. Sauté the onion, celery, salt, and pepper for 3 to 5 minutes or until the vegetables begin to soften. 3. Add the garlic and carrots, and stir to mix well. Hit Cancel. 4. Add the chicken to the pot, meat-side down. Add the broth, water, and soy sauce. Close and lock the lid of the pressure cooker. Set the valve to sealing. 5. Cook on high pressure for 20 minutes. 6. When the cooking is complete, hit Cancel and quick release the pressure. Unlock and remove the lid. 7. Using tongs, remove the chicken breasts to a cutting board. Hit Sauté/More and bring the soup to a boil. 8. Add the noodles and cook for 4 to 5 minutes or until the noodles are al dente. 9. While the noodles are cooking, use two forks to shred the chicken. Add the meat back to the pot and save the bones to make more bone broth. 10. Season with additional pepper, if desired, and serve.
Per Serving:
calories: 294 | fat: 13.92g | protein: 26.68g | carbs: 15.28g | sugars: 2.8g | fiber: 2.7g | sodium: 640mg

Summer Vegetable Soup

Prep time: 10 minutes | Cook time: 6 minutes | Serves 6

3 cups finely sliced leeks
6 cups chopped rainbow chard, stems and leaves separated
1 cup chopped celery

2 tablespoons minced garlic, divided
1 teaspoon dried oregano
1 teaspoon salt

2 teaspoons freshly ground black pepper
3 cups chicken broth, plus more as needed
2 cups sliced yellow summer squash, ½-inch slices
¼ cup chopped fresh parsley
¾ cup heavy (whipping) cream
4 to 6 tablespoons grated Parmesan cheese

1. Put the leeks, chard, celery, 1 tablespoon of garlic, oregano, salt, pepper, and broth into the inner cooking pot of the Instant Pot. 2. Lock the lid into place. Select Manual and adjust the pressure to High. Cook for 3 minutes. When the cooking is complete, quick-release the pressure. Unlock the lid. 3. Add more broth if needed. 4. Turn the pot to Sauté and adjust the heat to high. Add the yellow squash, parsley, and remaining 1 tablespoon of garlic. 5. Allow the soup to cook for 2 to 3 minutes, or until the squash is softened and cooked through. 6. Stir in the cream and ladle the soup into bowls. Sprinkle with the Parmesan cheese and serve.

Per Serving:
calories: 210 | fat: 14g | protein: 10g | carbs: 12g | net carbs: 8g | fiber: 4g

Favorite Chili

Prep time: 10 minutes | Cook time: 35 minutes | Serves 5

1 pound extra-lean ground beef
1 teaspoon salt
½ teaspoons black pepper
1 tablespoon olive oil
1 small onion, chopped
2 cloves garlic, minced
1 green pepper, chopped
2 tablespoons chili powder
½ teaspoons cumin
1 cup water
16-ounce can chili beans
15-ounce can low-sodium crushed tomatoes

1. Press Sauté button and adjust once to Sauté More function. Wait until indicator says "hot." 2. Season the ground beef with salt and black pepper. 3. Add the olive oil into the inner pot. Coat the whole bottom of the pot with the oil. 4. Add ground beef into the inner pot. The ground beef will start to release moisture. Allow the ground beef to brown and crisp slightly, stirring occasionally to break it up. Taste and adjust the seasoning with more salt and ground black pepper. 5. Add diced onion, minced garlic, chopped pepper, chili powder, and cumin. Sauté for about 5 minutes, until the spices start to release their fragrance. Stir frequently. 6. Add water and 1 can of chili beans, not drained. Mix well. Pour in 1 can of crushed tomatoes. 7. Close and secure lid, making sure vent is set to sealing, and pressure cook on Manual at high pressure for 10 minutes. 8. Let the pressure release naturally when cooking time is up. Open the lid carefully.

Per Serving:
calories: 213 | fat: 10g | protein: 18g | carbs: 11g | sugars: 4g | fiber: 4g | sodium: 385mg

Turkey and Pinto Chili

Prep time: 0 minutes | Cook time: 60 minutes | Serves 8

2 tablespoons cold-pressed avocado oil
4 garlic cloves, diced
1 large yellow onion, diced
4 jalapeño chiles, seeded and diced
2 carrots, diced
4 celery stalks, diced
2 teaspoons fine sea salt
2 pounds 93 percent lean ground turkey
Two 4-ounce cans fire-roasted diced green chiles
4 tablespoons chili powder
2 teaspoons ground cumin
2 teaspoons ground coriander
1 teaspoon dried oregano
1 teaspoon dried sage
1 cup low-sodium chicken broth
3 cups drained cooked pinto
beans, or two 15-ounce cans pinto beans, drained and rinsed
Two 14½-ounce cans no-salt petite diced tomatoes and their liquid
¼ cup tomato paste

1. Select the Sauté setting on the Instant Pot and heat the oil and garlic for 3 minutes, until the garlic is bubbling but not browned. Add the onion, jalapeños, carrots, celery, and salt and sauté for 5 minutes, until the onion begins to soften. Add the turkey and sauté, using a wooden spoon or spatula to break up the meat as it cooks, for 6 minutes, until cooked through and no streaks of pink remain. Stir in the green chiles, chili powder, cumin, coriander, oregano, sage, and broth, using a wooden spoon or spatula to nudge any browned bits from the bottom of the pot. 2. Pour in the beans in a layer on top of the turkey. Pour in the tomatoes and their liquid and add the tomato paste in a dollop on top. Do not stir in the beans, tomatoes, or tomato paste. 3. Secure the lid and set the Pressure Release to Sealing. Press the Cancel button to reset the cooking program, then select the Pressure Cook or Manual setting and set the cooking time for 15 minutes at high pressure. (The pot will take about 15 minutes to come up to pressure before the cooking program begins.) 4. When the cooking program ends, let the pressure release naturally for at least 20 minutes, then move the Pressure Release to Venting to release any remaining steam. Open the pot and stir the chili to mix all of the ingredients. 5. Press the Cancel button to reset the cooking program, then select the Sauté setting and set the cooking time for 10 minutes. Allow the chili to reduce and thicken. Do not stir the chili while it is cooking, as this will cause it to sputter more. 6. When the cooking program ends, the pot will turn off. Wearing heat-resistant mitts, remove the inner pot from the housing. Wait for about 2 minutes to allow the chili to stop simmering, then give it a final stir. 7. Ladle the chili into bowls and serve hot.

Per Serving:
calories: 354 | fat: 14g | protein: 30g | carbs: 28g | sugars: 6g | fiber: 9g | sodium: 819mg

Chicken Rice Soup

Prep time: 10 minutes | Cook time: 10 minutes | Serves 8

1 teaspoon vegetable oil
2 ribs celery, chopped in ½"-thick pieces
1 medium onion, chopped
1 cup wild rice, uncooked
½ cup long-grain rice, uncooked
1 pound boneless skinless chicken breasts, cut into ¾" cubes
5¼ cups fat-free, low-sodium chicken broth
2 teaspoons dried thyme leaves
¼ teaspoon red pepper flakes

1. Using the Sauté function on the Instant Pot, heat the teaspoon of vegetable oil. Sauté the celery and onion until the onions are slightly translucent (3–5 minutes). Once cooked, press Cancel. 2. Add the remaining ingredients to the inner pot. 3. Secure the lid and make sure the vent is set to sealing. Using the Manual function, set the time to 10 minutes. 4. When cook time is over, let the pressure release naturally for 10 minutes, then perform a quick release.

Per Serving:
calories: 160 | fat: 2g | protein: 16g | carbs: 18g | sugars: 2g | fiber: 1g | sodium: 375mg

Beef Oxtail Soup with White Beans, Tomatoes, and Aleppo Pepper

Prep time: 20 minutes | Cook time: 1 hour 10 minutes | Serves 6 to 8

4 pounds (1.8 kg) oxtails, trimmed
1 teaspoon table salt
1 tablespoon extra-virgin olive oil
1 onion, chopped fine
2 carrots, peeled and chopped fine
¼ cup ground dried Aleppo pepper
6 garlic cloves, minced
2 tablespoons tomato paste
¾ teaspoon dried oregano
½ teaspoon ground cinnamon
½ teaspoon ground cumin
6 cups water
1 (28-ounce / 794-g) can diced tomatoes, drained
1 (15-ounce / 425-g) can navy beans, rinsed
1 tablespoon sherry vinegar
¼ cup chopped fresh parsley
½ preserved lemon, pulp and white pith removed, rind rinsed and minced (2 tablespoons)

1. Pat oxtails dry with paper towels and sprinkle with salt. Using highest sauté function, heat oil in Instant Pot for 5 minutes (or until just smoking). Brown half of oxtails, 4 to 6 minutes per side; transfer to plate. Set aside remaining uncooked oxtails. 2. Add onion and carrots to fat left in pot and cook, using highest sauté function, until softened, about 5 minutes. Stir in Aleppo pepper, garlic, tomato paste, oregano, cinnamon, and cumin and cook until fragrant, about 30 seconds. Stir in water, scraping up any browned bits, then stir in tomatoes. Nestle remaining uncooked oxtails into pot along with browned oxtails and add any accumulated juices. 3. Lock lid in place and close pressure release valve. Select high pressure cook function and cook for 45 minutes. Turn off Instant Pot and quick-release pressure. Carefully remove lid, allowing steam to escape away from you. 4. Transfer oxtails to cutting board, let cool slightly, then shred into bite-size pieces using 2 forks; discard bones and excess fat. Strain broth through fine-mesh strainer into large container; return solids to now-empty pot. Using wide, shallow spoon, skim excess fat from surface of liquid; return to pot. 5. Stir shredded oxtails and any accumulated juices and beans into pot. Using highest sauté function, cook until soup is heated through, about 5 minutes. Stir in vinegar and parsley and season with salt and pepper to taste. Serve, passing preserved lemon separately.
Per Serving:
calories: 380 | fat: 18g | protein: 38g | carbs: 17g | fiber: 5g | sodium: 890mg

Vegetable and Chickpea Stew

Prep time: 25 minutes | Cook time: 30 minutes | Serves 6 to 8

¼ cup extra-virgin olive oil, plus extra for drizzling
2 red bell peppers, stemmed, seeded, and cut into 1-inch pieces
1 onion, chopped fine
½ teaspoon table salt
½ teaspoon pepper
1½ tablespoons baharat
4 garlic cloves, minced
1 tablespoon tomato paste
4 cups vegetable or chicken broth
1 (28-ounce / 794-g) can whole peeled tomatoes, drained with juice reserved, chopped
1 pound (454 g) Yukon Gold potatoes, peeled and cut into ½-inch pieces
2 zucchini, quartered lengthwise and sliced 1 inch thick
1 (15-ounce / 425-g) can chickpeas, rinsed
⅓ cup chopped fresh mint

1. Using highest sauté function, heat oil in Instant Pot until shimmering. Add bell pepper, onion, salt, and pepper and cook until vegetables are softened and lightly browned, 5 to 7 minutes. Stir in baharat, garlic, and tomato paste and cook until fragrant, about 1 minute. Stir in broth and tomatoes and reserved juice, scraping up any browned bits, then stir in potatoes. 2. Lock lid in place and close pressure release valve. Select high pressure cook function and cook for 9 minutes. Turn off Instant Pot and quick-release pressure. Carefully remove lid, allowing steam to escape away from you. 3. Stir zucchini and chickpeas into stew and cook, using highest sauté function, until zucchini is tender, 10 to 15 minutes. Turn off multicooker. Season with salt and pepper to taste. Drizzle individual portions with extra oil, and sprinkle with mint before serving.
Per Serving:
calories: 200 | fat: 8g | protein: 5g | carbs: 28g | fiber: 5g | sodium: 740mg

Beef and Spinach Stew

Prep time: 20 minutes | Cook time: 30 minutes | Serves 4

1 pound (454 g) beef sirloin, chopped
2 cups spinach, chopped
3 cups chicken broth
1 cup coconut milk
1 teaspoon allspices
1 teaspoon coconut aminos

1. Put all ingredients in the Instant Pot. Stir to mix well. 2. Close the lid. Set the Manual mode and set cooking time for 30 minutes on High Pressure. 3. When timer beeps, use a natural pressure release for 10 minutes, then release any remaining pressure. Open the lid. 4. Blend with an immersion blender until smooth. 5. Serve warm.
Per Serving:
calories: 383 | fat: 22g | protein: 40g | carbs: 5g | net carbs: 3g | fiber: 2g

Mushroom Pizza Soup

Prep time: 10 minutes | Cook time: 22 minutes | Serves 3

1 teaspoon coconut oil
¼ cup cremini mushrooms, sliced
5 ounces (142 g) Italian sausages, chopped
½ jalapeño pepper, sliced
½ teaspoon Italian seasoning
1 teaspoon unsweetened tomato purée
1 cup water
4 ounces (113 g) Mozzarella, shredded

1. Melt the coconut oil in the Instant Pot on Sauté mode. 2. Add the mushrooms and cook for 10 minutes. 3. Add the chopped sausages, sliced jalapeño, Italian seasoning, and unsweetened tomato purée. Pour in the water and stir to mix well. 4. Close the lid and select Manual mode. Set cooking time for 12 minutes on High Pressure. 5. When timer beeps, use a quick pressure release and open the lid. 6. Ladle the soup in the bowls. Top it with Mozzarella. Serve warm.
Per Serving:
calories: 289 | fat: 23.2g | protein: 17.7g | carbs: 2.5g | net carbs: 2.3g | fiber: 0.2g

Chicken and Vegetable Soup

1 pound (454 g) boneless, skinless chicken thighs, diced small
1 (10-ounce / 283-g) bag frozen vegetables
2 cups water
1 teaspoon poultry seasoning
1 tablespoon powdered chicken broth base
1 teaspoon salt
1 teaspoon freshly ground black pepper
1 cup heavy (whipping) cream

1. Put the chicken, vegetables, water, poultry seasoning, chicken broth base, salt, and pepper in the inner cooking pot of your Instant Pot. 2. Lock the lid into place. Select Manual and adjust the pressure to High. Cook for 2 minutes. When the cooking is complete, quick-release the pressure (you may want to do this in short bursts so the soup doesn't spurt out). Unlock the lid. 3. Add the cream, stir, and serve. Or, if you prefer, you can mash up the chicken with the back of a wooden spoon to break it into shreds before adding the cream.
Per Serving:
calories: 327 | fat: 19g | protein: 26g | carbs: 13g | net carbs: 10g | fiber: 3g

Hearty Hamburger and Lentil Stew

Prep time: 0 minutes | Cook time: 55 minutes | Serves 8

2 tablespoons cold-pressed avocado oil
2 garlic cloves, chopped
1 large yellow onion, diced
2 carrots, diced
2 celery stalks, diced
2 pounds 95 percent lean ground beef
½ cup small green lentils
2 cups low-sodium roasted beef bone broth or vegetable broth
1 tablespoon Italian seasoning
1 tablespoon paprika
1½ teaspoons fine sea salt
1 extra-large russet potato, diced
1 cup frozen green peas
1 cup frozen corn
One 14½-ounce can no-salt petite diced tomatoes and their liquid
¼ cup tomato paste

1. Select the Sauté setting on the Instant Pot and heat the oil and garlic for 3 minutes, until the garlic is bubbling but not browned. Add the onion, carrots, and celery and sauté for 5 minutes, until the onion begins to soften. Add the beef and sauté, using a wooden spoon or spatula to break up the meat as it cooks, for 6 minutes, until cooked through and no streaks of pink remain. 2. Stir in the lentils, broth, Italian seasoning, paprika, and salt. Add the potato, peas, corn, and tomatoes and their liquid in layers on top of the lentils and beef, then add the tomato paste in a dollop on top. Do not stir in the vegetables and tomato paste. 3. Secure the lid and set the Pressure Release to Sealing. Press the Cancel button to reset the cooking program, then select the Pressure Cook or Manual setting and set the cooking time for 20 minutes at high pressure. (The pot will take about 20 minutes to come up to pressure before the cooking program begins.) 4. When the cooking program ends, let the pressure release naturally for at least 15 minutes, then move the Pressure Release to Venting to release any remaining steam. Open the pot and stir the stew to mix all of the ingredients. 5. Ladle the stew into bowls and serve hot.
Per Serving:
calories: 334 | fat: 8g | protein: 34g | carbs: 30g | sugars: 6g | fiber: 7g | sodium: 902mg

Garlic Beef Soup

Prep time: 12 minutes | Cook time: 42 minutes | Serves 8

10 strips bacon, chopped
1 medium white onion, chopped
Cloves squeezed from 3 heads roasted garlic, or 6 cloves garlic, minced
1 to 2 jalapeño peppers, seeded and chopped (optional)
2 pounds (907 g) boneless beef chuck roast, cut into 4 equal-sized pieces
5 cups beef broth
1 cup chopped fresh cilantro, plus more for garnish
2 teaspoons fine sea salt
1 teaspoon ground black pepper
For Garnish:
1 avocado, peeled, pitted, and diced
2 radishes, very thinly sliced
2 tablespoons chopped fresh chives

1. Place the bacon in the Instant Pot and press Sauté. Cook, stirring occasionally, for 4 minutes, or until the bacon is crisp. Remove the bacon with a slotted spoon, leaving the drippings in the pot. Set the bacon on a paper towel-lined plate to drain. 2. Add the onion, garlic, and jalapeños, if using, to the Instant Pot and sauté for 3 minutes, or until the onion is soft. Press Cancel to stop the Sauté. 3. Add the beef, broth, cilantro, salt, and pepper. Stir to combine. 4. Seal the lid, press Manual, and set the timer for 35 minutes. Once finished, let the pressure release naturally. 5. Remove the lid and shred the beef with two forks. Taste the liquid and add more salt, if needed. 6. Ladle the soup into bowls. Garnish with the reserved bacon, avocado, radishes, chives, and more cilantro.
Per Serving:
calories: 456 | fat: 36g | protein: 25g | carbs: 6g | net carbs: 4g | fiber: 2g

Avocado and Serrano Chile Soup

Prep time: 10 minutes | Cook time: 7 minutes | Serves 4

2 avocados
1 small fresh tomatillo, quartered
2 cups chicken broth
2 tablespoons avocado oil
1 tablespoon butter
2 tablespoons finely minced onion
1 clove garlic, minced
½ Serrano chile, deseeded and ribs removed, minced, plus thin slices for garnish
¼ teaspoon sea salt
Pinch of ground white pepper
½ cup full-fat coconut milk
Fresh cilantro sprigs, for garnish

1. Scoop the avocado flesh into a food processor. Add the tomatillo and chicken broth and purée until smooth. Set aside. 2. Set the Instant Pot to Sauté mode and add the avocado oil and butter. When the butter melts, add the onion and garlic and sauté for a minute or until softened. Add the Serrano chile and sauté for 1 minute more. 3. Pour the puréed avocado mixture into the pot, add the salt and pepper, and stir to combine. 4. Secure the lid. Press the Manual button and set cooking time for 5 minutes on High Pressure. 5. When timer beeps, use a quick pressure release. Open the lid and stir in the coconut milk. 6. Serve hot topped with thin slices of Serrano chile, and cilantro sprigs.
Per Serving:
calories: 333 | fat: 32.1g | protein: 3.8g | carbs: 14.5g | net carbs: 6.6g | fiber: 7.9g

Jalapeño Popper Chicken Soup

Prep time: 5 minutes | Cook time: 25 minutes | Serves 4

2 tablespoons butter
½ medium diced onion
¼ cup sliced pickled jalapeños
¼ cup cooked crumbled bacon
2 cups chicken broth
2 cups cooked diced chicken
4 ounces (113 g) cream cheese
1 teaspoon salt
½ teaspoon pepper
¼ teaspoon garlic powder
⅓ cup heavy cream
1 cup shredded sharp Cheddar cheese

1. Press the Sauté button. Add butter, onion, and sliced jalapeños to Instant Pot. Sauté for 5 minutes, until onions are translucent. Add bacon and press the Cancel button. 2. Add broth, cooked chicken, cream cheese, salt, pepper, and garlic to Instant Pot. Click lid closed. Press the Soup button and adjust time for 20 minutes. 3. When timer beeps, quick-release the steam. Stir in heavy cream and Cheddar. Continue stirring until cheese is fully melted. Serve warm.

Per Serving:
calories: 524 | fat: 36g | protein: 35g | carbs: 9g | net carbs: 8g | fiber: 1g

Pancetta and Jalapeño Soup

Prep time: 10 minutes | Cook time: 10 minutes | Serves 4

3 ounces (85 g) pancetta, chopped
1 teaspoon coconut oil
2 jalapeño peppers, sliced
½ teaspoon garlic powder
½ teaspoon smoked paprika
½ cup heavy cream
2 cups water
½ cup Monterey Jack cheese, shredded

1. Toss the pancetta in the Instant Pot, then add the coconut oil and cook for 4 minutes on Sauté mode. Stir constantly. 2. Add the sliced jalapeños, garlic powder, and smoked paprika. Sauté for 1 more minute. 3. Pour in the heavy cream and water. Add the Monterey Jack cheese and stir to mix well. 4. Close the lid and select Manual mode and set cooking time on High Pressure. 5. When timer beeps, make a quick pressure release. Open the lid. 6. Serve warm.

Per Serving:
calories: 234 | fat: 20.0g | protein: 11.8g | carbs: 1.7g | net carbs: 1.3g | fiber: 0.4g

French Market Soup

Prep time: 20 minutes | Cook time: 1 hour | Serves 8

2 cups mixed dry beans, washed with stones removed
7 cups water
1 ham hock, all visible fat removed
1 teaspoon salt
¼ teaspoon pepper
16-ounce can low-sodium tomatoes
1 large onion, chopped
1 garlic clove, minced
1 chile, chopped, or 1 teaspoon chili powder
¼ cup lemon juice

1. Combine all ingredients in the inner pot of the Instant Pot. 2. Secure the lid and make sure vent is set to sealing. Using Manual, set the Instant Pot to cook for 60 minutes. 3. When cooking time is over, let the pressure release naturally. When the Instant Pot is ready, unlock the lid, then remove the bone and any hard or fatty pieces.

Pull the meat off the bone and chop into small pieces. Add the ham back into the Instant Pot.

Per Serving:
calories: 191 | fat: 4g | protein: 12g | carbs: 29g | sugars: 5g | fiber: 7g | sodium: 488mg

Pork and Daikon Stew

Prep time: 15 minutes | Cook time: 3 minutes | Serves 6

1 pound (454 g) pork tenderloin, chopped
1 ounce (28 g) green onions, chopped
½ cup daikon, chopped
1 lemon slice
1 tablespoon heavy cream
1 tablespoon butter
1 teaspoon ground black pepper
3 cups water

1. Put all ingredients in the Instant Pot and stir to mix with a spatula. 2. Seal the lid. Set Manual mode and set cooking time for 20 minutes on High Pressure. 3. When cooking is complete, use a natural pressure release for 15 minutes, then release any remaining pressure. Open the lid. 4. Serve warm.

Per Serving:
calories: 137 | fat: 5.5g | protein: 20.1g | carbs: 0.9g | net carbs: 0.6g | fiber: 0.3g

Ground Turkey Stew

Prep time: 5 minutes | Cook time: 25 minutes | Serves 5

1 tablespoon olive oil
1 onion, chopped
1 pound ground turkey
½ teaspoon garlic powder
1 teaspoon chili powder
¾ teaspoon cumin
2 teaspoons coriander
1 teaspoon dried oregano
½ teaspoon salt
1 green pepper, chopped
1 red pepper, chopped
1 tomato, chopped
1½ cups reduced-sodium tomato sauce
1 tablespoon low-sodium soy sauce
1 cup water
2 handfuls cilantro, chopped
15-ounce can reduced-salt black beans

1. Press the Sauté function on the control panel of the Instant Pot. 2. Add the olive oil to the inner pot and let it get hot. Add onion and sauté for a few minutes, or until light golden. 3. Add ground turkey. Break the ground meat using a wooden spoon to avoid formation of lumps. Sauté for a few minutes, until the pink color has faded. 4. Add garlic powder, chili powder, cumin, coriander, dried oregano, and salt. Combine well. Add green pepper, red pepper, and chopped tomato. Combine well. 5. Add tomato sauce, soy sauce, and water; combine well. 6. Close and secure the lid. Click on the Cancel key to cancel the Sauté mode. Make sure the pressure release valve on the lid is in the sealing position. 7. Click on Manual function first and then select high pressure. Click the + button and set the time to 15 minutes. 8. You can either have the steam release naturally (it will take around 20 minutes) or, after 10 minutes, turn the pressure release valve on the lid to venting and release steam. Be careful as the steam is very hot. After the pressure has released completely, open the lid. 9. If the stew is watery, turn on the Sauté function and let it cook for a few more minutes with the lid off. 10. Add cilantro and can of black beans, combine well, and let cook for a few minutes.

Per Serving:
calories: 209 | fat: 3g | protein: 24g | carbs: 21g | sugars: 8g | fiber: 6g | sodium: 609mg

Beef and Cauliflower Soup

Prep time: 10 minutes | Cook time: 14 minutes | Serves 4

1 cup ground beef
½ cup cauliflower, shredded
1 teaspoon unsweetened tomato purée
¼ cup coconut milk
1 teaspoon minced garlic
1 teaspoon dried oregano
½ teaspoon salt
4 cups water

1. Put all ingredients in the Instant Pot and stir well. 2. Close the lid. Select Manual mode and set cooking time for 14 minutes on High Pressure. 3. When timer beeps, make a quick pressure release and open the lid. 4. Blend with an immersion blender until smooth. 5. Serve warm.

Per Serving:
calories: 106 | fat: 7.7g | protein: 7.3g | carbs: 2.2g | net carbs: 1.3g | fiber: 0.9g

Beef and Okra Stew

Prep time: 15 minutes | Cook time: 25 minutes | Serves 3

8 ounces (227 g) beef sirloin, chopped
¼ teaspoon cumin seeds
1 teaspoon dried basil
1 tablespoon avocado oil
¼ cup coconut cream
1 cup water
6 ounces (170 g) okra, chopped

1. Sprinkle the beef sirloin with cumin seeds and dried basil and put in the Instant Pot. 2. Add avocado oil and roast the meat on Sauté mode for 5 minutes. Flip occasionally. 3. Add coconut cream, water, and okra. 4. Close the lid and select Manual mode. Set cooking time for 25 minutes on High Pressure. 5. When timer beeps, use a natural pressure release for 10 minutes, the release any remaining pressure. Open the lid. 6. Serve warm.

Per Serving:
calories: 216 | fat: 10.2g | protein: 24.6g | carbs: 5.7g | net carbs: 3.2g | fiber: 2.5g

Vegetarian Chili

Prep time: 25 minutes | Cook time: 10 minutes | Serves 6

2 teaspoons olive oil
3 garlic cloves, minced
2 onions, chopped
1 green bell pepper, chopped
1 cup textured vegetable protein (T.V.P.)
1-pound can beans of your choice, drained
1 jalapeño pepper, seeds removed, chopped
28-ounce can diced Italian tomatoes
1 bay leaf
1 tablespoon dried oregano
½ teaspoons salt
¼ teaspoons pepper

1. Set the Instant Pot to the Sauté function. As it's heating, add the olive oil, garlic, onions, and bell pepper. Stir constantly for about 5 minutes as it all cooks. Press Cancel. 2. Place all of the remaining ingredients into the inner pot of the Instant pot and stir. 3. Secure the lid and make sure vent is set to sealing. Cook on Manual mode for 10 minutes. 4. When cook time is up, let the steam release naturally for 5 minutes and then manually release the rest.

Per Serving:
calories: 242 | fat: 2g | protein: 17g | carbs: 36g | sugars: 9g | fiber: 12g | sodium: 489mg

Nancy's Vegetable Beef Soup

Prep time: 25 minutes | Cook time: 8 hours | Serves 8

2-pound roast, cubed, or 2 pounds stewing meat
15-ounce can corn
15-ounce can green beans
1-pound bag frozen peas
40-ounce can no-added-salt
stewed tomatoes
5 teaspoons salt-free beef bouillon powder
Tabasco, to taste
½ teaspoons salt

1. Combine all ingredients in the Instant Pot. Do not drain vegetables. 2. Add water to fill inner pot only to the fill line. 3. Secure the lid, or use the glass lid and set the Instant Pot on Slow Cook mode, Low for 8 hours, or until meat is tender and vegetables are soft.

Per Serving:
calories: 229 | fat: 5g | protein: 23g | carbs: 24g | sugars: 10g | fiber: 6g | sodium: 545mg

Chicken Brunswick Stew

Prep time: 0 minutes | Cook time: 30 minutes | Serves 6

2 tablespoons extra-virgin olive oil
2 garlic cloves, chopped
1 large yellow onion, diced
2 pounds boneless, skinless chicken (breasts, tenders, or thighs), cut into bite-size pieces
1 teaspoon dried thyme
1 teaspoon smoked paprika
1 teaspoon fine sea salt
½ teaspoon freshly ground black pepper
1 cup low-sodium chicken
broth
1 tablespoon hot sauce (such as Tabasco or Crystal)
1 tablespoon raw apple cider vinegar
1½ cups frozen corn
1½ cups frozen baby lima beans
One 14½-ounce can fire-roasted diced tomatoes and their liquid
2 tablespoons tomato paste
Cornbread, for serving

1. Select the Sauté setting on the Instant Pot and heat the oil and garlic for 2 minutes, until the garlic is bubbling but not browned. Add the onion and sauté for 3 minutes, until it begins to soften. Add the chicken and sauté for 3 minutes more, until mostly opaque. The chicken does not have to be cooked through. Add the thyme, paprika, salt, and pepper and sauté for 1 minute more. 2. Stir in the broth, hot sauce, vinegar, corn, and lima beans. Add the diced tomatoes and their liquid in an even layer and dollop the tomato paste on top. Do not stir them in. 3. Secure the lid and set the Pressure Release to Sealing. Press the Cancel button to reset the cooking program, then select the Pressure Cook or Manual setting and set the cooking time for 5 minutes at high pressure. (The pot will take about 15 minutes to come up to pressure before the cooking program begins.) 4. When the cooking program ends, let the pressure release naturally for at least 10 minutes, then move the Pressure Release to Venting to release any remaining steam. Open the pot and stir the stew to mix all of the ingredients. 5. Ladle the stew into bowls and serve hot, with cornbread alongside.

Per Serving:
calories: 349 | fat: 7g | protein: 40g | carbs: 17g | sugars: 7g | fiber: 7g | sodium: 535mg

Turkey Barley Vegetable Soup

Prep time: 5 minutes | Cook time: 20 minutes | Serves 8

2 tablespoons avocado oil
1 pound ground turkey
4 cups Chicken Bone Broth, low-sodium store-bought chicken broth, or water
1 (28-ounce) carton or can diced tomatoes
2 tablespoons tomato paste
1 (15-ounce) package frozen chopped carrots (about 2½ cups)
1 (15-ounce) package frozen peppers and onions (about 2½ cups)
⅓ cup dry barley
1 teaspoon kosher salt
¼ teaspoon freshly ground black pepper
2 bay leaves

1. Set the electric pressure cooker to the Sauté/More setting. When the pot is hot, pour in the avocado oil. 2. Add the turkey to the pot and sauté, stirring frequently to break up the meat, for about 7 minutes or until the turkey is no longer pink. Hit Cancel. 3. Add the broth, tomatoes and their juices, and tomato paste. Stir in the carrots, peppers and onions, barley, salt, pepper, and bay leaves. 4. Close and lock the lid of the pressure cooker. Set the valve to sealing. 5. Cook on high pressure for 20 minutes. 6. When the cooking is complete, hit Cancel and allow the pressure to release naturally for 10 minutes, then quick release any remaining pressure. 7. Once the pin drops, unlock and remove the lid. Discard the bay leaves. 8. Spoon into bowls and serve.

Per Serving:
calories: 203 | fat: 8.73g | protein: 14.62g | carbs: 18.17g | sugars: 7.62g | fiber: 5.6g | sodium: 793mg

Beef Meatball Minestrone

Prep time: 5 minutes | Cook time: 35 minutes | Serves 6

1 pound (454 g) ground beef
1 large egg
1½ tablespoons golden flaxseed meal
⅓ cup shredded Mozzarella cheese
¼ cup unsweetened tomato purée
1½ tablespoons Italian seasoning, divided
1½ teaspoons garlic powder, divided
1½ teaspoons sea salt, divided
1 tablespoon olive oil
2 garlic cloves, minced
½ medium yellow onion, minced
¼ cup pancetta, diced
1 cup sliced yellow squash
1 cup sliced zucchini
½ cup sliced turnips
4 cups beef broth
14 ounces (397 g) can diced tomatoes
½ teaspoon ground black pepper
3 tablespoons shredded Parmesan cheese

1. Preheat the oven to 400°F (205°C) and line a large baking sheet with aluminum foil. 2. In a large bowl, combine the ground beef, egg, flaxseed meal, Mozzarella, unsweetened tomato purée, ½ tablespoon of Italian seasoning, ½ teaspoon of garlic powder, and ½ teaspoon of sea salt. Mix the ingredients until well combined. 3. Make the meatballs by shaping 1 heaping tablespoon of the ground beef mixture into a meatball. Repeat with the remaining mixture and then transfer the meatballs to the prepared baking sheet. 4. Place the meatballs in the oven and bake for 15 minutes. When the baking time is complete, remove from the oven and set aside. 5. Select Sauté mode of the Instant Pot. Once the pot is hot, add the olive oil, garlic, onion, and pancetta. Sauté for 2 minutes or until the garlic becomes fragrant and the onions begin to soften. 6. Add the yellow squash, zucchini, and turnips to the pot. Sauté for 3 more minutes. 7. Add the beef broth, diced tomatoes, black pepper, and remaining garlic powder, sea salt, and Italian seasoning to the pot. Stir to combine and then add the meatballs. 8. Lock the lid. Select Manual mode and set cooking time for 15 minutes on High Pressure. 9. When cooking is complete, allow the pressure to release naturally for 10 minutes and then release the remaining pressure. 10. Open the lid and gently stir the soup. Ladle into serving bowls and top with Parmesan. Serve hot.

Per Serving:
calories: 373 | fat: 18.8g | protein: 34.7g | carbs: 15.0g | net carbs: 11.3g | fiber: 3.7g

Pasta e Fagioli with Ground Beef

Prep time: 0 minutes | Cook time: 30 minutes | Serves 8

2 tablespoons extra-virgin olive oil
4 garlic cloves, minced
1 yellow onion, diced
2 large carrots, diced
4 celery stalks, diced
1½ pounds 95 percent extra-lean ground beef
4 cups low-sodium vegetable broth
2 teaspoons Italian seasoning
½ teaspoon freshly ground black pepper
1¼ cups chickpea-based elbow pasta or whole-wheat elbow pasta
1½ cups drained cooked kidney beans, or one 15-ounce can kidney beans, rinsed and drained
One 28-ounce can whole San Marzano tomatoes and their liquid
2 tablespoons chopped fresh flat-leaf parsley

1. Select the Sauté setting on the Instant Pot and heat the oil and garlic for 2 minutes, until the garlic is bubbling but not browned. Add the onion, carrots, and celery and sauté for 5 minutes, until the onion begins to soften. Add the beef and sauté, using a wooden spoon or spatula to break up the meat as it cooks, for 5 minutes; it's fine if some streaks of pink remain, the beef does not need to be cooked through. 2. Stir in the broth, Italian seasoning, pepper, and pasta, making sure all of the pasta is submerged in the liquid. Add the beans and stir to mix. Add the tomatoes and their liquid, crushing the tomatoes with your hands as you add them to the pot. Do not stir them in. 3. Secure the lid and set the Pressure Release to Sealing. Press the Cancel button to reset the cooking program, then select the Pressure Cook or Manual setting and set the cooking time for 2 minutes at low pressure. (The pot will take about 15 minutes to come up to pressure before the cooking program begins.) 4. When the cooking program ends, let the pressure release naturally for 10 minutes, then move the Pressure Release to Venting to release any remaining steam. Open the pot and stir the soup to mix all of the ingredients. 5. Ladle the soup into bowls, sprinkle with the parsley, and serve right away.

Per Serving:
calories: 278 | fat: 9g | protein: 26g | carbs: 25g | sugars: 4g | fiber: 6g | sodium: 624mg

French Onion Soup

Prep time: 10 minutes | Cook time: 20 minutes | Serves 10

½ cup light, soft tub margarine
8–10 large onions, sliced
3 14-ounce cans 98% fat-free, lower-sodium beef broth

2½ cups water
3 teaspoons sodium-free chicken bouillon powder
1½ teaspoons Worcestershire
sauce
3 bay leaves
10 (1-ounce) slices French bread, toasted

1. Turn the Instant Pot to the Sauté function and add in the margarine and onions. Cook about 5 minutes, or until the onions are slightly soft. Press Cancel. 2. Add the beef broth, water, bouillon powder, Worcestershire sauce, and bay leaves and stir. 3. Secure the lid and make sure vent is set to sealing. Cook on Manual mode for 20 minutes. 4. Let the pressure release naturally for 15 minutes, then do a quick release. Open the lid and discard bay leaves. 5. Ladle into bowls. Top each with a slice of bread and some cheese if you desire.

Per Serving:
calories: 178 | fat: 4g | protein: 6g | carbs: 31g | sugars: 10g | fiber: 4g | sodium: 476mg

Swiss Chard and Chicken Soup

Prep time: 10 minutes | Cook time: 5 minutes | Serves 4

1 onion, chopped
6 garlic cloves, peeled
1 (2-inch) piece fresh ginger, chopped
1 (10-ounce / 283-g) can tomatoes with chiles
1½ cups full-fat coconut milk, divided
1 tablespoon powdered chicken broth base
1 pound (454 g) boneless chicken thighs, cut into large bite-size pieces
1½ cups chopped celery
2 cups chopped Swiss chard
1 teaspoon ground turmeric

1. To a blender jar, add the onion, garlic, ginger, tomatoes, ½ cup of coconut milk, and chicken broth base. Purée the ingredients into a sauce. 2. Pour the mixture into the inner cooking pot of the Instant Pot. Add the chicken, celery, and chard. 3. Lock the lid into place. Select Manual and adjust the pressure to High. Cook for 5 minutes. When the cooking is complete, let the pressure release naturally for 10 minutes, then quick-release any remaining pressure. 4. Unlock the lid and add the remaining 1 cup of coconut milk and turmeric. Stir to heat through and serve.

Per Serving:
calories: 338 | fat: 22g | protein: 25g | carbs: 10g | net carbs: 7g | fiber: 3g

Broccoli and Bacon Cheese Soup

Prep time: 6 minutes | Cook time: 10 minutes | Serves 6

3 tablespoons butter
2 stalks celery, diced
½ yellow onion, diced
3 garlic cloves, minced
3½ cups chicken stock
4 cups chopped fresh broccoli florets
3 ounces (85 g) block-style cream cheese, softened and cubed
½ teaspoon ground nutmeg
½ teaspoon sea salt
1 teaspoon ground black pepper
3 cups shredded Cheddar cheese
½ cup shredded Monterey Jack cheese
2 cups heavy cream
4 slices cooked bacon, crumbled
1 tablespoon finely chopped chives

1. Select Sauté mode. Once the Instant Pot is hot, add the butter and heat until the butter is melted. 2. Add the celery, onions, and garlic. Continue sautéing for 5 minutes or until the vegetables are softened. 3. Add the chicken stock and broccoli florets to the pot. Bring the liquid to a boil. 4. Lock the lid,. Select Manual mode and set cooking time for 5 minutes on High Pressure. 5. When cooking is complete, allow the pressure to release naturally for 10 minutes and then release the remaining pressure. 6. Open the lid and add the cream cheese, nutmeg, sea salt, and black pepper. Stir to combine. 7. Select Sauté mode. Bring the soup to a boil and then slowly stir in the Cheddar and Jack cheeses. Once the cheese has melted, stir in the heavy cream. 8. Ladle the soup into serving bowls and top with bacon and chives. Serve hot.

Per Serving:
calories: 681 | fat: 59.0g | protein: 27.4g | carbs: 11.6g | net carbs: 10.3g | fiber: 1.3g

Savory Beef Stew with Mushrooms and Turnips

Prep time: 0 minutes | Cook time: 55 minutes | Serves 6

1½ pounds beef stew meat
¾ teaspoon fine sea salt
¾ teaspoon freshly ground black pepper
1 tablespoon cold-pressed avocado oil
3 garlic cloves, minced
1 yellow onion, diced
2 celery stalks, diced
8 ounces cremini mushrooms, quartered
1 cup low-sodium roasted beef bone broth
2 tablespoons Worcestershire
sauce
1 tablespoon Dijon mustard
1 teaspoon dried rosemary, crumbled
1 bay leaf
3 tablespoons tomato paste
8 ounces carrots, cut into 1-inch-thick rounds
1 pound turnips, cut into 1-inch pieces
1 pound parsnips, halved lengthwise, then cut crosswise into 1-inch pieces

1. Sprinkle the beef all over with the salt and pepper. 2. Select the Sauté setting on the Instant Pot and heat the oil and garlic for 2 minutes, until the garlic is bubbling but not browned. Add the onion, celery, and mushrooms and sauté for 5 minutes, until the onion begins to soften and the mushrooms are giving up their liquid. Stir in the broth, Worcestershire sauce, mustard, rosemary, and bay leaf. Stir in the beef. Add the tomato paste in a dollop on top. Do not stir it in. 3. Secure the lid and set the Pressure Release to Sealing. Press the Cancel button to reset the cooking program, then select the Meat/Stew, Pressure Cook, or Manual setting and set the cooking time for 20 minutes at high pressure. (The pot will take about 10 minutes to come up to pressure before the cooking program begins.) 4. When the cooking program ends, perform a quick pressure release by moving the Pressure Release to Venting, or let the pressure release naturally. Open the pot, remove and discard the bay leaf, and stir in the tomato paste. Place the carrots, turnips, and parsnips on top of the meat. 5. Secure the lid and set the Pressure Release to Sealing. Press the Cancel button to reset the cooking program, then select the Pressure Cook or Manual setting and set the cooking time for 3 minutes at low pressure. (The pot will take about 15 minutes to come up to pressure before the cooking program begins.) 6. When the cooking program ends, perform a quick pressure release by moving the Pressure Release to Venting. Open the pot and stir to combine all of the ingredients. 7. Ladle the stew into bowls and serve hot.

Per Serving:
calories: 304 | fat: 8g | protein: 29g | carbs: 30g | sugars: 10g | fiber: 8g | sodium: 490mg

Broccoli Brie Soup

Prep time: 5 minutes | Cook time: 14 minutes | Serves 6

1 tablespoon coconut oil or unsalted butter
1 cup finely diced onions
1 head broccoli, cut into small florets
2½ cups chicken broth or vegetable broth
8 ounces (227 g) Brie cheese, cut off rind and cut into chunks
1 cup unsweetened almond milk or heavy cream, plus more for drizzling
Fine sea salt and ground black pepper, to taste
Extra-virgin olive oil, for drizzling
Coarse sea salt, for garnish

1. Place the coconut oil in the Instant Pot and press Sauté. Once hot, add the onions and sauté for 4 minutes, or until soft. Press Cancel to stop the Sauté. 2. Add the broccoli and broth. Seal the lid, press Manual, and set the timer for 10 minutes. Once finished, let the pressure release naturally. 3. Remove the lid and add the Brie and almond milk to the pot. Transfer the soup to a food processor or blender and process until smooth, or purée the soup right in the pot with a stick blender. 4. Season with salt and pepper to taste. Ladle the soup into bowls and drizzle with almond milk and olive oil. Garnish with coarse sea salt and freshly ground pepper.

Per Serving:
calories: 210 | fat: 16g | protein: 9g | carbs: 7g | net carbs: 6g | fiber: 1g

Hot and Sour Soup

Prep time: 0 minutes | Cook time: 30 minutes | Serves 6

4 cups boiling water
1 ounce dried shiitake mushrooms
2 tablespoons cold-pressed avocado oil
3 garlic cloves, chopped
4 ounces cremini or button mushrooms, sliced
1 pound boneless pork loin, sirloin, or tip, thinly sliced against the grain into ¼-inch-thick, ½-inch-wide, 2-inch-long strips
1 teaspoon ground ginger
½ teaspoon ground white pepper
2 cups low-sodium chicken
broth or vegetable broth
One 8-ounce can sliced bamboo shoots, drained and rinsed
2 tablespoons low-sodium soy sauce
1 tablespoon chile garlic sauce
1 teaspoon toasted sesame oil
2 teaspoons Lakanto Monkfruit Sweetener Classic
2 large eggs
¼ cup rice vinegar
2 tablespoons cornstarch
4 green onions, white and green parts, thinly sliced
¼ cup chopped fresh cilantro

1. In a large liquid measuring cup or heatproof bowl, pour the boiling water over the shiitake mushrooms. Cover and let soak for 30 minutes. Drain the mushrooms, reserving the soaking liquid. Remove and discard the stems and thinly slice the caps. 2. Select the Sauté setting on the Instant Pot and heat the avocado oil and garlic for 2 minutes, until the garlic is bubbling but not browned. Add the cremini and shiitake mushrooms and sauté for 3 minutes, until the mushrooms are beginning to wilt. Add the pork, ginger, and white pepper and sauté for about 5 minutes, until the pork is opaque and cooked through. 3. Pour the mushroom soaking liquid into the pot, being careful to leave behind any sediment at the bottom of the measuring cup or bowl. Using a wooden spoon, nudge any browned

bits from the bottom of the pot. Stir in the broth, bamboo shoots, soy sauce, chile garlic sauce, sesame oil, and sweetener. 4. Secure the lid and set the Pressure Release to Sealing. Press the Cancel button to reset the cooking program, then select the Pressure Cook or Manual setting and set the cooking time for 5 minutes at high pressure. (The pot will take about 10 minutes to come up to pressure before the cooking program begins.) 5. While the soup is cooking, in a small bowl, beat the eggs until no streaks of yolk remain. 6. When the cooking program ends, let the pressure release naturally for at least 15 minutes, then move the Pressure Release to Venting to release any remaining steam. 7. In a small bowl, stir together the vinegar and cornstarch until the cornstarch dissolves. Open the pot and stir the vinegar mixture into the soup. Press the Cancel button to reset the cooking program, then select the Sauté setting. Bring the soup to a simmer and cook, stirring occasionally, for about 3 minutes, until slightly thickened. While stirring the soup constantly, pour in the beaten eggs in a thin stream. Press the Cancel button to turn off the pot and then stir in the green onions and cilantro. 8. Ladle the soup into bowls and serve hot.

Per Serving:
calories: 231 | fat: 13g | protein: 21g | carbs: 14g | sugars: 2g | fiber: 3g | sodium: 250mg

Unstuffed Cabbage Soup

Prep time: 15 minutes | Cook time: 20 minutes | Serves 5

2 tablespoons coconut oil
1 pound ground sirloin or turkey
1 medium onion, diced
2 cloves garlic, minced
1 small head cabbage, chopped, cored, cut into roughly 2-inch pieces.
6-ounce can low-sodium tomato paste
32-ounce can low-sodium diced tomatoes, with liquid
2 cups low-sodium beef broth
1½ cups water
¾ cup brown rice
1–2 teaspoons salt
½ teaspoon black pepper
1 teaspoon oregano
1 teaspoon parsley

1. Melt coconut oil in the inner pot of the Instant Pot using Sauté function. Add ground meat. Stir frequently until meat loses color, about 2 minutes. 2. Add onion and garlic and continue to sauté for 2 more minutes, stirring frequently. 3. Add chopped cabbage. 4. On top of cabbage layer tomato paste, tomatoes with liquid, beef broth, water, rice, and spices. 5. Secure the lid and set vent to sealing. Using Manual setting, select 20 minutes. 6. When time is up, let the pressure release naturally for 10 minutes, then do a quick release.

Per Serving:
calories: 282 | fat: 6g | protein: 23g | carbs: 34g | sugars: 6g | fiber: 3g | sodium: 898mg

Italian Vegetable Soup

Prep time: 20 minutes | Cook time: 5 to 9 hours | Serves 6

3 small carrots, sliced
1 small onion, chopped
2 small potatoes, diced
2 tablespoons chopped parsley
1 garlic clove, minced
3 teaspoons sodium-free beef
bouillon powder
1¼ teaspoons dried basil
¼ teaspoon pepper
16-ounce can red kidney beans, undrained
3 cups water

14½-ounce can stewed tomatoes, with juice	1 cup diced, extra-lean, lower-sodium cooked ham

1. In the inner pot of the Instant Pot, layer the carrots, onion, potatoes, parsley, garlic, beef bouillon, basil, pepper, and kidney beans. Do not stir. Add water. 2. Secure the lid and cook on the Low Slow Cook mode for 8–9 hours, or on high 4½–5½ hours, until vegetables are tender. 3. Remove the lid and stir in the tomatoes and ham. Secure the lid again and cook on high Slow Cook mode for 10–15 minutes more.

Per Serving:
calories: 156 | fat: 1g | protein: 9g | carbs: 29g | sugars: 8g | fiber: 5g | sodium: 614mg

Cauliflower Rice and Chicken Thigh Soup

Prep time: 15 minutes | Cook time: 13 minutes | Serves 5

2 cups cauliflower florets	pepper
1 pound (454 g) boneless, skinless chicken thighs	½ cup sliced zucchini
	⅓ cup sliced turnips
4½ cups chicken broth	1 teaspoon dried parsley
½ yellow onion, chopped	3 celery stalks, chopped
2 garlic cloves, minced	1 teaspoon ground turmeric
1 tablespoon unflavored gelatin powder	½ teaspoon dried marjoram
	1 teaspoon dried thyme
2 teaspoons sea salt	½ teaspoon dried oregano
½ teaspoon ground black	

1. Add the cauliflower florets to a food processor and pulse until a ricelike consistency is achieved. Set aside. 2. Add the chicken thighs, chicken broth, onions, garlic, gelatin powder, sea salt, and black pepper to the pot. Gently stir to combine. 3. Lock the lid. Select Manual mode and set cooking time for 10 minutes on High Pressure. 4. When cooking is complete, quick release the pressure and open the lid. 5. Transfer the chicken thighs to a cutting board. Chop the chicken into bite-sized pieces and then return the chopped chicken to the pot. 6. Add the cauliflower rice, zucchini, turnips, parsley, celery, turmeric, marjoram, thyme, and oregano to the pot. Stir to combine. 7. Lock the lid. Select Manual mode and set cooking time for 3 minutes on High Pressure. 8. When cooking is complete, quick release the pressure. 9. Open the lid. Ladle the soup into serving bowls. Serve hot.

Per Serving:
calories: 247 | fat: 10.4g | protein: 30.2g | carbs: 8.3g | net carbs: 6.1g | fiber: 2.2g

Beef and Mushroom Stew

Prep time: 15 minutes | Cook time: 30 minutes | Serves 4

2 tablespoons coconut oil	½ cup chopped celery
1 pound (454 g) cubed chuck roast	1 tablespoon sugar-free tomato paste
1 cup sliced button mushrooms	1 teaspoon thyme
½ medium onion, chopped	2 garlic cloves, minced
2 cups beef broth	½ teaspoon xanthan gum

1. Press the Sauté button and add coconut oil to Instant Pot. Brown cubes of chuck roast until golden, working in batches if necessary. (If the pan is overcrowded, they will not brown properly.) Set aside after browning is completed. 2. Add mushrooms and onions to pot. Sauté until mushrooms begin to brown and onions are translucent. Press the Cancel button. 3. Add broth to Instant Pot. Use wooden spoon to scrape bits from bottom if necessary. Add celery, tomato paste, thyme, and garlic. Click lid closed. Press the Manual button and adjust time for 35 minutes. When timer beeps, allow a natural release. 4. When pressure valve drops, stir in xanthan gum and allow to thicken. Serve warm.

Per Serving:
calories: 354 | fat: 25g | protein: 24g | carbs: 4g | net carbs: 2g | fiber: 2g

Creamy Chicken Wild Rice Soup

Prep time: 15 minutes | Cook time: 15 minutes | Serves 5

2 tablespoons margarine	Long Grain & Wild Rice Fast Cook
½ cup yellow onion, diced	
¾ cup carrots, diced	2 14-ounce cans low-sodium chicken broth
¾ cup sliced mushrooms (about 3–4 mushrooms)	
	1 cup skim milk
½ pound chicken breast, diced into 1-inch cubes	1 cup evaporated skim milk
	2 ounces fat-free cream cheese
6.2-ounce box Uncle Ben's	2 tablespoons cornstarch

1. Select the Sauté feature and add the margarine, onion, carrots, and mushrooms to the inner pot. Sauté for about 5 minutes until onions are translucent and soft. 2. Add the cubed chicken and seasoning packet from the Uncle Ben's box and stir to combine. 3. Add the rice and chicken broth. Select Manual, high pressure, then lock the lid and make sure the vent is set to sealing. Set the time for 5 minutes. 4. After the cooking time ends, allow it to stay on Keep Warm for 5 minutes and then quick release the pressure. 5. Remove the lid; change the setting to the Sauté function again. 6. Add the skim milk, evaporated milk, and cream cheese. Stir to melt. 7. In a small bowl, mix the cornstarch with a little bit of water to dissolve, then add to the soup to thicken.

Per Serving:
calories: 316 | fat: 7g | protein: 27g | carbs: 35g | sugars: 10g | fiber: 1g | sodium: 638mg

Broccoli Cheddar Soup

Prep time: 5 minutes | Cook time: 10 minutes | Serves 4

2 tablespoons butter	1 cup chopped broccoli
⅛ cup onion, diced	1 tablespoon cream cheese, softened
½ teaspoon garlic powder	
½ teaspoon salt	¼ cup heavy cream
¼ teaspoon pepper	1 cup shredded Cheddar cheese
2 cups chicken broth	

1. Press the Sauté button and add butter to Instant Pot. Add onion and sauté until translucent. Press the Cancel button and add garlic powder, salt, pepper, broth, and broccoli to pot. 2. Click lid closed. Press the Soup button and set time for 5 minutes. When timer beeps, stir in heavy cream, cream cheese, and Cheddar.

Per Serving:
calories: 250 | fat: 20g | protein: 9g | carbs: 4g | net carbs: 3g | fiber: 1g

Curried Chicken Soup

Prep time: 10 minutes | Cook time: 10 minutes | Serves 6

1 pound (454 g) boneless, skinless chicken thighs
1½ cups unsweetened coconut milk
½ onion, finely diced
3 or 4 garlic cloves, crushed
1 (2-inch) piece ginger, finely chopped

1 cup sliced mushrooms, such as cremini and shiitake
4 ounces (113 g) baby spinach
1 teaspoon salt
½ teaspoon ground turmeric
½ teaspoon cayenne
1 teaspoon garam masala
¼ cup chopped fresh cilantro

1. In the inner cooking pot of your Instant Pot, add the chicken, coconut milk, onion, garlic, ginger, mushrooms, spinach, salt, turmeric, cayenne, garam masala, and cilantro. 2. Lock the lid into place. Select Manual and adjust the pressure to High. Cook for 10 minutes. When the cooking is complete, let the pressure release naturally. Unlock the lid. 3. Use tongs to transfer the chicken to a bowl. Shred the chicken, then stir it back into the soup. 4. Eat and rejoice.
Per Serving:
calories: 378 | fat: 26g | protein: 26g | carbs: 6g | net carbs: 2g | fiber: 4g

Cream of Mushroom Soup

Prep time: 10 minutes | Cook time: 10 minutes | Serves 4

1 pound (454 g) sliced button mushrooms
3 tablespoons butter
2 tablespoons diced onion
2 cloves garlic, minced

2 cups chicken broth
½ teaspoon salt
¼ teaspoon pepper
½ cup heavy cream
¼ teaspoon xanthan gum

1. Press the Sauté button and then press the Adjust button to set heat to Less. Add mushrooms, butter, and onion to pot. Sauté for 5 to 8 minutes or until onions and mushrooms begin to brown. Add garlic and sauté until fragrant. Press the Cancel button. 2. Add broth, salt, and pepper. Click lid closed. Press the Manual button and adjust time for 3 minutes. When timer beeps, quick-release the pressure. Stir in heavy cream and xanthan gum. Allow a few minutes to thicken and serve warm.
Per Serving:
calories: 220 | fat: 19g | protein: 5g | carbs: 6g | net carbs: 5g | fiber: 1g

Green Garden Soup

Prep time: 20 minutes | Cook time: 29 minutes | Serves 5

1 tablespoon olive oil
1 garlic clove, diced
½ cup cauliflower florets
1 cup kale, chopped

2 tablespoons chives, chopped
1 teaspoon sea salt
6 cups beef broth

1. Heat the olive oil in the Instant Pot on Sauté mode for 2 minutes and add the garlic. Sauté for 2 minutes or until fragrant. 2. Add cauliflower, kale, chives, sea salt, and beef broth. 3. Close the lid.

Select Manual mode and set cooking time for 5 minutes on High Pressure. 4. When timer beeps, use a quick pressure release and open the lid. 5. Ladle the soup into the bowls. Serve warm.
Per Serving:
calories: 80 | fat: 4.5g | protein: 6.5g | carbs: 2.3g | net carbs: 1.8g | fiber: 0.5g

Spanish-Style Turkey Meatball Soup

Prep time: 10 minutes | Cook time: 15 minutes | Serves 6 to 8

1 slice hearty white sandwich bread, torn into quarters
¼ cup whole milk
1 ounce (28 g) Manchego cheese, grated (½ cup), plus extra for serving
5 tablespoons minced fresh parsley, divided
½ teaspoon table salt
1 pound (454 g) ground turkey
1 tablespoon extra-virgin olive

oil
1 onion, chopped
1 red bell pepper, stemmed, seeded, and cut into ¾-inch pieces
4 garlic cloves, minced
2 teaspoons smoked paprika
½ cup dry white wine
8 cups chicken broth
8 ounces (227 g) kale, stemmed and chopped

1. Using fork, mash bread and milk together into paste in large bowl. Stir in Manchego, 3 tablespoons parsley, and salt until combined. Add turkey and knead mixture with your hands until well combined. Pinch off and roll 2-teaspoon-size pieces of mixture into balls and arrange on large plate (you should have about 35 meatballs); set aside. 2. Using highest sauté function, heat oil in Instant Pot until shimmering. Add onion and bell pepper and cook until softened and lightly browned, 5 to 7 minutes. Stir in garlic and paprika and cook until fragrant, about 30 seconds. Stir in wine, scraping up any browned bits, and cook until almost completely evaporated, about 5 minutes. Stir in broth and kale, then gently submerge meatballs. 3. Lock lid in place and close pressure release valve. Select high pressure cook function and cook for 3 minutes. Turn off Instant Pot and quick-release pressure. Carefully remove lid, allowing steam to escape away from you. 4. Stir in remaining 2 tablespoons parsley and season with salt and pepper to taste. Serve, passing extra Manchego separately.
Per Serving:
calories: 170 | fat: 5g | protein: 21g | carbs: 9g | fiber: 2g | sodium: 750mg

Butternut Squash Soup

Prep time: 30 minutes | Cook time: 15 minutes | Serves 4

2 tablespoons margarine
1 large onion, chopped
2 cloves garlic, minced
1 teaspoon thyme
½ teaspoon sage
Salt and pepper to taste

2 large butternut squash, peeled, seeded, and cubed (about 4 pounds)
4 cups low-sodium chicken stock

1. In the inner pot of the Instant Pot, melt the margarine using Sauté function. 2. Add onion and garlic and cook until soft, 3 to 5 minutes. 3. Add thyme and sage and cook another minute. Season with salt and pepper. 4. Stir in butternut squash and add chicken stock. 5. Secure the lid and make sure vent is at sealing. Using Manual setting, cook

squash and seasonings 10 minutes, using high pressure. 6. When time is up, do a quick release of the pressure. 7. Puree the soup in a food processor or use immersion blender right in the inner pot. If soup is too thick, add more stock. Adjust salt and pepper as needed.

Per Serving:
calories: 279 | fat: 7g | protein: 6g | carbs: 56g | sugars: 10g | fiber: 9g | sodium: 144mg

Chapter 7: Vegetables and Sides

Asparagus and Mushroom Soup

Prep time: 10 minutes | Cook time: 7 minutes | Serves 4

2 tablespoons coconut oil
½ cup chopped shallots
2 cloves garlic, minced
1 pound (454 g) asparagus, washed, trimmed, and chopped
4 ounces (113 g) button mushrooms, sliced
4 cups vegetable broth
2 tablespoons balsamic vinegar
Himalayan salt, to taste
¼ teaspoon ground black pepper
¼ teaspoon paprika
¼ cup vegan sour cream

1. Press the Sauté button to heat up your Instant Pot. Heat the oil and cook the shallots and garlic for 2 to 3 minutes. 2. Add the remaining ingredients, except for sour cream, to the Instant Pot. 3. Secure the lid. Choose Manual mode and High Pressure; cook for 4 minutes. Once cooking is complete, use a quick pressure release; carefully remove the lid. 4. Spoon into four soup bowls; add a dollop of sour cream to each serving and serve immediately. Bon appétit!
Per Serving:
calories: 171 | fat: 12g | protein: 10g | carbs: 9g | net carbs: 6g | fiber: 3g

Indian Okra

Prep time: 8 minutes | Cook time: 7 minutes | Serves 6

1 pound (454 g) young okra
4 tablespoons ghee or avocado oil
½ teaspoon cumin seeds
¼ teaspoon ground turmeric
Pinch of ground cinnamon
½ medium onion, diced
2 cloves garlic, minced
2 teaspoons minced fresh
ginger
1 serrano chile, seeded and ribs removed, minced
1 small tomato, diced
½ teaspoon sea salt
¼ teaspoon cayenne pepper (optional)
1 cup vegetable stock or filtered water

1. Rinse and thoroughly dry the okra. Slice it on a diagonal into slices ½ to ¾ inch thick, discarding the stems. 2. Set the Instant Pot to Sauté. Once hot, add the ghee and heat until melted. Stir in the cumin seeds, turmeric, and cinnamon and cook until they are fragrant, about 1 minute. This may cause the cumin seeds to jump and pop. Add the onion and cook, stirring frequently, until soft and translucent, about 3 minutes. Add the garlic, ginger, and serrano chile and sauté for an additional minute. Press Cancel. 3. Stir in the tomato, okra, salt, cayenne (if using), and stock. Secure the lid and set the steam release valve to Sealing. Press the Manual button and set the cook time to 2 minutes. 4. When the Instant Pot beeps, carefully switch the steam release valve to Venting to quick-release the pressure. When fully released, open the lid. Stir gently and allow the okra to rest on the Keep Warm setting for a few minutes before serving.
Per Serving:
calories: 114 | fat: 9g | protein: 2g | carbs: 9g | net carbs: 6g | fiber: 3g

Falafel and Lettuce Salad

Prep time: 10 minutes | Cook time: 6 to 8 minutes | Serves 4

1 cup shredded cauliflower
⅓ cup coconut flour
1 teaspoon grated lemon zest
1 egg, beaten
2 tablespoons coconut oil
2 cups chopped lettuce
1 cucumber, chopped
1 tablespoon olive oil
1 teaspoon lemon juice
½ teaspoon cayenne pepper

1. In a bowl, combine the cauliflower, coconut flour, grated lemon zest and egg. Form the mixture into small balls. 2. Set the Instant Pot to the Sauté mode and melt the coconut oil. Place the balls in the pot in a single layer. Cook for 3 to 4 minutes per side, or until they are golden brown. 3. In a separate bowl, stir together the remaining ingredients. 4. Place the cooked balls on top and serve.
Per Serving:
calories: 175 | fat: 13.4g | protein: 4.7g | carbs: 11.1g | net carbs: 5.9g | fiber: 5.2g

Cauliflower Rice Curry

Prep time: 5 minutes | Cook time: 2 minutes | Serves 4

1 (9-ounce / 255-g) head cauliflower, chopped
½ teaspoon garlic powder
½ teaspoon freshly ground black pepper
½ teaspoon ground turmeric
½ teaspoon curry powder
½ teaspoon kosher salt
½ teaspoon fresh paprika
¼ small onion, thinly sliced

1. Pour 1 cup of filtered water into the inner pot of the Instant Pot, then insert the trivet. In a well-greased, Instant Pot-friendly dish, add the cauliflower. Sprinkle the garlic powder, black pepper, turmeric, curry powder, salt, paprika, and onion over top. 2. Place the dish onto the trivet, and cover loosely with aluminum foil. Close the lid, set the pressure release to Sealing and select Manual. Set the Instant Pot to 2 minutes on High Pressure, and let cook. 3. Once cooked, perform a quick release. 4. Open the Instant Pot, and remove the dish. Serve, and enjoy!
Per Serving:
calories: 24 | fat: 0g | protein: 2g | carbs: 5g | net carbs: 3g | fiber: 2g

Braised Whole Cauliflower with North African Spices

Prep time: 15 minutes | Cook time: 10 minutes | Serves 4

2 tablespoons extra-virgin olive oil
6 garlic cloves, minced
3 anchovy fillets, rinsed and minced (optional)
2 teaspoons ras el hanout
⅛ teaspoon red pepper flakes
1 (28-ounce / 794-g) can whole peeled tomatoes, drained with
juice reserved, chopped coarse
1 large head cauliflower (3 pounds / 1.4 kg)
½ cup pitted brine-cured green olives, chopped coarse
¼ cup golden raisins
¼ cup fresh cilantro leaves
¼ cup pine nuts, toasted

1. Using highest sauté function, cook oil, garlic, anchovies (if using), ras el hanout, and pepper flakes in Instant Pot until fragrant, about 3 minutes. Turn off Instant Pot, then stir in tomatoes and reserved juice. 2. Trim outer leaves of cauliflower and cut stem flush with bottom florets. Using paring knife, cut 4-inch-deep cross in stem. Nestle cauliflower stem side down into pot and spoon some of sauce over top. Lock lid in place and close pressure release valve. Select high pressure cook function and cook for 3 minutes. 3. Turn off Instant Pot and quick-release pressure. Carefully remove lid, allowing steam to escape away from you. Using tongs and slotted

spoon, transfer cauliflower to serving dish and tent with aluminum foil. Stir olives and raisins into sauce and cook, using highest sauté function, until sauce has thickened slightly, about 5 minutes. Season with salt and pepper to taste. Cut cauliflower into wedges and spoon some of sauce over top. Sprinkle with cilantro and pine nuts. Serve, passing remaining sauce separately.

Per Serving:

calories: 265 | fat: 16g | protein: 8g | carbs: 29g | fiber: 9g | sodium: 319mg

Perfect Sweet Potatoes

Prep time: 5 minutes | Cook time: 15 minutes | Serves 4 to 6

4–6 medium sweet potatoes   1 cup of water

1. Scrub skin of sweet potatoes with a brush until clean. Pour water into inner pot of the Instant Pot. Place steamer basket in the bottom of the inner pot. Place sweet potatoes on top of steamer basket. 2. Secure the lid and turn valve to seal. 3. Select the Manual mode and set to pressure cook on high for 15 minutes. 4. Allow pressure to release naturally (about 10 minutes). 5. Once the pressure valve lowers, remove lid and serve immediately.

Per Serving:

calories: 112 | fat: 0g | protein: 2g | carbs: 26g | sugars: 5g | fiber: 4g | sodium: 72mg

Asparagus with Copoundy Cheese

Prep time: 5 minutes | Cook time: 1 minute | Serves 4

1½ pounds (680 g) fresh asparagus
1 cup water
2 tablespoons olive oil
4 garlic cloves, minced

Sea salt, to taste
¼ teaspoon ground black pepper
½ cup shredded Copoundy cheese

1. Pour the water into the Instant Pot and put the steamer basket in the pot. 2. Place the asparagus in the steamer basket. Drizzle the asparagus with the olive oil and sprinkle with the garlic on top. Season with salt and black pepper. 3. Close and secure the lid. Select the Manual mode and set the cooking time for 1 minute at High Pressure. Once cooking is complete, do a quick pressure release. Carefully open the lid. 4. Transfer the asparagus to a platter and served topped with the shredded cheese.

Per Serving:

calories: 151 | fat: 11.3g | protein: 7.4g | carbs: 7.8g | net carbs: 4.1g | fiber: 3.7g

Steamed Tomato with Halloumi Cheese

Prep time: 5 minutes | Cook time: 3 minutes | Serves 4

8 tomatoes, sliced
1 cup water
½ cup crumbled Halloumi cheese
2 tablespoons extra-virgin olive

oil
2 tablespoons snipped fresh basil
2 garlic cloves, smashed

1. Pour the water into the Instant Pot and put the trivet in the pot. Place the tomatoes in the trivet. 2. Lock the lid. Select the Manual

mode and set the cooking time for 3 minutes on High Pressure. When the timer goes off, perform a quick pressure release. Carefully open the lid. 3. Toss the tomatoes with the remaining ingredients and serve.

Per Serving:

calories: 141 | fat: 10.8g | protein: 4.5g | carbs: 8.1g | net carbs: 5.9g | fiber: 2.2g

Broccoli and Mushroom Bake

Prep time: 10 minutes | Cook time: 3 minutes | Serves 4

½ cup sunflower seeds, soaked overnight
2 tablespoons sesame seeds
1 cup water
1 cup unsweetened almond milk
¼ teaspoon grated nutmeg
½ teaspoon sea salt
1 tablespoon nutritional yeast
2 tablespoons rice vinegar

1 pound (454 g) broccoli, broken into florets
½ cup chopped spring onions
10 ounces (283 g) white fresh mushrooms, sliced
Sea salt and white pepper, to taste
1 tablespoon cayenne pepper
¼ teaspoon dried dill
¼ teaspoon ground bay leaf

1. Add sunflower seeds, sesame seeds, water, milk, nutmeg, ½ teaspoon of sea salt, nutritional yeast, and vinegar to your blender. 2. Blend until smooth and uniform. 3. Spritz a casserole dish with a nonstick cooking spray. Add broccoli, spring onions and mushrooms. 4. Sprinkle with salt, white pepper, cayenne pepper, dill, and ground bay leaf. Pour the prepared vegan béchamel over your casserole. 5. Add 1 cup of water and a metal rack to your Instant Pot. Place the dish on the rack. 6. Secure the lid. Choose Manual mode and High Pressure; cook for 3 minutes. Once cooking is complete, use a quick pressure release; carefully remove the lid. 7. Allow the dish to stand for 5 to 10 minutes before slicing and serving. Bon appétit!

Per Serving:

calories: 130 | fat: 8g | protein: 8g | carbs: 9g | net carbs: 3g | fiber: 6g

Vinegary Broccoli with Cheese

Prep time: 5 minutes | Cook time: 5 minutes | Serves 4

1 pound (454 g) broccoli, cut into florets
1 cup water
2 garlic cloves, minced
1 cup crumbled Cottage cheese

2 tablespoons balsamic vinegar
1 teaspoon cumin seeds
1 teaspoon mustard seeds
Salt and pepper, to taste

1. Pour the water into the Instant Pot and put the steamer basket in the pot. Place the broccoli in the steamer basket. 2. Close and secure the lid. Select the Manual setting and set the cooking time for 5 minutes at High Pressure. Once the timer goes off, do a quick pressure release. Carefully open the lid. 3. Stir in the remaining ingredients. 4. Serve immediately.

Per Serving:

calories: 105 | fat: 3.0g | protein: 9.5g | carbs: 11.9g | net carbs: 8.7g | fiber: 3.2g

Beet and Watercress Salad with Orange and Dill

Prep time: 20 minutes | Cook time: 8 minutes | Serves 4

2 pounds (907 g) beets, scrubbed, trimmed, and cut into ¾-inch pieces
½ cup water
1 teaspoon caraway seeds
½ teaspoon table salt
1 cup plain Greek yogurt
1 small garlic clove, minced to paste
5 ounces (142 g) watercress, torn into bite-size pieces
1 tablespoon extra-virgin olive oil, divided, plus extra for drizzling
1 tablespoon white wine vinegar, divided
1 teaspoon grated orange zest plus 2 tablespoons juice
¼ cup hazelnuts, toasted, skinned, and chopped
¼ cup coarsely chopped fresh dill
Coarse sea salt

1. Combine beets, water, caraway seeds, and table salt in Instant Pot. Lock lid in place and close pressure release valve. Select high pressure cook function and cook for 8 minutes. Turn off Instant Pot and quick-release pressure. Carefully remove lid, allowing steam to escape away from you. 2. Using slotted spoon, transfer beets to plate; set aside to cool slightly. Combine yogurt, garlic, and 3 tablespoons beet cooking liquid in bowl; discard remaining cooking liquid. In large bowl toss watercress with 2 teaspoons oil and 1 teaspoon vinegar. Season with table salt and pepper to taste. 3. Spread yogurt mixture over surface of serving dish. Arrange watercress on top of yogurt mixture, leaving 1-inch border of yogurt mixture. Add beets to now-empty large bowl and toss with orange zest and juice, remaining 2 teaspoons vinegar, and remaining 1 teaspoon oil. Season with table salt and pepper to taste. Arrange beets on top of watercress mixture. Drizzle with extra oil and sprinkle with hazelnuts, dill, and sea salt. Serve.

Per Serving:
calories: 240 | fat: 15g | protein: 9g | carbs: 19g | fiber: 5g | sodium: 440mg

Green Beans with Potatoes and Basil

Prep time: 20 minutes | Cook time: 10 minutes | Serves 4

2 tablespoons extra-virgin olive oil, plus extra for drizzling
1 onion, chopped fine
2 tablespoons minced fresh oregano or 2 teaspoons dried
2 tablespoons tomato paste
4 garlic cloves, minced
1 (14½-ounce / 411-g) can whole peeled tomatoes, drained with juice reserved, chopped
1 cup water
1 teaspoon table salt
¼ teaspoon pepper
1½ pounds (680 g) green beans, trimmed and cut into 2-inch lengths
1 pound (454 g) Yukon Gold potatoes, peeled and cut into 1-inch pieces
3 tablespoons chopped fresh basil or parsley
2 tablespoons toasted pine nuts
Shaved Parmesan cheese

1. Using highest sauté function, heat oil in Instant Pot until shimmering. Add onion and cook until softened, about 5 minutes. Stir in oregano, tomato paste, and garlic and cook until fragrant, about 30 seconds. Stir in tomatoes and their juice, water, salt, and pepper, then stir in green beans and potatoes. Lock lid in place and close pressure

release valve. Select high pressure cook function and cook for 5 minutes. 2. Turn off Instant Pot and quick-release pressure. Carefully remove lid, allowing steam to escape away from you. Season with salt and pepper to taste. Sprinkle individual portions with basil, pine nuts, and Parmesan and drizzle with extra oil. Serve.

Per Serving:
calories: 280 | fat: 10g | protein: 7g | carbs: 42g | fiber: 8g | sodium: 880mg

Italian Wild Mushrooms

Prep time: 30 minutes | Cook time: 3 minutes | Serves 10

2 tablespoons canola oil
2 large onions, chopped
4 garlic cloves, minced
3 large red bell peppers, chopped
3 large green bell peppers, chopped
12-ounce package oyster mushrooms, cleaned and chopped
3 fresh bay leaves
10 fresh basil leaves, chopped
1 teaspoon salt
1½ teaspoons pepper
28-ounce can Italian plum tomatoes, crushed or chopped

1. Press Sauté on the Instant Pot and add in the oil. Once the oil is heated, add the onions, garlic, peppers, and mushroom to the oil. Sauté just until mushrooms begin to turn brown. 2. Add remaining ingredients. Stir well. 3. Secure the lid and make sure vent is set to sealing. Press Manual and set time for 3 minutes. 4. When cook time is up, release the pressure manually. Discard bay leaves.

Per Serving:
calories: 82 | fat: 3g | protein: 3g | carbs: 13g | sugars: 8g | fiber: 4g | sodium: 356mg

Lemon Garlic Asparagus

Prep time: 6 minutes | Cook time: 5 minutes | Serves 4

1 large bunch asparagus, woody ends cut off (medium-thick spears if possible)
1 cup water
2 tablespoons salted butter
2 large cloves garlic, minced
2 teaspoons fresh lemon juice (from ½ lemon)
¾ cup finely shredded Parmesan cheese (optional)
Salt, to taste

1. Cut the asparagus spears on a diagonal into 3 equal pieces, or trim the whole spears to fit your Instant Pot. 2. Pour the water into the Instant Pot. Place a metal steaming basket inside. Place the asparagus in the basket. Secure the lid and set the steam release valve to Sealing. Press the Manual button and set the cook time to 1 minute for tender (for softer, increase to 2 minutes; for crisp, decrease to 0). While it cooks, prepare a bowl with ice water. 3. When the Instant Pot beeps, carefully switch the steam release valve to Venting to quick-release the pressure. When fully released, open the lid and use tongs to transfer the asparagus to the ice bath. Let it sit for a minute, then drain and place the asparagus on a clean kitchen towel and pat dry. 4. Carefully remove the pot insert. Remove the steaming basket, drain the water, and wipe the pot insert dry. 5. Return the pot insert to the Instant Pot and press the Sauté button. Put the butter in the pot. When it has melted and starts to foam, add the garlic and sauté, stirring, for 1 minute. 6. Return the asparagus to the pot and stir well to coat it with the garlic-butter mixture. Add the lemon juice. Sauté until it reaches the desired doneness, about 1 minute more. 7. Transfer the asparagus to a serving bowl and stir in the Parmesan.

Taste the asparagus and add salt to taste. Serve warm.
Per Serving:
calories: 70 | fat: 11g | protein: 10g | carbs: 4g | net carbs: 3g | fiber: 1g

Thyme Cabbage

Prep time: 10 minutes | Cook time: 5 minutes | Serves 4

1 pound (454 g) white cabbage
2 tablespoons butter
1 teaspoon dried thyme
½ teaspoon salt
1 cup water

1. Cut the white cabbage on medium size petals and sprinkle with the butter, dried thyme and salt. Place the cabbage petals in the Instant Pot pan. 2. Pour the water and insert the trivet in the Instant Pot. Put the pan on the trivet. 3. Set the lid in place. Select the Manual mode and set the cooking time for 5 minutes on High Pressure. When the timer goes off, do a quick pressure release. Carefully open the lid. 4. Serve immediately.
Per Serving:
calories: 81 | fat: 6.0g | protein: 1.6g | carbs: 6.6g | net carbs: 3.8g | fiber: 2.8g

Almond Butter Zucchini Noodles

Prep time: 10 minutes | Cook time: 4 minutes | Serves 4

2 tablespoons coconut oil
1 yellow onion, chopped
2 zucchini, julienned
1 cup shredded Chinese cabbage
2 garlic cloves, minced
2 tablespoons almond butter
Sea salt and freshly ground black pepper, to taste
1 teaspoon cayenne pepper

1. Press the Sauté button to heat up your Instant Pot. Heat the coconut oil and sweat the onion for 2 minutes. 2. Add the other ingredients. 3. Secure the lid. Choose Manual mode and High Pressure; cook for 2 minutes. Once cooking is complete, use a quick pressure release; carefully remove the lid. Bon appétit!
Per Serving:
calories: 145 | fat: 15g | protein: 1g | carbs: 4g | net carbs: 2g | fiber: 2g

Parmesan Zoodles

Prep time: 5 minutes | Cook time: 5 minutes | Serves 2

1 large zucchini, trimmed and spiralized
1 tablespoon butter
1 garlic clove, diced
½ teaspoon chili flakes
3 ounces (85 g) Parmesan cheese, grated

1. Set the Instant Pot on the Sauté mode and melt the butter. Add the garlic and chili flakes to the pot. Sauté for 2 minutes, or until fragrant. 2. Stir in the zucchini spirals and sauté for 2 minutes, or until tender. 3. Add the grated Parmesan cheese to the pot and stir well. Continue to cook it for 1 minute, or until the cheese melts. 4. Transfer to a plate and serve immediately
Per Serving:
calories: 217 | fat: 15.3g | protein: 15.7g | carbs: 7.4g | net carbs: 5.7g | fiber: 1.7g

Wild Rice Salad with Cranberries and Almonds

Prep time: 10 minutes | Cook time: 25 minutes | Serves 18

For the rice
2 cups wild rice blend, rinsed
1 teaspoon kosher salt
2½ cups Vegetable Broth or Chicken Bone Broth
For the dressing
¼ cup extra-virgin olive oil
¼ cup white wine vinegar
1½ teaspoons grated orange zest
Juice of 1 medium orange (about ¼ cup)
1 teaspoon honey or pure maple syrup
For the salad
¾ cup unsweetened dried cranberries
½ cup sliced almonds, toasted
Freshly ground black pepper

Make the Rice 1. In the electric pressure cooker, combine the rice, salt, and broth. 2. Close and lock the lid. Set the valve to sealing. 3. Cook on high pressure for 25 minutes. 4. When the cooking is complete, hit Cancel and allow the pressure to release naturally for 15 minutes, then quick release any remaining pressure. 5. Once the pin drops, unlock and remove the lid. 6. Let the rice cool briefly, then fluff it with a fork. Make the Dressing 7. While the rice cooks, make the dressing: In a small jar with a screw-top lid, combine the olive oil, vinegar, zest, juice, and honey. (If you don't have a jar, whisk the ingredients together in a small bowl.) Shake to combine. Make the Salad 8. In a large bowl, combine the rice, cranberries, and almonds. 9. Add the dressing and season with pepper. 10. Serve warm or refrigerate.
Per Serving:
calories: 129 | fat: 4.25g | protein: 3.46g | carbs: 20.34g | sugars: 5.08g | fiber: 1.7g | sodium: 200mg

Cauliflower Curry

Prep time: 10 minutes | Cook time: 3 minutes | Serves 6

1 pound (454 g) cauliflower, chopped
3 ounces (85 g) scallions, chopped
1 cup coconut milk
¼ cup crushed tomatoes
1 tablespoon coconut oil
1 teaspoon garam masala
1 teaspoon ground turmeric

1. Add all the ingredients to the Instant Pot and stir to combine. 2. Lock the lid. Select the Manual mode and set the cooking time for 3 minutes at High Pressure. When the timer goes off, use a natural pressure release for 5 minutes, then release any remaining pressure. Carefully open the lid. 3. Stir the cooked dish well before serving.
Per Serving:
calories: 142 | fat: 12.2g | protein: 3.1g | carbs: 8.2g | net carbs: 4.7g | fiber: 3.5g

Spicy Cauliflower Head

Prep time: 5 minutes | Cook time: 7 minutes | Serves 4

13 ounces (369 g) cauliflower head
1 cup water
1 tablespoon coconut cream
1 tablespoon avocado oil
1 teaspoon ground paprika
1 teaspoon ground turmeric
½ teaspoon ground cumin

½ teaspoon salt

1. Pour the water in the Instant Pot and insert the trivet. 2. In the mixing bowl, stir together the coconut cream, avocado oil, paprika, turmeric, cumin and salt. 3. Carefully brush the cauliflower head with the coconut cream mixture. Sprinkle the remaining coconut cream mixture over the cauliflower. 4. Transfer the cauliflower head onto the trivet. 5. Lock the lid. Select the Manual mode and set the cooking time for 7 minutes at High Pressure. When the timer goes off, use a natural pressure release for 10 minutes, then release any remaining pressure. Carefully open the lid. 6. Serve immediately.
Per Serving:
calories: 71 | fat: 5g | protein: 2g | carbs: 5g | net carbs: 2g | fiber: 3g

Individual Asparagus and Goat Cheese Frittatas

Prep time: 15 minutes | Cook time: 15 minutes | Serves 4

1 tablespoon extra-virgin olive oil	2 ounces (57 g) goat cheese, crumbled (½ cup)
8 ounces (227 g) asparagus, trimmed and sliced ¼ inch thick	1 tablespoon minced fresh tarragon
1 red bell pepper, stemmed, seeded, and chopped	1 teaspoon grated lemon zest
2 shallots, minced	8 large eggs
	½ teaspoon table salt

1. Using highest sauté function, heat oil in Instant Pot until shimmering. Add asparagus, bell pepper, and shallots; cook until softened, about 5 minutes. Turn off Instant Pot and transfer vegetables to bowl. Stir in goat cheese, tarragon, and lemon zest. 2. Arrange trivet included with Instant Pot in base of now-empty insert and add 1 cup water. Spray four 6-ounce ramekins with vegetable oil spray. Beat eggs, ¼ cup water, and salt in large bowl until thoroughly combined. Divide vegetable mixture between prepared ramekins, then pour egg mixture over top (you may have some left over). Set ramekins on trivet. Lock lid in place and close pressure release valve. Select high pressure cook function and cook for 10 minutes. 3. Turn off Instant Pot and quick-release pressure. Carefully remove lid, allowing steam to escape away from you. Using tongs, transfer ramekins to wire rack and let cool slightly. Run paring knife around inside edge of ramekins to loosen frittatas, then invert onto individual serving plates. Serve.
Per Serving:
calories: 240 | fat: 16g | protein: 17g | carbs: 6g | fiber: 2g | sodium: 500mg

Potatoes with Parsley

Prep time: 10 minutes | Cook time: 5 minutes | Serves 4

3 tablespoons margarine, divided	½ teaspoon salt
2 pounds medium red potatoes (about 2 ounces each), halved lengthwise	½ cup low-sodium chicken broth
1 clove garlic, minced	2 tablespoons chopped fresh parsley

1. Place 1 tablespoon margarine in the inner pot of the Instant Pot and select Sauté. 2. After margarine is melted, add potatoes, garlic, and salt, stirring well. 3. Sauté 4 minutes, stirring frequently. 4. Add chicken broth and stir well. 5. Seal lid, make sure vent is on sealing, then select Manual for 5 minutes on high pressure. 6. When cooking time is up, manually release the pressure. 7. Strain potatoes, toss with remaining 2 tablespoons margarine and chopped parsley, and serve immediately.
Per Serving:
calories: 237 | fat: 9g | protein: 5g | carbs: 37g | sugars: 3g | fiber: 4g | sodium: 389mg

Garlicky Broccoli with Roasted Almonds

Prep time: 10 minutes | Cook time: 4 minutes | Serves 4 to 6

6 cups broccoli florets	medium lemon
1 cup water	½ teaspoon kosher salt
1½ tablespoons olive oil	Freshly ground black pepper, to taste
8 garlic cloves, thinly sliced	¼ cup chopped roasted almonds
2 shallots, thinly sliced	
½ teaspoon crushed red pepper flakes	¼ cup finely slivered fresh basil
Grated zest and juice of 1	

1. Pour the water into the Instant Pot. Place the broccoli florets in a steamer basket and lower into the pot. 2. Close and secure the lid. Select the Steam setting and set the cooking time for 2 minutes at Low Pressure. Once the timer goes off, use a quick pressure release. Carefully open the lid. 3. Transfer the broccoli to a large bowl filled with cold water and ice. Once cooled, drain the broccoli and pat dry. 4. Select the Sauté mode on the Instant Pot and heat the olive oil. Add the garlic to the pot and sauté for 30 seconds, tossing constantly. Add the shallots and pepper flakes to the pot and sauté for 1 minute. 5. Stir in the cooked broccoli, lemon juice, salt and black pepper. Toss the ingredients together and cook for 1 minute. 6. Transfer the broccoli to a serving platter and sprinkle with the chopped almonds, lemon zest and basil. Serve immediately.
Per Serving:
calories: 127 | fat: 8.2g | protein: 5.1g | carbs: 12.2g | net carbs: 10.6g | fiber: 1.6g

Vegetable Medley

Prep time: 20 minutes | Cook time: 2 minutes | Serves 8

2 medium parsnips	1 teaspoon salt
4 medium carrots	3 tablespoons sugar
1 turnip, about 4½ inches diameter	2 tablespoons canola or olive oil
1 cup water	½ teaspoon salt

1. Clean and peel vegetables. Cut in 1-inch pieces. 2. Place the cup of water and 1 teaspoon salt into the Instant Pot's inner pot with the vegetables. 3. Secure the lid and make sure vent is set to sealing. Press Manual and set for 2 minutes. 4. When cook time is up, release the pressure manually and press Cancel. Drain the water from the inner pot. 5. Press Sauté and stir in sugar, oil, and salt. Cook until sugar is dissolved. Serve.
Per Serving:
calories: 63 | fat: 2g | protein: 1g | carbs: 12g | sugars: 6g | fiber: 2g | sodium: 327mg

Masala Cauliflower

Prep time: 6 minutes | Cook time: 5 minutes | Serves 4

2 tablespoons olive oil	pepper, to taste
½ cup chopped scallions	1 tablespoon chopped fresh
2 cloves garlic, pressed	coriander
1 tablespoon garam masala	2 tomatoes, puréed
1 teaspoon curry powder	1 pound (454 g) cauliflower,
1 red chili pepper, minced	broken into florets
½ teaspoon ground cumin	½ cup water
Sea salt and ground black	½ cup almond yogurt

1. Press the Sauté button to heat up your Instant Pot. Now, heat the oil and sauté the scallions for 1 minute. 2. Add garlic and continue to cook an additional 30 seconds or until aromatic. 3. Add garam masala, curry powder, chili pepper, cumin, salt, black pepper, coriander, tomatoes, cauliflower, and water. 4. Secure the lid. Choose Manual mode and High Pressure; cook for 3 minutes. Once cooking is complete, use a quick pressure release; carefully remove the lid. 5. Pour in the almond yogurt, stir well and serve warm. Bon appétit!
Per Serving:
calories: 140 | fat: 8g | protein: 6g | carbs: 11g | net carbs: 7g | fiber: 4g

Mushroom Stroganoff with Vodka

Prep time: 8 minutes | Cook time: 8 minutes | Serves 4

2 tablespoons olive oil	mushrooms, chopped
½ teaspoon crushed caraway	1 celery stalk, chopped
seeds	1 ripe tomato, puréed
½ cup chopped onion	1 teaspoon mustard seeds
2 garlic cloves, smashed	Sea salt and freshly ground
¼ cup vodka	pepper, to taste
¾ pound (340 g) button	2 cups vegetable broth

1. Press the Sauté button to heat up your Instant Pot. Now, heat the oil and sauté caraway seeds until fragrant, about 40 seconds. 2. Then, add the onion and garlic, and continue sautéing for 1 to 2 minutes more, stirring frequently. 3. After that, add the remaining ingredients and stir to combine. 4. Secure the lid. Choose Manual mode and High Pressure; cook for 5 minutes. Once cooking is complete, use a quick pressure release; carefully remove the lid. 5. Ladle into individual bowls and serve warm. Bon appétit!
Per Serving:
calories: 128 | fat: 9g | protein: 6g | carbs: 7g | net carbs: 4g | fiber: 3g

Chinese-Style Pe-Tsai with Onion

Prep time: 5 minutes | Cook time: 8 minutes | Serves 4

2 tablespoons sesame oil	1 tablespoon coconut aminos
1 yellow onion, chopped	1 teaspoon finely minced garlic
1 pound (454 g) pe-tsai	½ teaspoon salt
cabbage, shredded	¼ teaspoon Szechuan pepper
¼ cup rice wine vinegar	

1. Set the Instant Pot on the Sauté mode and heat the sesame oil. Add the onion to the pot and sauté for 5 minutes, or until tender. Stir in the remaining ingredients. 2. Lock the lid. Select the Manual mode and set the cooking time for 3 minutes on High Pressure. When the timer goes off, perform a quick pressure release. Carefully open the lid. 3. Transfer the cabbage mixture to a bowl and serve immediately.
Per Serving:
calories: 96 | fat: 7.1g | protein: 2.2g | carbs: 6.8g | net carbs:4.9 g | fiber: 1.9g

Instant Pot Zucchini Sticks

Prep time: 5 minutes | Cook time: 8 minutes | Serves 2

2 zucchinis, trimmed and cut	½ teaspoon white pepper
into sticks	½ teaspoon salt
2 teaspoons olive oil	1 cup water

1. Place the zucchini sticks in the Instant Pot pan and sprinkle with the olive oil, white pepper and salt. 2. Pour the water and put the trivet in the pot. Place the pan on the trivet. 3. Lock the lid. Select the Manual setting and set the cooking time for 8 minutes at High Pressure. Once the timer goes off, use a quick pressure release. Carefully open the lid. 4. Remove the zucchinis from the pot and serve.
Per Serving:
calories: 74 | fat: 5g | protein: 2g | carbs: 5g | net carbs: 2g | fiber: 3g

Sauerkraut and Mushroom Casserole

Prep time: 6 minutes | Cook time: 15 minutes | Serves 6

1 tablespoon olive oil	mushrooms, sliced
1 celery rib, diced	1 teaspoon caraway seeds
½ cup chopped leeks	1 teaspoon brown mustard
2 pounds (907 g) canned	1 bay leaf
sauerkraut, drained	1 cup dry white wine
6 ounces (170 g) brown	

1. Press the Sauté button to heat up your Instant Pot. Now, heat the oil and cook celery and leeks until softened. 2. Add the sauerkraut and mushrooms and cook for 2 minutes more. 3. Add the remaining ingredients and stir to combine well. 4. Secure the lid. Choose Manual mode and High Pressure; cook for 10 minutes. Once cooking is complete, use a natural pressure release; carefully remove the lid. Bon appétit!
Per Serving:
calories: 90 | fat: 3g | protein: 2g | carbs: 8g | net carbs: 3g | fiber: 5g

Curried Cauliflower and Tomatoes

Prep time: 10 minutes | Cook time: 2 minutes | Serves 4 to 6

1 medium head cauliflower, cut	2 tablespoons red curry paste
into bite-size pieces	1 teaspoon salt
1 (14-ounce / 397-g) can sugar-	1 teaspoon garlic powder
free diced tomatoes, undrained	½ teaspoon onion powder
1 bell pepper, thinly sliced	½ teaspoon ground ginger
1 (14-ounce / 397-g) can full-	¼ teaspoon chili powder
fat coconut milk	Freshly ground black pepper,
½ to 1 cup water	to taste

1. Add all the ingredients, except for the black pepper, to the Instant Pot and stir to combine. 2. Lock the lid. Select the Manual setting and set the cooking time for 2 minutes at High Pressure. Once the

timer goes off, use a quick pressure release. Carefully open the lid. 3. Sprinkle the black pepper and stir well. Serve immediately.

Per Serving:

calories: 262 | fat: 22.0g | protein: 6.3g | carbs: 16.8g | net carbs: 10.8g | fiber: 6.0g

Best Brown Rice

Prep time: 5 minutes | Cook time: 22 minutes | Serves 6 to 12

2 cups brown rice   2½ cups water

1. Rinse brown rice in a fine-mesh strainer. 2. Add rice and water to the inner pot of the Instant Pot. 3. Secure the lid and make sure vent is on sealing. 4. Use Manual setting and select 22 minutes cooking time on high pressure. 5. When cooking time is done, let the pressure release naturally for 10 minutes, then press Cancel and manually release any remaining pressure.

Per Serving:

calorie: 114 | fat: 1g | protein: 2g | carbs: 23g | sugars: 0g | fiber: 1g | sodium: 3mg

Braised Radishes with Sugar Snap Peas and Dukkah

Prep time: 20 minutes | Cook time: 5 minutes | Serves 4

¼ cup extra-virgin olive oil, divided
1 shallot, sliced thin
3 garlic cloves, sliced thin
1½ pounds (680 g) radishes, 2 cups greens reserved, radishes trimmed and halved if small or quartered if large
½ cup water
½ teaspoon table salt
8 ounces (227 g) sugar snap

peas, strings removed, sliced thin on bias
8 ounces (227 g) cremini mushrooms, trimmed and sliced thin
2 teaspoons grated lemon zest plus 1 teaspoon juice
1 cup plain Greek yogurt
½ cup fresh cilantro leaves
3 tablespoons dukkah

1. Using highest sauté function, heat 2 tablespoons oil in Instant Pot until shimmering. Add shallot and cook until softened, about 2 minutes. Stir in garlic and cook until fragrant, about 30 seconds. Stir in radishes, water, and salt. Lock lid in place and close pressure release valve. Select high pressure cook function and cook for 1 minute. 2. Turn off Instant Pot and quick-release pressure. Carefully remove lid, allowing steam to escape away from you. Stir in snap peas, cover, and let sit until heated through, about 3 minutes. Add radish greens, mushrooms, lemon zest and juice, and remaining 2 tablespoons oil and gently toss to combine. Season with salt and pepper to taste. 3. Spread ¼ cup yogurt over bottom of 4 individual serving plates. Using slotted spoon, arrange vegetable mixture on top and sprinkle with cilantro and dukkah. Serve.

Per Serving:

calories: 310 | fat: 23g | protein: 10g | carbs: 17g | fiber: 5g | sodium: 320mg

Spaghetti Squash Noodles with Tomatoes

Prep time: 15 minutes | Cook time: 14 to 16 minutes | Serves 4

1 medium spaghetti squash
1 cup water
2 tablespoons olive oil
1 small yellow onion, diced
6 garlic cloves, minced
2 teaspoons crushed red pepper flakes
2 teaspoons dried oregano
1 cup sliced cherry tomatoes

1 teaspoon kosher salt
½ teaspoon freshly ground black pepper
1 (14.5-ounce / 411-g) can sugar-free crushed tomatoes
¼ cup capers
1 tablespoon caper brine
½ cup sliced olives

1. With a sharp knife, halve the spaghetti squash crosswise. Using a spoon, scoop out the seeds and sticky gunk in the middle of each half. 2. Pour the water into the Instant Pot and place the trivet in the pot with the handles facing up. Arrange the squash halves, cut side facing up, on the trivet. 3. Lock the lid. Select the Manual mode and set the cooking time for 7 minutes on High Pressure. When the timer goes off, use a quick pressure release. Carefully open the lid. 4. Remove the trivet and pour out the water that has collected in the squash cavities. Using the tines of a fork, separate the cooked strands into spaghetti-like pieces and set aside in a bowl. 5. Pour the water out of the pot. Select the Sauté mode and heat the oil. 6. Add the onion to the pot and sauté for 3 minutes. Add the garlic, pepper flakes and oregano to the pot and sauté for 1 minute. 7. Stir in the cherry tomatoes, salt and black pepper and cook for 2 minutes, or until the tomatoes are tender. 8. Pour in the crushed tomatoes, capers, caper brine and olives and bring the mixture to a boil. Continue to cook for 2 to 3 minutes to allow the flavors to meld. 9. Stir in the spaghetti squash noodles and cook for 1 to 2 minutes to warm everything through. 10. Transfer the dish to a serving platter and serve.

Per Serving:

calories: 132 | fat: 9.3g | protein: 2.9g | carbs: 12.7g | net carbs: 7.8g | fiber: 4.9g

Stir Fried Asparagus and Kale

Prep time: 5 minutes | Cook time: 3 minutes | Serves 4

8 ounces (227 g) asparagus, chopped
2 cups chopped kale
2 bell peppers, chopped

1 tablespoon avocado oil
1 teaspoon apple cider vinegar
½ teaspoon minced ginger
½ cup water

1. Pour the water into the Instant Pot. 2. In the Instant Pot pan, stir together the remaining ingredients. 3. Insert the trivet and place the pan on it. 4. Set the lid in place. Select the Manual mode and set the cooking time for 3 minutes on High Pressure. When the timer goes off, perform a quick pressure release. Carefully open the lid. 5. Serve immediately.

Per Serving:

calories: 56 | fat: 4g | protein: 2g | carbs: 4g | net carbs: 2g | fiber: 2g

Lemony Brussels Sprouts with Poppy Seeds

Prep time: 10 minutes | Cook time: 2 minutes | Serves 4

1 pound (454 g) Brussels sprouts
2 tablespoons avocado oil, divided
1 cup vegetable broth or chicken bone broth

1 tablespoon minced garlic
½ teaspoon kosher salt
Freshly ground black pepper, to taste
½ medium lemon
½ tablespoon poppy seeds

1. Trim the Brussels sprouts by cutting off the stem ends and removing any loose outer leaves. Cut each in half lengthwise (through the stem). 2. Set the electric pressure cooker to the Sauté/More setting. When the pot is hot, pour in 1 tablespoon of the avocado oil. 3. Add half of the Brussels sprouts to the pot, cut-side down, and let them brown for 3 to 5 minutes without disturbing. Transfer to a bowl and add the remaining tablespoon of avocado oil and the remaining Brussels sprouts to the pot. Hit Cancel and return all of the Brussels sprouts to the pot. 4. Add the broth, garlic, salt, and a few grinds of pepper. Stir to distribute the seasonings. 5. Close and lock the lid of the pressure cooker. Set the valve to sealing. 6. Cook on high pressure for 2 minutes. 7. While the Brussels sprouts are cooking, zest the lemon, then cut it into quarters. 8. When the cooking is complete, hit Cancel and quick release the pressure. 9. Once the pin drops, unlock and remove the lid. 10. Using a slotted spoon, transfer the Brussels sprouts to a serving bowl. Toss with the lemon zest, a squeeze of lemon juice, and the poppy seeds. Serve immediately.
Per Serving:
calories: 125 | fat: 8g | protein: 4g | carbs: 13g | sugars: 3g | fiber: 5g | sodium: 504mg

Vegetable Curry

Prep time: 25 minutes | Cook time: 3 minutes | Serves 10

16-ounce package baby carrots
3 medium potatoes, unpeeled, cubed
1 pound fresh or frozen green beans, cut in 2-inch pieces
1 medium green pepper, chopped
1 medium onion, chopped
1–2 cloves garlic, minced

15-ounce can garbanzo beans, drained
28-ounce can crushed tomatoes
3 teaspoons curry powder
1½ teaspoons chicken bouillon granules
1¾ cups boiling water
3 tablespoons minute tapioca

1. Combine carrots, potatoes, green beans, pepper, onion, garlic, garbanzo beans, crushed tomatoes, and curry powder in the Instant Pot. 2. Dissolve bouillon in boiling water, then stir in tapicoa. Pour over the contents of the Instant Pot and stir. 3. Secure the lid and make sure vent is set to sealing. Press Manual and set for 3 minutes. 4. When cook time is up, manually release the pressure.
Per Serving:
calories: 166 | fat: 1g | protein: 6g | carbs: 35g | sugars: 10g | fiber: 8g | sodium: 436mg

Sesame Zoodles with Scallions

Prep time: 10 minutes | Cook time: 3 minutes | Serves 6

2 large zucchinis, trimmed and spiralized
¼ cup chicken broth
1 tablespoon chopped scallions

1 tablespoon coconut aminos
1 teaspoon sesame oil
1 teaspoon sesame seeds
¼ teaspoon chili flakes

1. Set the Instant Pot on the Sauté mode. Add the zucchini spirals to the pot and pour in the chicken broth. Sauté for 3 minutes and transfer to the serving bowls. 2. Sprinkle with the scallions, coconut aminos, sesame oil, sesame seeds and chili flakes. Gently stir the zoodles. 3. Serve immediately.
Per Serving:
calories: 28 | fat: 2g | protein: 2g | carbs: 0g | net carbs: 0g | fiber: 0g

Parmesan Cauliflower Mash

Prep time: 7 minutes | Cook time: 5 minutes | Serves 4

1 head cauliflower, cored and cut into large florets
½ teaspoon kosher salt
½ teaspoon garlic pepper
2 tablespoons plain Greek yogurt

¾ cup freshly grated Parmesan cheese
1 tablespoon unsalted butter or ghee (optional)
Chopped fresh chives

1. Pour 1 cup of water into the electric pressure cooker and insert a steamer basket or wire rack. 2. Place the cauliflower in the basket. 3. Close and lock the lid of the pressure cooker. Set the valve to sealing. 4. Cook on high pressure for 5 minutes. 5. When the cooking is complete, hit Cancel and quick release the pressure. 6. Once the pin drops, unlock and remove the lid. 7. Remove the cauliflower from the pot and pour out the water. Return the cauliflower to the pot and add the salt, garlic pepper, yogurt, and cheese. Use an immersion blender or potato masher to purée or mash the cauliflower in the pot. 8. Spoon into a serving bowl, and garnish with butter (if using) and chives.
Per Serving:
calories: 141 | fat: 6g | protein: 12g | carbs: 12g | sugars: 9g | fiber: 4g | sodium: 592mg

Garlic Brussels Sprouts with Almonds

Prep time: 5 minutes | Cook time: 15 minutes | Serves 4

1 pound (454 g) Brussels sprouts
1 teaspoon sea salt
1 teaspoon garlic powder
1 tablespoon butter
1 small onion, diced
2 cloves garlic, crushed

3 strips uncured bacon, cut into ½-inch pieces
1 tablespoon extra-fine blanched almond slivers
½ cup chicken broth
2 tablespoons chopped scallions, for garnish

1. Wash the Brussels sprouts well and discard any old and rotten leaves. Trim the ends off and cut the Brussels sprouts in half vertically. Put any loose leaves with the rest of the Brussels sprouts, sea salt and garlic powder in a large mixing bowl and mix. 2. Turn on the Instant Pot by pressing Sauté and set to More. Insert the inner pot and wait until the panel says "Hot." 3. Add the butter, onion and garlic and sauté for 2 minutes or until the onion is soft. Add the

bacon and sauté for 3 minutes or until the bacon starts to shrivel. If there's too much bacon grease, you can spoon out some of it now. You want some bacon grease, but not so much that the Brussels sprouts won't brown. 4. Push the bacon to the side and add half of the Brussels sprouts to brown. Place the Brussels sprouts with their flat sides down on the inner pot. Do not to crowd them and don't mix until the sides turn brown. 5. When most of the sides are browned, take them out, place them in a bowl and set aside. Add the remaining Brussels sprouts to the inner pot to brown the sides. If needed, add more bacon grease back so as not to burn the Brussels sprouts. When they are browned, add the first batch of the browned Brussels sprouts back to the inner pot and add the almonds and the chicken broth and mix while scraping the bottom of the inner pot to loosen up all the bits and pieces. 6. Hit Cancel, then press the Manual button and set the timer for 8 minutes on High Pressure. 7. Close the lid tightly and move the steam release handle to Sealing. When the timer goes off, turn the steam release handle to the Venting position carefully for the steam to escape and the float valve to drop down. Press Cancel. Open the lid. 8. Garnish with the chopped scallions and serve immediately.

Per Serving:

calories: 128 | fat: 6g | protein: 7g | carbs: 15g | net carbs: 10g | fiber: 5g

Braised Cabbage with Ginger

Prep time: 10 minutes | Cook time: 8 minutes | Serves 6

1 tablespoon avocado oil
1 tablespoon butter or ghee (or more avocado oil)
½ medium onion, diced
1 medium bell pepper (any color), diced
1 teaspoon sea salt
½ teaspoon ground black pepper
1 clove garlic, minced
1-inch piece fresh ginger, grated
1 pound (454 g) green or red cabbage, cored and leaves chopped
½ cup bone broth or vegetable broth

1. Set the Instant Pot to Sauté and heat the oil and butter together. When the butter has stopped foaming, add the onion, bell pepper, salt, and black pepper. Sauté, stirring frequently, until just softened, about 3 minutes. Add the garlic and ginger and cook 1 minute longer. Add the cabbage and stir to combine. Pour in the broth. 2. Secure the lid and set the steam release valve to Sealing. Press the Manual button and set the cook time to 2 minutes. 3. When the Instant Pot beeps, carefully switch the steam release valve to Venting to quick-release the pressure. When fully released, open the lid. Stir the cabbage and transfer it to a serving dish. Serve warm.

Per Serving:

calories: 73 | fat: 5g | protein: 2g | carbs: 7g | net carbs: 5g | fiber: 2g

Chapter 8 Desserts

Flourless Chocolate Tortes

Prep time: 7 minutes | Cook time: 10 minutes | Serves 8

7 ounces (198 g) unsweetened baking chocolate, finely chopped
¾ cup plus 2 tablespoons unsalted butter (or butter-flavored coconut oil for dairy-free)
1¼ cups Swerve, or more to taste
5 large eggs
1 tablespoon coconut flour
2 teaspoons ground cinnamon
Seeds scraped from 1 vanilla bean (about 8 inches long), or 2 teaspoons vanilla extract
Pinch of fine sea salt

1. Grease 8 ramekins. Place the chocolate and butter in a pan over medium heat and stir until the chocolate is completely melted, about 3 minutes. 2. Remove the pan from the heat, then add the remaining ingredients and stir until smooth. Taste and adjust the sweetness to your liking. Pour the batter into the greased ramekins. 3. Place a trivet in the bottom of the Instant Pot and pour in 1 cup of cold water. Place four of the ramekins on the trivet. 4. Lock the lid. Select the Manual mode and set the cooking time for 7 minutes at High Pressure. 5. When the timer beeps, use a quick pressure release. Carefully remove the lid. 6. Use tongs to remove the ramekins. Repeat with the remaining ramekins. 7. Serve the tortes warm or chilled.

Per Serving:
calories: 328 | fat: 27.5g | protein: 8.4g | carbs: 11.7g | net carbs: 7.2g | fiber: 4.5g

Greek Yogurt Strawberry Pops

Prep time: 5 minutes | Cook time: 0 minutes | Serves 6

2 ripe bananas, peeled, cut into ½-inch pieces, and frozen
½ cup plain 2 percent Greek yogurt
1 cup chopped fresh strawberries

1. In a food processor, combine the bananas and yogurt and process at high speed for 2 minutes, until mostly smooth (it's okay if a few small chunks remain). Scrape down the sides of the bowl, add the strawberries, and process for 1 minute, until smooth. 2. Divide the mixture evenly among six ice-pop molds. Tap each mold on a countertop a few times to get rid of any air pockets, then place an ice-pop stick into each mold and transfer the molds to the freezer. Freeze for at least 4 hours, or until frozen solid. 3. To unmold each ice pop, run it under cold running water for 5 seconds, taking care not to get water inside the mold, then remove the ice pop from the mold. Eat the ice pops right away or store in a ziplock plastic freezer bag in the freezer for up to 2 months.

Per Serving:
calories: 57 | fat: 1g | protein: 3g | carbs: 12g | sugars: 6g | fiber: 2g | sodium: 8mg

Tapioca Berry Parfaits

Prep time: 10 minutes | Cook time: 6 minutes | Serves 4

2 cups unsweetened almond milk
½ cup small pearl tapioca, rinsed and still wet
1 teaspoon almond extract
1 tablespoon pure maple syrup
2 cups berries
¼ cup slivered almonds

1. Pour the almond milk into the electric pressure cooker. Stir in the tapioca and almond extract. 2. Close and lock the lid of the pressure cooker. Set the valve to sealing. 3. Cook on High pressure for 6 minutes. 4. When the cooking is complete, hit Cancel. Allow the pressure to release naturally for 10 minutes, then quick release any remaining pressure. 5. Once the pin drops, unlock and remove the lid. Remove the pot to a cooling rack. 6. Stir in the maple syrup and let the mixture cool for about an hour. 7. In small glasses, create several layers of tapioca, berries, and almonds. Refrigerate for 1 hour. 8. Serve chilled.

Per Serving:
(½ cup): calories: 174 | fat: 5g | protein: 3g | carbs: 32g | sugars: 11g | fiber: 3g | sodium: 77mg

Daikon and Almond Cake

Prep time: 10 minutes | Cook time: 45 minutes | Serves 12

5 eggs, beaten
½ cup heavy cream
1 cup almond flour
1 daikon, diced
1 teaspoon ground cinnamon
2 tablespoon erythritol
1 tablespoon butter, melted
1 cup water

1. In the mixing bowl, mix up eggs, heavy cream, almond flour, ground cinnamon, and erythritol. 2. When the mixture is smooth, add daikon and stir it carefully with the help of the spatula. 3. Pour the mixture in the cake pan. 4. Then pour water and insert the trivet in the instant pot. 5. Place the cake in the instant pot. 6. Set the lid in place. Select the Manual mode and set the cooking time for 45 minutes on High Pressure. When the timer goes off, do a quick pressure release. Carefully open the lid. 7. Serve immediately.

Per Serving:
calories: 66 | fat: 5.7g | protein: 3.1g | carbs: 3.5g | net carbs: 3.0g | fiber: 0.5g

Pumpkin Pie Spice Pots De Crème

Prep time: 5 minutes | Cook time: 7 minutes | Serves 4

2 cups heavy cream (or full-fat coconut milk for dairy-free)
4 large egg yolks
¼ cup Swerve, or more to taste
2 teaspoons pumpkin pie spice
1 teaspoon vanilla extract
Pinch of fine sea salt
1 cup cold water

1. Heat the cream in a pan over medium-high heat until hot, about 2 minutes. 2. Place the remaining ingredients except the water in a medium bowl and stir until smooth. 3. Slowly pour in the hot cream while stirring. Taste and adjust the sweetness to your liking. Scoop the mixture into four ramekins with a spatula. Cover the ramekins with aluminum foil. 4. Place a trivet in the Instant Pot and pour in the water. Place the ramekins on the trivet. 5. Lock the lid. Select the Manual mode and set the cooking time for 5 minutes at High Pressure. 6. When the timer beeps, use a quick pressure release. Carefully remove the lid. 7. Remove the foil and set the foil aside. Let the pots de crème cool for 15 minutes. Cover the ramekins with the foil again and place in the refrigerator to chill completely, about 2 hours. 8. Serve.

Per Serving:
calories: 289 | fat: 27.1g | protein: 7.6g | carbs: 4.0g | net carbs: 3.9g | fiber: 0.1g

Lush Chocolate Cake

Prep time: 10 minutes | Cook time: 35 minutes | Serves 8

For Cake:
2 cups almond flour
⅓ cup unsweetened cocoa powder
1½ teaspoons baking powder
1 cup granulated erythritol
Pinch of salt
4 eggs
1 teaspoon vanilla extract
½ cup butter, melted and cooled
6 tablespoons strong coffee,
cooled
½ cup water
For Frosting:
4 ounces (113 g) cream cheese, softened
½ cup butter, softened
¼ teaspoon vanilla extract
2½ tablespoons powdered erythritol
2 tablespoons unsweetened cocoa powder

1. To make the cake: In a large bowl, whisk together the almond flour, cocoa powder, baking powder, granulated erythritol, and salt. Whisk well to remove any lumps. 2. Add the eggs and vanilla and mix with a hand mixer until combined. 3. With the mixer still on low speed, slowly add the melted butter and mix until well combined. 4. Add the coffee and mix on low speed until the batter is thoroughly combined. Scrape the sides and bottom of the bowl to make sure everything is well mixed. 5. Spray the cake pan with cooking spray. Pour the batter into the pan. Cover tightly with aluminum foil. 6. Add the water to the pot. Place the cake pan on the trivet and carefully lower then pan into the pot. 7. Close the lid. Select Manual mode and set cooking time for 35 minutes on High Pressure. 8. When timer beeps, use a quick pressure release and open the lid. 9. Carefully remove the cake pan from the pot and place on a wire rack to cool. Flip the cake onto a plate once it is cool enough to touch. Cool completely before frosting. 10. To make the frosting: In a medium bowl, use the mixer to whip the cream cheese, butter, and vanilla until light and fluffy, 1 to 2 minutes. With the mixer running, slowly add the powdered erythritol and cocoa powder. Mix until everything is well combined. 11. Once the cake is completely cooled, spread the frosting on the top and down the sides.

Per Serving:
calories: 475 | fat: 44.2g | protein: 11.0g | carbs: 8.6g | net carbs: 4.2g | fiber: 4.4g

Espresso Cheesecake with Raspberries

Prep time: 5 minutes | Cook time: 35 minutes | Serves 8

1 cup blanched almond flour
½ cup plus 2 tablespoons Swerve
3 tablespoons espresso powder, divided
2 tablespoons butter
1 egg
½ cup full-fat heavy cream
16 ounces (454 g) cream cheese
1 cup water
6 ounces (170 g) dark chocolate (at least 80% cacao)
8 ounces (227 g) full-fat heavy whipping cream
2 cups raspberries

1. In a small mixing bowl, combine the almond flour, 2 tablespoons of Swerve, 1 tablespoon of espresso powder and the butter. 2. Line the bottom of a springform pan with parchment paper. Press the almond flour dough flat on the bottom and about 1 inch on the sides. Set aside. 3. In a food processor, mix the egg, heavy cream, cream cheese, remaining Swerve and remaining espresso powder until smooth. 4. Pour the cream cheese mixture into the springform pan. Loosely cover with aluminum foil. 5. Put the water in the Instant Pot and place the trivet inside. 6. Close the lid. Select Manual button and set the timer for 35 minutes on High pressure. 7. When timer beeps, use a natural pressure release for 15 minutes, then release any remaining pressure. Open the lid. 8. Remove the springform pan and place it on a cooling rack for 2 to 3 hours or until it reaches room temperature. Refrigerate overnight. 9. Melt the chocolate and heavy whipping cream in the double boiler. Cool for 15 minutes and drizzle on top of the cheesecake, allowing the chocolate to drip down the sides. 10. Add the raspberries on top of the cheesecake before serving.

Per Serving:
calories: 585 | fat: 53.8g | protein: 12.2g | carbs: 14.9g | net carbs: 10.8g | fiber: 4.1g

Traditional Kentucky Butter Cake

Prep time: 5 minutes | Cook time: 35 minutes | Serves 4

2 cups almond flour
¾ cup granulated erythritol
1½ teaspoons baking powder
4 eggs
1 tablespoon vanilla extract
½ cup butter, melted
Cooking spray
½ cup water

1. In a medium bowl, whisk together the almond flour, erythritol, and baking powder. Whisk well to remove any lumps. 2. Add the eggs and vanilla and whisk until combined. 3. Add the butter and whisk until the batter is mostly smooth and well combined. 4. Grease the pan with cooking spray and pour in the batter. Cover tightly with aluminum foil. 5. Add the water to the pot. Place the Bundt pan on the trivet and carefully lower it into the pot using. 6. Set the lid in place. Select the Manual mode and set the cooking time for 35 minutes on High Pressure. When the timer goes off, do a quick pressure release. Carefully open the lid. 7. Remove the pan from the pot. Let the cake cool in the pan before flipping out onto a plate.

Per Serving:
calories: 179 | fat: 15.9g | protein: 2.1g | carbs: 2.0g | net carbs: 2.0g | fiber: 0g

Chai Pear-Fig Compote

Prep time: 20 minutes | Cook time: 3 minutes | Serves 4

1 vanilla chai tea bag
1 (3-inch) cinnamon stick
1 strip lemon peel (about 2-by-½ inches)
1½ pounds pears, peeled and chopped (about 3 cups)
½ cup chopped dried figs
2 tablespoons raisins

1. Pour 1 cup of water into the electric pressure cooker and hit Sauté/More. When the water comes to a boil, add the tea bag and cinnamon stick. Hit Cancel. Let the tea steep for 5 minutes, then remove and discard the tea bag. 2. Add the lemon peel, pears, figs, and raisins to the pot. 3. Close and lock the lid of the pressure cooker. Set the valve to sealing. 4. Cook on high pressure for 3 minutes. 5. When the cooking is complete, hit Cancel and quick release the pressure. 6. Once the pin drops, unlock and remove the lid. 7. Remove the lemon peel and cinnamon stick. Serve warm or cool to room temperature and refrigerate.

Per Serving:
calories: 167 | fat: 1g | protein: 2g | carbs: 44g | sugars: 29g | fiber: 9g | sodium: 4mg

Egg Custard Tarts

Prep time: 10 minutes | Cook time: 20 minutes | Serves 2

¼ cup almond flour	1 tablespoon erythritol
1 tablespoon coconut oil	1 teaspoon vanilla extract
2 egg yolks	1 cup water, for cooking
¼ cup coconut milk	

1. Make the dough: Mix up almond flour and coconut oil. 2. Then place the dough into 2 mini tart molds and flatten well in the shape of cups. 3. Pour water in the instant pot. Insert the steamer rack. 4. Place the tart mold in the instant pot. Close and seal the lid. 5. Cook them for 3 minutes on Manual mode (High Pressure). Make a quick pressure release. 6. Then whisk together vanilla extract, erythritol, coconut milk, and egg yolks. 7. Pour the liquid in the tart molds and close the lid. 8. Cook the dessert for 7 minutes on Manual mode (High Pressure). 9. Then allow the natural pressure release for 10 minutes more.

Per Serving:

calories: 208 | fat: 20g | protein: 4g | carbs: 3g | net carbs: 2g | fiber: 1g

Vanilla Poppy Seed Cake

Prep time: 10 minutes | Cook time: 25 minutes | Serves 6

1 cup almond flour	¼ cup heavy cream
2 eggs	⅛ cup sour cream
½ cup erythritol	½ teaspoon baking powder
2 teaspoons vanilla extract	1 cup water
1 teaspoon lemon extract	¼ cup powdered erythritol, for garnish
1 tablespoon poppy seeds	
4 tablespoons melted butter	

1. In large bowl, mix almond flour, eggs, erythritol, vanilla, lemon, and poppy seeds. 2. Add butter, heavy cream, sour cream, and baking powder. 3. Pour into 7-inch round cake pan. Cover with foil. 4. Pour water into Instant Pot and place steam rack in bottom. Place baking pan on steam rack and click lid closed. Press the Cake button and press the Adjust button to set heat to Less. Set time for 25 minutes. 5. When timer beeps, allow a 15-minute natural release, then quick-release the remaining pressure. Let cool completely. Sprinkle with powdered erythritol for serving.

Per Serving:

calories: 221 | fat: 21g | protein: 3g | carbs: 5g | net carbs: 3g | fiber: 2g

Fudgy Walnut Brownies

Prep time: 10 minutes | Cook time: 1 hour | Serves 12

¾ cup walnut halves and pieces	1 cup Lakanto Monkfruit Sweetener Golden
½ cup unsalted butter, melted and cooled	¼ teaspoon fine sea salt
4 large eggs	¾ cup almond flour
1½ teaspoons instant coffee crystals	¾ cup natural cocoa powder
1½ teaspoons vanilla extract	¾ cup stevia-sweetened chocolate chips

1. In a dry small skillet over medium heat, toast the walnuts, stirring often, for about 5 minutes, until golden. Transfer the walnuts to a bowl to cool. 2. Pour 1 cup water into the Instant Pot. Line the base of a 7 by 3-inch round cake pan with a circle of parchment paper. Butter the sides of the pan and the parchment or coat with nonstick cooking spray. 3. Pour the butter into a medium bowl. One at a time, whisk in the eggs, then whisk in the coffee crystals, vanilla, sweetener, and salt. Finally, whisk in the flour and cocoa powder just until combined. Using a rubber spatula, fold in the chocolate chips and walnuts. 4. Transfer the batter to the prepared pan and, using the spatula, spread it in an even layer. Cover the pan tightly with aluminum foil. Place the pan on a long-handled silicone steam rack, then, holding the handles of the steam rack, lower it into the Instant Pot. 5. Secure the lid and set the Pressure Release to Sealing. Select the Cake, Pressure Cook, or Manual setting and set the cooking time for 45 minutes at high pressure. (The pot will take about 10 minutes to come up to pressure before the cooking program begins.) 6. When the cooking program ends, let the pressure release naturally for 10 minutes, then move the Pressure Release to Venting to release any remaining steam. Open the pot and, wearing heat-resistant mitts, grasp the handles of the steam rack and lift it out of the pot. Uncover the pan, taking care not to get burned by the steam or to drip condensation onto the brownies. Let the brownies cool in the pan on a cooling rack for about 2 hours, to room temperature. 7. Run a butter knife around the edge of the pan to make sure the brownies are not sticking to the pan sides. Invert the brownies onto the rack, lift off the pan, and peel off the parchment paper. Invert the brownies onto a serving plate and cut into twelve wedges. The brownies will keep, stored in an airtight container in the refrigerator for up to 5 days, or in the freezer for up to 4 months.

Per Serving:

calories: 199 | fat: 19g | protein: 5g | carbs: 26g | sugars: 10g | fiber: 20g | sodium: 56mg

Vanilla Crème Brûlée

Prep time: 7 minutes | Cook time: 9 minutes | Serves 4

1 cup heavy cream (or full-fat coconut milk for dairy-free)	bean (about 8 inches long), or 1 teaspoon vanilla extract
2 large egg yolks	1 cup cold water
2 tablespoons Swerve, or more to taste	4 teaspoons Swerve, for topping
Seeds scraped from ½ vanilla	

1. Heat the cream in a pan over medium-high heat until hot, about 2 minutes. 2. Place the egg yolks, Swerve, and vanilla seeds in a blender and blend until smooth. 3. While the blender is running, slowly pour in the hot cream. Taste and adjust the sweetness to your liking. 4. Scoop the mixture into four ramekins with a spatula. Cover the ramekins with aluminum foil. 5. Add the water to the Instant Pot and insert a trivet. Place the ramekins on the trivet. 6. Lock the lid. Select the Manual mode and set the cooking time for 7 minutes at High Pressure. 7. When the timer beeps, perform a quick pressure release. Carefully remove the lid. 8. Keep the ramekins covered with the foil and place in the refrigerator for about 2 hours until completely chilled. 9. Sprinkle 1 teaspoon of Swerve on top of each crème brûlée. Use the oven broiler to melt the sweetener. 10. Allow the topping to cool in the fridge for 5 minutes before serving.

Per Serving:

calories: 138 | fat: 13.4g | protein: 2.0g | carbs: 2.3g | net carbs: 2.3g | fiber: 0g

Cardamom Rolls with Cream Cheese

Prep time: 20 minutes | Cook time: 18 minutes | Serves 5

½ cup coconut flour
1 tablespoon ground cardamom
2 tablespoon Swerve
1 egg, whisked

¼ cup almond milk
1 tablespoon butter, softened
1 tablespoon cream cheese
⅓ cup water

1. Combine together coconut flour, almond milk, and softened butter. 2. Knead the smooth dough. 3. Roll up the dough with the help of the rolling pin. 4. Then combine together Swerve and ground cardamom. 5. Sprinkle the surface of the dough with the ground cardamom mixture. 6. Roll the dough into one big roll and cut them into servings. 7. Place the rolls into the instant pot round mold. 8. Pour water in the instant pot (⅓ cup) and insert the mold inside. 9. Set Manual mode (High Pressure) for 18 minutes. 10. Then use the natural pressure release method for 15 minutes. 11. Chill the rolls to the room temperature and spread with cream cheese.
Per Serving:
calories: 128 | fat: 6g | protein: 5g | carbs: 12g | net carbs: 8g | fiber: 4g

Apple Crunch

Prep time: 13 minutes | Cook time: 2 minutes | Serves 4

3 apples, peeled, cored, and sliced (about 1½ pounds)
1 teaspoon pure maple syrup
1 teaspoon apple pie spice or

ground cinnamon
¼ cup unsweetened apple juice, apple cider, or water
¼ cup low-sugar granola

1. In the electric pressure cooker, combine the apples, maple syrup, apple pie spice, and apple juice. 2. Close and lock the lid of the pressure cooker. Set the valve to sealing. 3. Cook on high pressure for 2 minutes. 4. When the cooking is complete, hit Cancel and quick release the pressure. 5. Once the pin drops, unlock and remove the lid. 6. Spoon the apples into 4 serving bowls and sprinkle each with 1 tablespoon of granola.
Per Serving:
calories: 103 | fat: 1g | protein: 1g | carbs: 26g | sugars: 18g | fiber: 4g | sodium: 13mg

Almond Butter Keto Fat Bombs

Prep time: 3 minutes | Cook time: 3 minutes | Serves 6

¼ cup coconut oil
¼ cup no-sugar-added almond butter

2 tablespoons cacao powder
¼ cup powdered erythritol

1. Press the Sauté button and add coconut oil to Instant Pot. Let coconut oil melt completely and press the Cancel button. Stir in remaining ingredients. Mixture will be liquid. 2. Pour into 6 silicone molds and place into freezer for 30 minutes until set. Store in fridge.
Per Serving:
calories: 142 | fat: 14g | protein: 3g | carbs: 9g | net carbs: 7g | fiber: 2g

Spiced Pear Applesauce

Prep time: 15 minutes | Cook time: 5 minutes | Makes: 3½ cups

1 pound pears, peeled, cored, and sliced
2 teaspoons apple pie spice or

cinnamon
Pinch kosher salt
Juice of ½ small lemon

1. In the electric pressure cooker, combine the apples, pears, apple pie spice, salt, lemon juice, and ¼ cup of water. 2. Close and lock the lid of the pressure cooker. Set the valve to sealing. 3. Cook on high pressure for 5 minutes. 4. When the cooking is complete, hit Cancel and let the pressure release naturally. 5. Once the pin drops, unlock and remove the lid. 6. Mash the apples and pears with a potato masher to the consistency you like. 7. Serve warm, or cool to room temperature and refrigerate.
Per Serving:
(½ cup): calories: 108 | fat: 1g | protein: 1g | carbs: 29g | sugars: 20g | fiber: 6g | sodium: 15mg

Crustless Key Lime Cheesecake

Prep time: 15 minutes | Cook time: 35 minutes | Serves 8

Nonstick cooking spray
16 ounces light cream cheese (Neufchâtel), softened
⅔ cup granulated erythritol sweetener
¼ cup unsweetened Key lime juice (I like Nellie & Joe's

Famous Key West Lime Juice)
½ teaspoon vanilla extract
¼ cup plain Greek yogurt
1 teaspoon grated lime zest
2 large eggs
Whipped cream, for garnish (optional)

1. Spray a 7-inch springform pan with nonstick cooking spray. Line the bottom and partway up the sides of the pan with foil. 2. Put the cream cheese in a large bowl. Use an electric mixer to whip the cream cheese until smooth, about 2 minutes. Add the erythritol, lime juice, vanilla, yogurt, and zest, and blend until smooth. Stop the mixer and scrape down the sides of the bowl with a rubber spatula. With the mixer on low speed, add the eggs, one at a time, blending until just mixed. (Don't overbeat the eggs.) 3. Pour the mixture into the prepared pan. Drape a paper towel over the top of the pan, not touching the cream cheese mixture, and tightly wrap the top of the pan in foil. (Your goal here is to keep out as much moisture as possible.) 4. Pour 1 cup of water into the electric pressure cooker. 5. Place the foil-covered pan onto the wire rack and carefully lower it into the pot. 6. Close and lock the lid of the pressure cooker. Set the valve to sealing. 7. Cook on high pressure for 35 minutes. 8. When the cooking is complete, hit Cancel. Allow the pressure to release naturally for 20 minutes, then quick release any remaining pressure. 9. Once the pin drops, unlock and remove the lid. 10. Using the handles of the wire rack, carefully transfer the pan to a cooling rack. Cool to room temperature, then refrigerate for at least 3 hours. 11. When ready to serve, run a thin rubber spatula around the rim of the cheesecake to loosen it, then remove the ring. 12. Slice into wedges and serve with whipped cream (if using).
Per Serving:
calories: 127 | fat: 2g | protein: 11g | carbs: 17g | sugars: 14g | fiber: 0g | sodium: 423mg

Chocolate Chip Brownies

Prep time: 10 minutes | Cook time: 33 minutes | Serves 8

1½ cups almond flour
⅓ cup unsweetened cocoa powder
¾ cup granulated erythritol
1 teaspoon baking powder
2 eggs
1 tablespoon vanilla extract
5 tablespoons butter, melted
¼ cup sugar-free chocolate chips
½ cup water

1. In a large bowl, add the almond flour, cocoa powder, erythritol, and baking powder. Use a hand mixer on low speed to combine and smooth out any lumps. 2. Add the eggs and vanilla and mix until well combined. 3. Add the butter and mix on low speed until well combined. Scrape the bottom and sides of the bowl and mix again if needed. Fold in the chocolate chips. 4. Grease a baking dish with cooking spray. Pour the batter into the dish and smooth with a spatula. Cover tightly with aluminum foil. 5. Pour the water into the pot. Place the trivet in the pot and carefully lower the baking dish onto the trivet. 6. Close the lid. Select Manual mode and set cooking time for 33 minutes on High Pressure. 7. When timer beeps, use a quick pressure release and open the lid. 8. Use the handles to carefully remove the trivet from the pot. Remove the foil from the dish. 9. Let the brownies cool for 10 minutes before turning out onto a plate.

Per Serving:
calories: 235 | fat: 20.2g | protein: 7.0g | carbs: 6.7g | net carbs: 2.7g | fiber: 4.0g

Pumpkin Walnut Cheesecake

Prep time: 15 minutes | Cook time: 50 minutes | Serves 6

2 cups walnuts
3 tablespoons melted butter
1 teaspoon cinnamon
16 ounces (454 g) cream cheese, softened
1 cup powdered erythritol
⅓ cup heavy cream
⅔ cup pumpkin purée
2 teaspoons pumpkin spice
1 teaspoon vanilla extract
2 eggs
1 cup water

1. Preheat oven to 350ºF (180ºC). Add walnuts, butter, and cinnamon to food processor. Pulse until ball forms. Scrape down sides as necessary. Dough should hold together in ball. 2. Press into greased 7-inch springform pan. Bake for 10 minutes or until it begins to brown. Remove and set aside. While crust is baking, make cheesecake filling. 3. In large bowl, stir cream cheese until completely smooth. Using rubber spatula, mix in erythritol, heavy cream, pumpkin purée, pumpkin spice, and vanilla. 4. In small bowl, whisk eggs. Slowly add them into large bowl, folding gently until just combined. 5. Pour mixture into crust and cover with foil. Pour water into Instant Pot and place steam rack on bottom. Place pan onto steam rack and click lid closed. Press the Cake button and press the Adjust button to set heat to More. Set timer for 40 minutes. 6. When timer beeps, allow a full natural release. When pressure indicator drops, carefully remove pan and place on counter. Remove foil. Let cool for additional hour and then refrigerate. Serve chilled.

Per Serving:
calories: 578 | fat: 54g | protein: 12g | carbs: 11g | net carbs: 8g | fiber: 3g

Coconut Almond Cream Cake

Prep time: 10 minutes | Cook time: 40 minutes | Serves 8

Nonstick cooking spray
1 cup almond flour
½ cup unsweetened shredded coconut
⅓ cup Swerve
1 teaspoon baking powder
1 teaspoon apple pie spice
2 eggs, lightly whisked
¼ cup unsalted butter, melted
½ cup heavy (whipping) cream

1. Grease a 6-inch round cake pan with the cooking spray. 2. In a medium bowl, mix together the almond flour, coconut, Swerve, baking powder, and apple pie spice. 3. Add the eggs, then the butter, then the cream, mixing well after each addition. 4. Pour the batter into the pan and cover with aluminum foil. 5. Pour 2 cups of water into the inner cooking pot of the Instant Pot, then place a trivet in the pot. Place the pan on the trivet. 6. Lock the lid into place. Select Manual and adjust the pressure to High. Cook for 40 minutes. When the cooking is complete, let the pressure release naturally for 10 minutes, then quick-release any remaining pressure. Unlock the lid. 7. Carefully take out the pan and let it cool for 15 to 20 minutes. Invert the cake onto a plate. Sprinkle with shredded coconut, almond slices, or powdered sweetener, if desired, and serve.

Per Serving:
calories: 231 | fat: 19g | protein: 3g | carbs: 12g | net carbs: 10g | fiber: 2g

Chocolate Chip Banana Cake

Prep time: 15 minutes | Cook time: 25 minutes | Serves 8

Nonstick cooking spray
3 ripe bananas
½ cup buttermilk
3 tablespoons honey
1 teaspoon vanilla extract
2 large eggs, lightly beaten
3 tablespoons extra-virgin olive oil
1½ cups whole wheat pastry flour
⅛ teaspoon ground nutmeg
1 teaspoon ground cinnamon
¼ teaspoon salt
1 teaspoon baking soda
⅓ cup dark chocolate chips

1. Spray a 7-inch Bundt pan with nonstick cooking spray. 2. In a large bowl, mash the bananas. Add the buttermilk, honey, vanilla, eggs, and olive oil, and mix well. 3. In a medium bowl, whisk together the flour, nutmeg, cinnamon, salt, and baking soda. 4. Add the flour mixture to the banana mixture and mix well. Stir in the chocolate chips. Pour the batter into the prepared Bundt pan. Cover the pan with foil. 5. Pour 1 cup of water into the electric pressure cooker. Place the pan on the wire rack and lower it into the pressure cooker. 6. Close and lock the lid of the pressure cooker. Set the valve to sealing. 7. Cook on high pressure for 25 minutes. 8. When the cooking is complete, hit Cancel and quick release the pressure. 9. Once the pin drops, unlock and remove the lid. 10. Carefully transfer the pan to a cooling rack, uncover, and let it cool for 10 minutes. 11. Invert the cake onto the rack and let it cool for about an hour. 12. Slice and serve the cake.

Per Serving:
(1 slice): calories: 261 | fat: 11g | protein: 6g | carbs: 39g | sugars: 16g | fiber: 4g | sodium: 239mg

Cinnamon Roll Cheesecake

Prep time: 15 minutes | Cook time: 35 minutes | Serves 12

Crust:
3½ tablespoons unsalted butter or coconut oil
1½ ounces (43 g) unsweetened baking chocolate, chopped
1 large egg, beaten
⅓ cup Swerve
2 teaspoons ground cinnamon
1 teaspoon vanilla extract
¼ teaspoon fine sea salt
Filling:
4 (8-ounce / 227-g) packages cream cheese, softened
¾ cup Swerve
½ cup unsweetened almond milk (or hemp milk for nut-free)
1 teaspoon vanilla extract
¼ teaspoon almond extract (omit for nut-free)
¼ teaspoon fine sea salt
3 large eggs
Cinnamon Swirl:
6 tablespoons (¾ stick) unsalted butter (or butter flavored coconut oil for dairy-free)
½ cup Swerve
Seeds scraped from ½ vanilla bean (about 8 inches long), or 1 teaspoon vanilla extract
1 tablespoon ground cinnamon
¼ teaspoon fine sea salt
1 cup cold water

1. Line a baking pan with two layers of aluminum foil. 2. Make the crust: Melt the butter in a pan over medium-low heat. Slowly add the chocolate and stir until melted. Stir in the egg, sweetener, cinnamon, vanilla extract, and salt. 3. Transfer the crust mixture to the prepared baking pan, spreading it with your hands to cover the bottom completely. 4. Make the filling: In the bowl of a stand mixer, add the cream cheese, sweetener, milk, extracts, and salt and mix until well blended. Add the eggs, one at a time, mixing on low speed after each addition just until blended. Then blend until the filling is smooth. Pour half of the filling over the crust. 5. Make the cinnamon swirl: Heat the butter over high heat in a pan until the butter froths and brown flecks appear, stirring occasionally. Stir in the sweetener, vanilla seeds, cinnamon, and salt. Remove from the heat and allow to cool slightly. 6. Spoon half of the cinnamon swirl on top of the cheesecake filling in the baking pan. Use a knife to cut the cinnamon swirl through the filling several times for a marbled effect. Top with the rest of the cheesecake filling and cinnamon swirl. Cut the cinnamon swirl through the cheesecake filling again several times. 7. Place a trivet in the bottom of the Instant Pot and pour in the water. Use a foil sling to lower the baking pan onto the trivet. Cover the cheesecake with 3 large sheets of paper towel to ensure that condensation doesn't leak onto it. Tuck in the sides of the sling. 8. Lock the lid. Select the Manual mode and set the cooking time for 26 minutes at High Pressure. 9. When the timer beeps, use a natural pressure release for 10 minutes. Carefully remove the lid. 10. Use the foil sling to lift the pan out of the Instant Pot. 11. Let the cheesecake cool, then place in the refrigerator for 4 hours to chill and set completely before slicing and serving.

Per Serving:
calories: 363 | fat: 34.2g | protein: 7.0g | carbs: 7.6g | net carbs: 6.4g | fiber: 1.2g

Coconut Cupcakes

Prep time: 5 minutes | Cook time: 10 minutes | Serves 6

4 eggs, beaten
4 tablespoons coconut milk
4 tablespoons coconut flour
½ teaspoon vanilla extract
2 tablespoons erythritol
1 teaspoon baking powder
1 cup water

1. In the mixing bowl, mix up eggs, coconut milk, coconut flour, vanilla extract, erythritol, and baking powder. 2. Then pour the batter in the cupcake molds. 3. Pour the water and insert the trivet in the instant pot. 4. Place the cupcakes on the trivet. 5. Lock the lid. Select the Manual mode and set the cooking time for 10 minutes on High Pressure. Once the timer goes off, perform a natural pressure release for 5 minutes, then release any remaining pressure. Carefully open the lid. 6. Serve immediately.

Per Serving:
calories: 85 | fat: 5.7g | protein: 4.7g | carbs: 9.1g | net carbs: 6.8g | fiber: 2.3g

Crustless Creamy Berry Cheesecake

Prep time: 10 minutes | Cook time: 40 minutes | Serves 12

16 ounces (454 g) cream cheese, softened
1 cup powdered erythritol
¼ cup sour cream
2 teaspoons vanilla extract
2 eggs
2 cups water
¼ cup blackberries and strawberries, for topping

1. In large bowl, beat cream cheese and erythritol until smooth. Add sour cream, vanilla, and eggs and gently fold until combined. 2. Pour batter into 7-inch springform pan. Gently shake or tap pan on counter to remove air bubbles and level batter. Cover top of pan with tinfoil. Pour water into Instant Pot and place steam rack in pot. 3. Carefully lower pan into pot. Press the Cake button and press the Adjust button to set heat to More. Set time for 40 minutes. When timer beeps, allow a full natural release. Using sling, carefully lift pan from Instant Pot and allow to cool completely before refrigerating. 4. Place strawberries and blackberries on top of cheesecake and serve.

Per Serving:
calories: 153 | fat: 13g | protein: 3g | carbs: 14g | net carbs: 14g | fiber: 0g

Glazed Pumpkin Bundt Cake

Prep time: 7 minutes | Cook time: 35 minutes | Serves 12

Cake:
3 cups blanched almond flour
1 teaspoon baking soda
½ teaspoon fine sea salt
2 teaspoons ground cinnamon
1 teaspoon ground nutmeg
1 teaspoon ginger powder
¼ teaspoon ground cloves
6 large eggs
2 cups pumpkin purée
1 cup Swerve
¼ cup (½ stick) unsalted butter (or coconut oil for dairy-free), softened
Glaze:
1 cup (2 sticks) unsalted butter (or coconut oil for dairy-free), melted
½ cup Swerve

1. In a large bowl, stir together the almond flour, baking soda, salt, and spices. In another large bowl, add the eggs, pumpkin, sweetener, and butter and stir until smooth. Pour the wet ingredients into the dry ingredients and stir well. 2. Grease a 6-cup Bundt pan. Pour the batter into the prepared pan and cover with a paper towel and then with aluminum foil. 3. Place a trivet in the bottom of the Instant Pot and pour in 2 cups of cold water. Place the Bundt pan on the trivet. 4. Lock the lid. Select the Manual mode and set the cooking time for

35 minutes at High Pressure. 5. When the timer beeps, use a natural pressure release for 10 minutes. Carefully remove the lid. 6. Let the cake cool in the pot for 10 minutes before removing. 7. While the cake is cooling, make the glaze: In a small bowl, mix the butter and sweetener together. Spoon the glaze over the warm cake. 8. Allow to cool for 5 minutes before slicing and serving.

Per Serving:
calories: 332 | fat: 21.9g | protein: 6.8g | carbs: 27.4g | net carbs: 26.2g | fiber: 1.2g

Hearty Crème Brûlée

Prep time: 5 minutes | Cook time: 30 minutes | Serves 4

5 egg yolks
5 tablespoons powdered erythritol
1½ cups heavy cream
2 teaspoons vanilla extract
2 cups water

1. In a small bowl, use a fork to break up the egg yolks. Stir in the erythritol. 2. Pour the cream into a small saucepan over medium-low heat and let it warm up for 3 to 4 minutes. Remove the saucepan from the heat. 3. Temper the egg yolks by slowly adding a small spoonful of the warm cream, keep whisking. Do this three times to make sure the egg yolks are fully tempered. 4. Slowly add the tempered eggs to the cream, whisking the whole time. Add the vanilla and whisk again. 5. Pour the cream mixture into the ramekins. Each ramekin should have ½ cup liquid. Cover each with aluminum foil. 6. Place the trivet inside the Instant Pot. Add the water. Carefully place the ramekins on top of the trivet. 7. Close the lid. Select Manual mode and set cooking time for 11 minutes on High Pressure. 8. When timer beeps, use a natural release for 15 minutes, then release any remaining pressure. Open the lid. 9. Carefully remove a ramekin from the pot. Remove the foil and check for doneness. The custard should be mostly set with a slightly jiggly center. 10. Place all the ramekins in the fridge for 2 hours to chill and set. Serve chilled.

Per Serving:
calories: 229 | fat: 22.2g | protein: 4.4g | carbs: 2.2g | net carbs: 2.2g | fiber: 0g

Goat Cheese–Stuffed Pears

Prep time: 6 minutes | Cook time: 2 minutes | Serves 4

2 ounces goat cheese, at room temperature
2 teaspoons pure maple syrup
2 ripe, firm pears, halved
lengthwise and cored
2 tablespoons chopped pistachios, toasted

1. Pour 1 cup of water into the electric pressure cooker and insert a wire rack or trivet. 2. In a small bowl, combine the goat cheese and maple syrup. 3. Spoon the goat cheese mixture into the cored pear halves. Place the pears on the rack inside the pot, cut-side up. 4. Close and lock the lid of the pressure cooker. Set the valve to sealing. 5. Cook on high pressure for 2 minutes. 6. When the cooking is complete, hit Cancel and quick release the pressure. 7. Once the pin drops, unlock and remove the lid. 8. Using tongs, carefully transfer the pears to serving plates. 9. Sprinkle with pistachios and serve immediately.

Per Serving:
(½ pear): calories: 120 | fat: 5g | protein: 4g | carbs: 17g | sugars: 11g | fiber: 3g | sodium: 54mg

Blackberry Crisp

Prep time: 5 minutes | Cook time: 5 minutes | Serves 1

10 blackberries
½ teaspoon vanilla extract
2 tablespoons powdered erythritol
⅛ teaspoon xanthan gum
1 tablespoon butter
¼ cup chopped pecans
3 teaspoons almond flour
½ teaspoon cinnamon
2 teaspoons powdered erythritol
1 cup water

1. Place blackberries, vanilla, erythritol, and xanthan gum in 4-inch ramekin. Stir gently to coat blackberries. 2. In small bowl, mix remaining ingredients. Sprinkle over blackberries and cover with foil. Press the Manual button and set time for 4 minutes. When timer beeps, quick-release the pressure. Serve warm. Feel free to add scoop of whipped cream on top.

Per Serving:
calories: 346 | fat: 31g | protein: 3g | carbs: 13g | net carbs: 5g | fiber: 8g

Caramelized Pumpkin Cheesecake

Prep time: 15 minutes | Cook time: 45 minutes | Serves 8

Crust:
1½ cups almond flour
4 tablespoons butter, melted
1 tablespoon Swerve
1 tablespoon granulated erythritol
½ teaspoon ground cinnamon
Cooking spray
Filling:
16 ounces (454 g) cream cheese, softened
½ cup granulated erythritol
2 eggs
¼ cup pumpkin purée
3 tablespoons Swerve
1 teaspoon vanilla extract
¼ teaspoon pumpkin pie spice
1½ cups water

1. To make the crust: In a medium bowl, combine the almond flour, butter, Swerve, erythritol, and cinnamon. Use a fork to press it all together. 2. Spray the pan with cooking spray and line the bottom with parchment paper. 3. Press the crust evenly into the pan. Work the crust up the sides of the pan, about halfway from the top, and make sure there are no bare spots on the bottom. 4. Place the crust in the freezer for 20 minutes while you make the filling. 5. To make the filling: In a large bowl using a hand mixer on medium speed, combine the cream cheese and erythritol. Beat until the cream cheese is light and fluffy, 2 to 3 minutes. 6. Add the eggs, pumpkin purée, Swerve, vanilla, and pumpkin pie spice. Beat until well combined. 7. Remove the crust from the freezer and pour in the filling. Cover the pan with aluminum foil and place it on the trivet. 8. Add the water to the pot and carefully lower the trivet into the pot. 9. Set the lid in place. Select the Manual mode and set the cooking time for 45 minutes on High Pressure. When the timer goes off, do a quick pressure release. Carefully open the lid. 10. Remove the trivet and cheesecake from the pot. Remove the foil from the pan. The center of the cheesecake should still be slightly jiggly. 11. Let the cheesecake cool for 30 minutes on the counter before placing it in the refrigerator to set. Leave the cheesecake in the refrigerator for at least 6 hours before removing the sides and serving.

Per Serving:
calories: 407 | fat: 35.8g | protein: 10.3g | carbs: 6.8g | net carbs: 4.3g | fiber: 2.5g

Pumpkin Pie Pudding

Prep time: 10 minutes | Cook time: 20 minutes | Serves 6

Nonstick cooking spray	pumpkin purée
2 eggs	1 teaspoon pumpkin pie spice
½ cup heavy (whipping) cream or almond milk (for dairy-free)	1 teaspoon vanilla extract
¾ cup Swerve	For Serving:
1 (15-ounce / 425-g) can	½ cup heavy (whipping) cream

1. Grease a 6-by-3-inch pan extremely well with the cooking spray, making sure it gets into all the nooks and crannies. 2. In a medium bowl, whisk the eggs. Add the cream, Swerve, pumpkin purée, pumpkin pie spice, and vanilla, and stir to mix thoroughly. 3. Pour the mixture into the prepared pan and cover it with a silicone lid or aluminum foil. 4. Pour 2 cups of water into the inner cooking pot of the Instant Pot, then place a trivet in the pot. Place the covered pan on the trivet. 5. Lock the lid into place. Select Manual and adjust the pressure to High. Cook for 20 minutes. When the cooking is complete, let the pressure release naturally for 10 minutes, then quick-release any remaining pressure. Unlock the lid. 6. Remove the pan and place it in the refrigerator. Chill for 6 to 8 hours. 8. When ready to serve, finish by making the whipped cream. Using a hand mixer, beat the heavy cream until it forms soft peaks. Do not overbeat and turn it to butter. Serve each pudding with a dollop of whipped cream.

Per Serving:
calories: 188 | fat: 17g | protein: 4g | carbs: 8g | net carbs:6 g | fiber: 2g

Chocolate Pecan Clusters

Prep time: 5 minutes | Cook time: 5 minutes | Makes 8 clusters

3 tablespoons butter	1 cup chopped pecans
¼ cup heavy cream	¼ cup low-carb chocolate chips
1 teaspoon vanilla extract	

1. Press the Sauté button and add butter to Instant Pot. Allow butter to melt and begin to turn golden brown. Once it begins to brown, immediately add heavy cream. Press the Cancel button. 2. Add vanilla and chopped pecans to Instant Pot. Allow to cool for 10 minutes, stirring occasionally. Spoon mixture onto parchment-lined baking sheet to form eight clusters, and scatter chocolate chips over clusters. Place in fridge to cool.

Per Serving:
calories: 194 | fat: 18g | protein: 2g | carbs: 7g | net carbs: 6g | fiber: 1g

Chocolate Macadamia Bark

Prep time: 5 minutes | Cook time: 20 minutes | Serves 20

16 ounces (454 g) raw dark chocolate	2 cups chopped macadamia nuts
3 tablespoons raw coconut butter	1 tablespoon almond butter
2 tablespoons coconut oil	½ teaspoon salt
	⅓ cup Swerve, or more to taste

1. In a large bowl, mix together the chocolate, coconut butter, coconut oil, macadamia nuts, almond butter, salt, and Swerve. Combine them very thoroughly, until a perfectly even mixture is obtained. 2. Pour 1 cup of filtered water into the Instant Pot, and insert the trivet. Transfer the mixture from the bowl into a well-greased, Instant Pot-friendly dish. 3. Place the dish onto the trivet, and cover loosely with aluminum foil. Close the lid, set the pressure release to Sealing, and select Manual. Set the Instant Pot to 20 minutes on High Pressure, and let cook. 4. Once cooked, let the pressure naturally disperse from the Instant Pot for about 10 minutes, then carefully switch the pressure release to Venting. 5. Open the Instant Pot and remove the dish. Cool in the refrigerator until set. Break into pieces, serve, and enjoy! Store remaining bark in the refrigerator or freezer.

Per Serving:
calories: 258 | fat: 22g | protein: 2g | carbs: 15g | net carbs: 12g | fiber: 3g

Chipotle Black Bean Brownies

Prep time: 15 minutes | Cook time: 30 minutes | Serves 8

Nonstick cooking spray	⅓ cup honey
½ cup dark chocolate chips, divided	1 teaspoon vanilla extract
¾ cup cooked calypso beans or black beans	⅓ cup white wheat flour
½ cup extra-virgin olive oil	½ teaspoon chipotle chili powder
2 large eggs	½ teaspoon ground cinnamon
¼ cup unsweetened dark chocolate cocoa powder	½ teaspoon baking powder
	½ teaspoon kosher salt

1. Spray a 7-inch Bundt pan with nonstick cooking spray. 2. Place half of the chocolate chips in a small bowl and microwave them for 30 seconds. Stir and repeat, if necessary, until the chips have completely melted. 3. In a food processor, blend the beans and oil together. Add the melted chocolate chips, eggs, cocoa powder, honey, and vanilla. Blend until the mixture is smooth. 4. In a large bowl, whisk together the flour, chili powder, cinnamon, baking powder, and salt. Pour the bean mixture from the food processor into the bowl and stir with a wooden spoon until well combined. Stir in the remaining chocolate chips. 5. Pour the batter into the prepared Bundt pan. Cover loosely with foil. 6. Pour 1 cup of water into the electric pressure cooker. 7. Place the Bundt pan onto the wire rack and lower it into the pressure cooker. 8. Close and lock the lid of the pressure cooker. Set the valve to sealing. 9. Cook on high pressure for 30 minutes. 10. When the cooking is complete, hit Cancel and quick release the pressure. 11. Once the pin drops, unlock and remove the lid. 12. Carefully transfer the pan to a cooling rack for about 10 minutes, then invert the cake onto the rack and let it cool completely. 13. Cut into slices and serve.

Per Serving:
(1 slice): calories: 296 | fat: 20g | protein: 5g | carbs: 29g | sugars: 16g | fiber: 4g | sodium: 224mg

Coconut Squares

Prep time: 15 minutes | Cook time: 4 minutes | Serves 2

⅓ cup coconut flakes	1 egg, beaten
1 tablespoon butter	1 cup water, for cooking

1. Mix up together coconut flakes, butter, and egg. 2. Then put the

mixture into the square shape mold and flatten well. 3. Pour water and insert the steamer rack in the instant pot. 4. Put the mold with dessert on the rack. Close and seal the lid. 5. Cook the meal on Manual mode (High Pressure) for 4 minutes. Make a quick pressure release. 6. Cool the cooked dessert little and cut into the squares.
Per Serving:
calories: 130 | fat: 12g | protein: 3g | carbs: 2g | net carbs: 1g | fiber: 1g

Southern Almond Pie

Prep time: 10 minutes | Cook time: 35 minutes | Serves 12

2 cups almond flour	1 egg
1½ cups powdered erythritol	1 teaspoon vanilla extract
1 teaspoon baking powder	Cooking spray
Pinch of salt	1½ teaspoons ground cinnamon
½ cup sour cream	1½ teaspoons Swerve
4 tablespoons butter, melted	1 cup water

1. In a large bowl, whisk together the almond flour, powdered erythritol, baking powder, and salt. 2. Add the sour cream, butter, egg, and vanilla and whisk until well combined. The batter will be very thick, almost like cookie dough. 3. Grease the baking dish with cooking spray. Line with parchment paper, if desired. 4. Transfer the batter to the dish and level with an offset spatula. 5. In a small bowl, combine the cinnamon and Swerve. Sprinkle over the top of the batter. 6. Cover the dish tightly with aluminum foil. Add the water to the pot. Set the dish on the trivet and carefully lower it into the pot. 7. Set the lid in place. Select the Manual mode and set the cooking time for 35 minutes on High Pressure. When the timer goes off, do a quick pressure release. Carefully open the lid. 8. Remove the trivet and pie from the pot. Remove the foil from the pan. The pie should be set but soft, and the top should be slightly cracked. 9. Cool completely before cutting.
Per Serving:
calories: 221 | fat: 19.0g | protein: 5.6g | carbs: 4.8g | net carbs: 2.4g | fiber: 2.4g

Candied Mixed Nuts

Prep time: 5 minutes | Cook time: 15 minutes | Serves 8

1 cup pecan halves	⅓ cup grass-fed butter
1 cup chopped walnuts	1 teaspoon ground cinnamon
⅓ cup Swerve, or more to taste	

1. Preheat your oven to 350ºF (180ºC), and line a baking sheet with aluminum foil. 2. While your oven is warming, pour ½ cup of filtered water into the inner pot of the Instant Pot, followed by the pecans, walnuts, Swerve, butter, and cinnamon. Stir nut mixture, close the lid, and then set the pressure valve to Sealing. Use the Manual mode to cook at High Pressure, for 5 minutes. 3. Once cooked, perform a quick release by carefully switching the pressure valve to Venting, and strain the nuts. Pour the nuts onto the baking sheet, spreading them out in an even layer. Place in the oven for 5 to 10 minutes (or until crisp, being careful not to overcook). Cool before serving. Store leftovers in the refrigerator or freezer.
Per Serving:
calories: 122 | fat: 12g | protein: 4g | carbs: 3g | net carbs: 1g | fiber: 2g

Vanilla Butter Curd

Prep time: 5 minutes | Cook time: 6 hours | Serves 3

4 egg yolks, whisked	½ cup organic almond milk
2 tablespoon butter	1 teaspoon vanilla extract
1 tablespoon erythritol	

1. Set the instant pot to Sauté mode and when the "Hot" is displayed, add butter. 2. Melt the butter but not boil it and add whisked egg yolks, almond milk, and vanilla extract. 3. Add erythritol. Whisk the mixture. 4. Cook the meal on Low for 6 hours.
Per Serving:
calories: 154 | fat: 14g | protein: 4g | carbs: 7g | net carbs: 7g | fiber: 0g

Almond Pie with Coconut

Prep time: 5 minutes | Cook time: 41 minutes | Serves 8

1 cup almond flour	1 tablespoon Truvia
½ cup coconut milk	¼ cup shredded coconut
1 teaspoon vanilla extract	1 cup water
2 tablespoons butter, softened	

1. In the mixing bowl, mix up almond flour, coconut milk, vanilla extract, butter, Truvia, and shredded coconut. 2. When the mixture is smooth, transfer it in the baking pan and flatten. 3. Pour water and insert the trivet in the instant pot. 4. Put the baking pan with cake on the trivet. 5. Lock the lid. Select the Manual mode and set the cooking time for 41 minutes on High Pressure. Once the timer goes off, perform a natural pressure release for 10 minutes, then release any remaining pressure. Carefully open the lid. 6. Serve immediately.
Per Serving:
calories: 89 | fat: 9.2g | protein: 1.3g | carbs: 2.5g | net carbs: 1.5g | fiber: 1.0g

Pine Nut Mousse

Prep time: 5 minutes | Cook time: 35 minutes | Serves 8

1 tablespoon butter	1 cup Swerve, reserve 1
1¼ cups pine nuts	tablespoon
1¼ cups full-fat heavy cream	1 c water
2 large eggs	1 cup full-fat heavy whipping
1 teaspoon vanilla extract	cream

1. Butter the bottom and the side of a pie pan and set aside. 2. In a food processor, blend the pine nuts and heavy cream. Add the eggs, vanilla extract and Swerve and pulse a few times to incorporate. 3. Pour the batter into the pan and loosely cover with aluminum foil. Pour the water in the Instant Pot and place the trivet inside. Place the pan on top of the trivet. 4. Close the lid. Select Manual mode and set the timer for 35 minutes on High pressure. 5. In a small mixing bowl, whisk the heavy whipping cream and 1 tablespoon of Swerve until a soft peak forms. 6. When timer beeps, use a natural pressure release for 15 minutes, then release any remaining pressure and open the lid. 7. Serve immediately with whipped cream on top.
Per Serving:
calories: 184 | fat: 18.8g | protein: 3.0g | carbs: 1.9g | net carbs: 1.8g | fiber: 0.1g

Lemon and Ricotta Torte

Prep time: 15 minutes | Cook time: 35 minutes | Serves 12

Cooking spray
Torte:
1⅓ cups Swerve
½ cup (1 stick) unsalted butter, softened
2 teaspoons lemon or vanilla extract
5 large eggs, separated
2½ cups blanched almond flour
1¼ (10-ounce / 284-g) cups whole-milk ricotta cheese
¼ cup lemon juice
1 cup cold water
Lemon Glaze:
½ cup (1 stick) unsalted butter
¼ cup Swerve
2 tablespoons lemon juice
2 ounces (57 g) cream cheese (¼ cup)
Grated lemon zest and lemon slices, for garnish

1. Line a baking pan with parchment paper and spray with cooking spray. Set aside. 2. Make the torte: In the bowl of a stand mixer, place the Swerve, butter, and extract and blend for 8 to 10 minutes until well combined. Scrape down the sides of the bowl as needed. 3. Add the egg yolks and continue to blend until fully combined. Add the almond flour and mix until smooth, then stir in the ricotta and lemon juice. 4. Whisk the egg whites in a separate medium bowl until stiff peaks form. Add the whites to the batter and stir well. Pour the batter into the prepared pan and smooth the top. 5. Place a trivet in the bottom of your Instant Pot and pour in the water. Use a foil sling to lower the baking pan onto the trivet. Tuck in the sides of the sling. 6. Seal the lid, press Pressure Cook or Manual, and set the timer for 30 minutes. Once finished, let the pressure release naturally. 7. Lock the lid. Select the Manual mode and set the cooking time for 30 minutes at High Pressure. 8. When the timer beeps, perform a natural pressure release for 10 minutes. Carefully remove the lid. 9. Use the foil sling to lift the pan out of the Instant Pot. Place the torte in the fridge for 40 minutes to chill before glazing. 10. Meanwhile, make the glaze: Place the butter in a large pan over high heat and cook for about 5 minutes until brown, stirring occasionally. Remove from the heat. While stirring the browned butter, add the Swerve. 11. Carefully add the lemon juice and cream cheese to the butter mixture. Allow the glaze to cool for a few minutes, or until it starts to thicken. 12. Transfer the chilled torte to a serving plate. Pour the glaze over the torte and return it to the fridge to chill for an additional 30 minutes. 13. Scatter the lemon zest on top of the torte and arrange the lemon slices on the plate around the torte. 14. Serve.

Per Serving:
calories: 367 | fat: 32.8g | protein: 11.5g | carbs: 10.0g | net carbs: 7.0g | fiber: 3.0g

Deconstructed Tiramisu

Prep time: 5 minutes | Cook time: 9 minutes | Serves 4

1 cup heavy cream (or full-fat coconut milk for dairy-free)
2 large egg yolks
2 tablespoons brewed decaf espresso or strong brewed coffee
2 tablespoons Swerve, or more to taste
1 teaspoon rum extract
1 teaspoon unsweetened cocoa powder, or more to taste
Pinch of fine sea salt
1 cup cold water
4 teaspoons Swerve, for topping

1. Heat the cream in a pan over medium-high heat until hot, about 2 minutes. 2. Place the egg yolks, coffee, sweetener, rum extract, cocoa powder, and salt in a blender and blend until smooth. 3. While the blender is running, slowly pour in the hot cream. Taste and adjust the sweetness to your liking. Add more cocoa powder, if desired. 4. Scoop the mixture into four ramekins with a spatula. Cover the ramekins with aluminum foil. 5. Place a trivet in the bottom of the Instant Pot and pour in the water. Place the ramekins on the trivet. 6. Lock the lid. Select the Manual mode and set the cooking time for 7 minutes at High Pressure. 7. When the timer beeps, use a quick pressure release. Carefully remove the lid. 8. Keep the ramekins covered with the foil and place in the refrigerator for about 2 hours until completely chilled. 9. Sprinkle 1 teaspoon of Swerve on top of each tiramisu. Use the oven broiler to melt the sweetener. 10. Put in the fridge to chill the topping, about 20 minutes. 11. Serve.

Per Serving:
calories: 139 | fat: 13.4g | protein: 2.1g | carbs: 2.6g | net carbs: 2.5g | fiber: 0.1g

Cocoa Custard

Prep time: 5 minutes | Cook time: 7 minutes | Serves 4

2 cups heavy cream (or full-fat coconut milk for dairy-free)
4 large egg yolks
¼ cup Swerve, or more to taste
1 tablespoon plus 1 teaspoon
unsweetened cocoa powder, or more to taste
½ teaspoon almond extract
Pinch of fine sea salt
1 cup cold water

1. Heat the cream in a pan over medium-high heat until hot, about 2 minutes. 2. Place the remaining ingredients except the water in a blender and blend until smooth. 3. While the blender is running, slowly pour in the hot cream. Taste and adjust the sweetness to your liking. Add more cocoa powder, if desired. 4. Scoop the custard mixture into four ramekins with a spatula. Cover the ramekins with aluminum foil. 5. Place a trivet in the Instant Pot and pour in the water. Place the ramekins on the trivet. 6. Lock the lid. Select the Manual mode and set the cooking time for 5 minutes at High Pressure. 7. When the timer beeps, use a quick pressure release. Carefully remove the lid. 8. Remove the foil and set the foil aside. Let the custard cool for 15 minutes. Cover the ramekins with the foil again and place in the refrigerator to chill completely, about 2 hours. 9. Serve.

Per Serving:
calories: 269 | fat: 26.9g | protein: 4.1g | carbs: 3.8g | net carbs: 3.6g | fiber: 0.2g

Lemon-Ricotta Cheesecake

Prep time: 10 minutes | Cook time: 30 minutes | Serves 6

Unsalted butter or vegetable oil, for greasing the pan
8 ounces (227 g) cream cheese, at room temperature
¼ cup plus 1 teaspoon Swerve, plus more as needed
⅓ cup full-fat or part-skim
ricotta cheese, at room temperature
Zest of 1 lemon
Juice of 1 lemon
½ teaspoon lemon extract
2 eggs, at room temperature
2 tablespoons sour cream

1. Grease a 6-inch springform pan extremely well. I find this easiest to do with a silicone basting brush so I can get into all the nooks and crannies. Alternatively, line the sides of the pan with parchment

paper. 2. In the bowl of a stand mixer, beat the cream cheese, ¼ cup of Swerve, the ricotta, lemon zest, lemon juice, and lemon extract on high speed until you get a smooth mixture with no lumps. 3. Taste to ensure the sweetness is to your liking and adjust if needed. 4. Add the eggs, reduce the speed to low and gently blend until the eggs are just incorporated. Overbeating at this stage will result in a cracked crust. 5. Pour the mixture into the prepared pan and cover with aluminum foil or a silicone lid. 6. Pour 2 cups of water into the inner cooking pot of the Instant Pot, then place a trivet in the pot. Place the covered pan on the trivet. 7. Lock the lid into place. Select Manual and adjust the pressure to High. Cook for 30 minutes. When the cooking is complete, let the pressure release naturally. Unlock the lid. 8. Carefully remove the pan from the pot, and remove the foil. 9. In a small bowl, mix together the sour cream and remaining 1 teaspoon of Swerve and spread this over the top of the warm cake. 10. Refrigerate the cheesecake for 6 to 8 hours. Do not be in a hurry! The cheesecake needs every bit of this time to be its best.

Per Serving:

calories: 217 | fat: 17g | protein: 6g | carbs: 10g | net carbs: 10g | fiber: 0g

Almond Butter Blondies

Prep time: 10 minutes | Cook time: 20 minutes | Serves 8

½ cup creamy natural almond butter, at room temperature
4 large eggs
¾ cup Lakanto Monkfruit Sweetener Golden
1 teaspoon pure vanilla extract
½ teaspoon fine sea salt
1¼ cups almond flour
¾ cup stevia-sweetened chocolate chips

1. Pour 1 cup water into the Instant Pot. Line the base of a 7 by 3-inch round cake pan with a circle of parchment paper. Butter the sides of the pan and the parchment or coat with nonstick cooking spray. 2. Put the almond butter into a medium bowl. One at a time, whisk the eggs into the almond butter, then whisk in the sweetener, vanilla, and salt. Stir in the flour just until it is fully incorporated, followed by the chocolate chips. 3. Transfer the batter to the prepared pan and, using a rubber spatula, spread it in an even layer. Cover the pan tightly with aluminum foil. Place the pan on a long-handled silicone steam rack, then, holding the handles of the steam rack, lower it into the Instant Pot. 4. Secure the lid and set the Pressure Release to Sealing. Select the Cake, Pressure Cook, or Manual setting and set the cooking time for 40 minutes at high pressure. (The pot will take about 10 minutes to come up to pressure before the cooking program begins.) 5. When the cooking program ends, let the pressure release naturally for 10 minutes, then move the Pressure Release to Venting to release any remaining steam. Open the pot and, wearing heat-resistant mitts, grasp the handles of the steam rack and lift it out of the pot. Uncover the pan, taking care not to get burned by the steam or to drip condensation onto the blondies. Let the blondies cool in the pan on a cooling rack for about 5 minutes. 6. Run a butter knife around the edge of pan to make sure the blondies are not sticking to the pan sides. Invert the blondies onto the rack, lift off the pan, and peel off the parchment paper. Let cool for 15 minutes, then invert the blondies onto a serving plate and cut into eight wedges. The blondies will keep, stored in an airtight container in the refrigerator for up to 5 days, or in the freezer for up to 4 months.

Per Serving:

calories: 211 | fat: 17g | protein: 8g | carbs: 20g | sugars: 10g | fiber: 17g | sodium: 186mg

Lime Muffins

Prep time: 10 minutes | Cook time: 15 minutes | Serves 6

1 teaspoon lime zest
1 tablespoon lemon juice
1 teaspoon baking powder
1 cup almond flour
2 eggs, beaten
1 tablespoon Swerve
¼ cup heavy cream
1 cup water, for cooking

1. In the mixing bowl, mix up lemon juice, baking powder, almond flour, eggs, Swerve, and heavy cream. 2. When the muffin batter is smooth, add lime zest and mix it up. 3. Fill the muffin molds with batter. 4. Then pour water and insert the rack in the instant pot. 5. Place the muffins on the rack. Close and seal the lid. 6. Cook the muffins on Manual (High Pressure) for 15 minutes. 7. Then allow the natural pressure release.

Per Serving:

calories: 153 | fat: 12g | protein: 6g | carbs: 5g | net carbs: 3g | fiber: 2g

Lemon Vanilla Cheesecake

Prep time: 15 minutes | Cook time: 20 minutes | Serves 6

2 teaspoons freshly squeezed lemon juice
2 teaspoons vanilla extract or almond extract
½ cup sour cream, divided, at room temperature
½ cup plus 2 teaspoons Swerve
8 ounces (227 g) cream cheese, at room temperature
2 eggs, at room temperature

1. Pour 2 cups of water into the inner cooking pot of the Instant Pot, then place a trivet (preferably with handles) in the pot. Line the sides of a 6-inch springform pan with parchment paper. 2. In a food processor, put the lemon juice, vanilla, ¼ cup of sour cream, ½ cup of Swerve, and the cream cheese. 3. Gently but thoroughly blend all the ingredients, scraping down the sides of the bowl as needed. 4. Add the eggs and blend only as long as you need to in order to get them well incorporated, 20 to 30 seconds. Your mixture will be pourable by now. 5. Pour the mixture into the prepared pan. Cover the pan with aluminum foil and place on the trivet. (If your trivet doesn't have handles, you may wish to use a foil sling to make removing the pan easier.) 6. Lock the lid into place. Select Manual and adjust the pressure to High. Cook for 20 minutes. When the cooking is complete, let the pressure release naturally. Unlock the lid. 7. Meanwhile, in a small bowl, mix together the remaining ¼ cup of sour cream and 2 teaspoons of Swerve for the topping. 8. Take out the cheesecake and remove the foil. Spread the topping over the top. Doing this while the cheesecake is still hot helps melt the topping into the cheesecake. 9. Put the cheesecake in the refrigerator and leave it alone. Seriously. Leave it alone and let it chill for at least 6 to 8 hours. It won't taste right hot. 10. When you're ready to serve, open the sides of the pan and peel off the parchment paper. Slice and serve.

Per Serving:

calories: 207 | fat: 19g | protein: 5g | carbs: 4g | net carbs: 4g | fiber: 0g

Strawberry Cheesecake

Prep time: 20 minutes | Cook time: 10 minutes | Serves 2

1 tablespoon gelatin
4 tablespoon water (for gelatin)
4 tablespoon cream cheese
1 strawberry, chopped
¼ cup coconut milk
1 tablespoon Swerve

1. Mix up gelatin and water and leave the mixture for 10 minutes. 2. Meanwhile, pour coconut milk in the instant pot. 3. Bring it to boil on Sauté mode, about 10 minutes. 4. Meanwhile, mash the strawberry and mix it up with cream cheese. 5. Add the mixture in the hot coconut milk and stir until smooth. 6. Cool the liquid for 10 minutes and add gelatin. Whisk it until gelatin is melted. 7. Then pour the cheesecake in the mold and freeze in the freezer for 3 hours.
Per Serving:
calories: 155 | fat: 14g | protein: 5g | carbs: 4g | net carbs: 3g | fiber: 1g

Chocolate Fondue

Prep time: 5 minutes | Cook time: 2 minutes | Serves 4

2 ounces (57 g) unsweetened baking chocolate, finely chopped, divided
1 cup heavy cream, divided
⅓ cup Swerve, divided
Fine sea salt
1 cup cold water
Special Equipment:
Set of fondue forks or wooden skewers

1. Divide the chocolate, cream, and sweetener evenly among four ramekins. Add a pinch of salt to each one and stir well. Cover the ramekins with aluminum foil. 2. Place a trivet in the bottom of your Instant Pot and pour in the water. Place the ramekins on the trivet. 3. Lock the lid. Select the Manual mode and set the cooking time for 2 minutes at High Pressure. 4. When the timer beeps, perform a natural pressure release for 10 minutes. Carefully remove the lid. 5. Use tongs to remove the ramekins from the pot. Use a fork to stir the fondue until smooth. 6. Use immediately.
Per Serving:
calories: 200 | fat: 18.5g | protein: 2.7g | carbs: 6.3g | net carbs: 3.9g | fiber: 2.4g

Coconut Lemon Squares

Prep time: 5 minutes | Cook time: 40 minutes | Serves 5 to 6

3 eggs
2 tablespoons grass-fed butter, softened
½ cup full-fat coconut milk
½ teaspoon baking powder
½ teaspoon vanilla extract
½ cup Swerve, or more to taste
¼ cup lemon juice
1 cup blanched almond flour

1. In a large bowl, mix together the eggs, butter, coconut milk, baking powder, vanilla, Swerve, lemon juice, and flour. Stir thoroughly, until a perfectly even mixture is obtained. 2. Next, pour 1 cup filtered water into the Instant Pot, and insert the trivet. Transfer the mixture from the bowl into a well-greased, Instant Pot-friendly pan (or dish). 3. Using a sling if desired, place the dish onto the trivet, and cover loosely with aluminum foil. Close the lid, set the pressure release to Sealing, and select Manual. Set the Instant Pot to 40 minutes on High Pressure, and let cook. 4. Once cooked, let the pressure naturally disperse from the Instant Pot for about 10 minutes, then carefully switch the pressure release to Venting. 5. Open the Instant Pot, and remove the dish. Let cool, cut into 6 squares, serve, and enjoy!
Per Serving:
calories: 166 | fat: 15g | protein: 6g | carbs: 3g | net carbs: 2g | fiber: 1g

Appendix 1: Measurement Conversion Chart

MEASUREMENT CONVERSION CHART

VOLUME EQUIVALENTS(DRY)

US STANDARD	METRIC (APPROXIMATE)
1/8 teaspoon	0.5 mL
1/4 teaspoon	1 mL
1/2 teaspoon	2 mL
3/4 teaspoon	4 mL
1 teaspoon	5 mL
1 tablespoon	15 mL
1/4 cup	59 mL
1/2 cup	118 mL
3/4 cup	177 mL
1 cup	235 mL
2 cups	475 mL
3 cups	700 mL
4 cups	1 L

VOLUME EQUIVALENTS(LIQUID)

US STANDARD	US STANDARD (OUNCES)	METRIC (APPROXIMATE)
2 tablespoons	1 fl.oz.	30 mL
1/4 cup	2 fl.oz.	60 mL
1/2 cup	4 fl.oz.	120 mL
1 cup	8 fl.oz.	240 mL
1 1/2 cup	12 fl.oz.	355 mL
2 cups or 1 pint	16 fl.oz.	475 mL
4 cups or 1 quart	32 fl.oz.	1 L
1 gallon	128 fl.oz.	4 L

TEMPERATURES EQUIVALENTS

FAHRENHEIT(F)	CELSIUS(C) (APPROXIMATE)
225 °F	107 °C
250 °F	120 °C
275 °F	135 °C
300 °F	150 °C
325 °F	160 °C
350 °F	180 °C
375 °F	190 °C
400 °F	205 °C
425 °F	220 °C
450 °F	235 °C
475 °F	245 °C
500 °F	260 °C

WEIGHT EQUIVALENTS

US STANDARD	METRIC (APPROXIMATE)
1 ounce	28 g
2 ounces	57 g
5 ounces	142 g
10 ounces	284 g
15 ounces	425 g
16 ounces (1 pound)	455 g
1.5 pounds	680 g
2 pounds	907 g

Appendix 2: Instant Pot Cooking Timetable

Instant Pot Cooking Timetable

Dried Beans, Legumes and Lentils

Dried Beans and Legume	Dry (Minutes)	Soaked (Minutes)
Soy beans	25 – 30	20 – 25
Scarlet runner	20 – 25	10 – 15
Pinto beans	25 – 30	20 – 25
Peas	15 – 20	10 – 15
Navy beans	25 – 30	20 – 25
Lima beans	20 – 25	10 – 15
Lentils, split, yellow (moong dal)	15 – 18	N/A
Lentils, split, red	15 – 18	N/A
Lentils, mini, green (brown)	15 – 20	N/A
Lentils, French green	15 – 20	N/A
Kidney white beans	35 – 40	20 – 25
Kidney red beans	25 – 30	20 – 25
Great Northern beans	25 – 30	20 – 25
Pigeon peas	20 – 25	15 – 20
Chickpeas (garbanzo bean chickpeas)	35 – 40	20 – 25
Cannellini beans	35 – 40	20 – 25
Black-eyed peas	20 – 25	10 – 15
Black beans	20 – 25	10 – 15

Fish and Seafood

Fish and Seafood	Fresh (minutes)	Frozen (minutes)
Shrimp or Prawn	1 to 2	2 to 3
Seafood soup or stock	6 to 7	7 to 9
Mussels	2 to 3	4 to 6
Lobster	3 to 4	4 to 6
Fish, whole (snapper, trout, etc.)	5 to 6	7 to 10
Fish steak	3 to 4	4 to 6
Fish fillet,	2 to 3	3 to 4
Crab	3 to 4	5 to 6

Fruits

Fruits	Fresh (in Minutes)	Dried (in Minutes)
Raisins	N/A	4 to 5
Prunes	2 to 3	4 to 5
Pears, whole	3 to 4	4 to 6
Pears, slices or halves	2 to 3	4 to 5
Peaches	2 to 3	4 to 5
Apricots, whole or halves	2 to 3	3 to 4
Apples, whole	3 to 4	4 to 6
Apples, in slices or pieces	2 to 3	3 to 4

Meat

Meat and Cuts	Cooking Time (minutes)	Meat and Cuts	Cooking Time (minutes)
Veal, roast	35 to 45	Duck, with bones, cut up	10 to 12
Veal, chops	5 to 8	Cornish Hen, whole	10 to 15
Turkey, drumsticks (leg)	15 to 20	Chicken, whole	20 to 25
Turkey, breast, whole, with bones	25 to 30	Chicken, legs, drumsticks, or thighs	10 to 15
Turkey, breast, boneless	15 to 20	Chicken, with bones, cut up	10 to 15
Quail, whole	8 to 10	Chicken, breasts	8 to 10
Pork, ribs	20 to 25	Beef, stew	15 to 20
Pork, loin roast	55 to 60	Beef, shanks	25 to 30
Pork, butt roast	45 to 50	Beef, ribs	25 to 30
Pheasant	20 to 25	Beef, steak, pot roast, round, rump, brisket or blade, small chunks, chuck,	25 to 30
Lamb, stew meat	10 to 15		
Lamb, leg	35 to 45	Beef, pot roast, steak, rump, round, chuck, blade or brisket, large	35 to 40
Lamb, cubes,	10 t0 15		
Ham slice	9 to 12	Beef, ox-tail	40 to 50
Ham picnic shoulder	25 to 30	Beef, meatball	10 to 15
Duck, whole	25 to 30	Beef, dressed	20 to 25

Appendix 3: Instant Pot Cooking Timetable

Vegetables (fresh/frozen)					
Vegetable	Fresh (minutes)	Frozen (minutes)	Vegetable	Fresh (minutes)	Frozen (minutes)
Zucchini, slices or chunks	2 to 3	3 to 4	Mixed vegetables	2 to 3	3 to 4
Yam, whole, small	10 to 12	12 to 14	Leeks	2 to 4	3 to 5
Yam, whole, large	12 to 15	15 to 19	Greens (collards, beet greens, spinach,	3 to 6	4 to 7
Yam, in cubes	7 to 9	9 to 11	kale, turnip greens, swiss chard) chopped		
Turnip, chunks	2 to 4	4 to 6	Green beans, whole	2 to 3	3 to 4
Tomatoes, whole	3 to 5	5 to 7	Escarole, chopped	1 to 2	2 to 3
Tomatoes, in quarters	2 to 3	4 to 5	Endive	1 to 2	2 to 3
Sweet potato, whole, small	10 to 12	12 to 14	Eggplant, chunks or slices	2 to 3	3 to 4
Sweet potato, whole, large	12 to 15	15 to 19	Corn, on the cob	3 to 4	4 to 5
Sweet potato, in cubes	7 to 9	9 to 11	Corn, kernels	1 to 2	2 to 3
Sweet pepper, slices or chunks	1 to 3	2 to 4	Collard	4 to 5	5 to 6
Squash, butternut, slices or chunks	8 to 10	10 to 12	Celery, chunks	2 to 3	3 to 4
Squash, acorn, slices or chunks	6 to 7	8 to 9	Cauliflower flowerets	2 to 3	3 to 4
Spinach	1 to 2	3 to 4	Carrots, whole or chunked	2 to 3	3 to 4
Rutabaga, slices	3 to 5	4 to 6	Carrots, sliced or shredded	1 to 2	2 to 3
Rutabaga, chunks	4 to 6	6 to 8	Cabbage, red, purple or green, wedges	3 to 4	4 to 5
Pumpkin, small slices or chunks	4 to 5	6 to 7	Cabbage, red, purple or green, shredded	2 to 3	3 to 4
Pumpkin, large slices or chunks	8 to 10	10 to 14	Brussel sprouts, whole	3 to 4	4 to 5
Potatoes, whole, large	12 to 15	15 to 19	Broccoli, stalks	3 to 4	4 to 5
Potatoes, whole, baby	10 to 12	12 to 14	Broccoli, flowerets	2 to 3	3 to 4
Potatoes, in cubes	7 to 9	9 to 11	Beets, small roots, whole	11 to 13	13 to 15
Peas, in the pod	1 to 2	2 to 3	Beets, large roots, whole	20 to 25	25 to 30
Peas, green	1 to 2	2 to 3	Beans, green/yellow or wax,	1 to 2	2 to 3
Parsnips, sliced	1 to 2	2 to 3	whole, trim ends and strings		
Parsnips, chunks	2 to 4	4 to 6	Asparagus, whole or cut	1 to 2	2 to 3
Onions, sliced	2 to 3	3 to 4	Artichoke, whole, trimmed without leaves	9 to 11	11 to 13
Okra	2 to 3	3 to 4	Artichoke, hearts	4 to 5	5 to 6

Rice and Grains					
Rice & Grain	Water Quantity (Grain: Water ratios)	Cooking Time (in Minutes)	Rice & Grain	Water Quantity (Grain: Water ratios)	Cooking Time (in Minutes)
Wheat berries	1:3	25 to 30	Oats, steel-cut	1:1	10
Spelt berries	1:3	15 to 20	Oats, quick cooking	1:1	6
Sorghum	1:3	20 to 25	Millet	1:1	10 to 12
Rice, wild	1:3	25 to 30	Kamut, whole	1:3	10 to 12
Rice, white	1:1.5	8	Couscous	1:2	5 to 8
Rice, Jasmine	1:1	4 to 10	Corn, dried, half	1:3	25 to 30
Rice, Brown	1:1.3	22 to 28	Congee, thin	1:6 ~ 1:7	15 to 20
Rice, Basmati	1:1.5	4 to 8	Congee, thick	1:4 ~ 1:5	15 to 20
Quinoa, quick cooking	1:2	8	Barley, pot	1:3 ~ 1:4	25 to 30
Porridge, thin	1:6 ~ 1:7	15 to 20	Barley, pearl	1:4	25 to 30

Made in the USA
Coppell, TX
18 April 2023